Trading For Canadians

FOR

DUMMIES®

by Michael Griffis, Lita Epstein, and Christopher Cottier

John Wiley & Sons Canada, Ltd.

Trading For Canadians For Dummies®

Published by
John Wiley & Sons Canada, Ltd
6045 Freemont Boulevard
Mississauga, Ontario, L5R 4J3

www.wiley.com

For general information on John Wiley & Sons Canada, Ltd., including all books published by Wiley Publishing, Inc., please call our distribution centre at 1-800-567-4797. For reseller information, including discounts and premium sales, please call our sales department at 416-646-7992. For press review copies, author interviews, or other publicity information, please contact our publicity department, Tel. 416-646-4582, Fax 416-236-4448.

For technical support, please visit www.wiley.com/techsupport.

Wiley also publishes its books in a variety of electronic formats. Some content that appears in print may not be available in electronic books.

Library and Archives Canada Cataloguing in Publication Data

Griffis, Michael

Trading for Canadians for dummies / Michael Griffis, Lita Epstein, Christopher Cottier.

Includes index.

ISBN 978-0-470-67744-5

1. Stocks—Canada. 2. Investments—Canada. 3. Investment
analysis—Canada. 4. Electronic trading of securities—Canada.
I. Cottier, Christopher II. Epstein, Lita III. Title.

HG5152.G75 2010   332.64'271   C2009-907404-4

Printed in the United States

3 4 5 BRR 14

WILEY

About the Authors

Michael Griffis became an active trader in the mid 1980s. He first traded commodities and precious metals after taking a commodities trading class as part of his MBA program at Rollins College. He turned his interest in trading into a profession and became a stockbroker in 1992, where he helped business and individuals manage investments in stocks, bonds, mutual funds, retirement plans, 401(k) employee-savings plans, and asset management programs. Today, he mostly trades stocks and exchange-traded funds for his own account.

In addition, Michael is an author and business owner and has written about stock trading for online audiences. Outside of the business and investment world, he is active in his community and volunteers his time and talents as a fundraiser for civic and nonprofit organizations.

Lita Epstein, who earned her MBA from Emory University's Goizueta Business School, enjoys helping people develop good financial, investing, and tax planning skills. She designs and teaches online courses on topics such as accounting, reading financial reports, investing for retirement, getting ready for tax time, and finance and investing for women. She has written more than 20 books, including *Bookkeeping For Dummies* and *Reading Financial Reports For Dummies,* both published by Wiley.

Lita was the content director for a financial services Web site, MostChoice. com, and managed the Investing for Women Web site. As a Congressional press secretary, Lita gained first-hand knowledge about how to work within and around the federal bureaucracy, which gives her great insight into how government programs work. In the past Lita has been a daily newspaper reporter, magazine editor, and fundraiser for The Carter Presidential Center. For fun, Lita enjoys scuba diving and is even certified as an underwater photographer. She hikes, canoes, and enjoys surfing the Web to find all its hidden treasures.

Christopher Cottier, BSc, MBA, is a senior investment adviser based in British Columbia. In 1982 he left the world of banking, where he traded foreign currencies, to join the investment industry in Vancouver so he could pursue his love of rugby. More than 25 years later, he's still managing money and still playing rugby. With Betty Jane Wylie, Christopher is the coauthor of *The Best Is Yet to Come: Enjoying a Financially Secure Retirement,* a pioneering Canadian book on financial planning. Christopher has also been the technical editor for other recent *For Canadians For Dummies* financial titles.

Authors' Acknowledgements

We would like to thank all the people who have been instrumental in making this new edition a reality. In particular, we'd like to thank Jessica Faust at BookEnds for getting us connected with Wiley. We'd also like to thank all of the wonderful *For Dummies* folks at Wiley, especially Michael Lewis and Corbin Collins in the U.S. and Robert Hickey in Canada for shepherding this project to completion and for advice and suggestions, and Russell Rhoads for keeping us accurate. Also, we appreciate the extraordinary efforts of Chip Anderson, owner of StockCharts.com, for his help providing the example charts used throughout this book. For this edition, we also thank Lindsay Humphreys for seeing the book through the process, and Kelli Howey for her careful copy editing.

Christopher would also like to offer special thanks again to Daniel Quon, a recipient of the Queen's Golden Jubilee Medal, who has been working with him for many years in the area of trading as well as research for this and other *For Canadians For Dummies* financial titles. Christopher acknowledges his inspiration from 3 guys: JC, JD, and Bex.

Publisher's Acknowledgements

We're proud of this book; please send us your comments at http://dummies.custhelp.com. For other comments, please contact our Customer Care Department within the U.S. at 877-762-2974, outside the U.S. at 317-572-3993 or fax 317-572-4002.

Some of the people who helped bring this book to market include the following:

Acquisitions and Editorial

U.S. Project Editor: Georgette Beatty

Acquiring Editor: Robert Hickey

Copy Editor: Kelli Howey

U.S. Technical Editor: Russell Rhoads

Project Coordinator, Canada:
Lindsay Humphreys

Editorial Assistant: Katie Wolsley

Cover photo: ©iStockphoto.com /
Adam Kazmierski

Cartoons: Rich Tennant
(www.the5thwave.com)

Composition

Project Coordinator, U.S.: Lynsey Stanford

Layout and Graphics: Wiley Indianapolis
Composition Services

Proofreaders: Leeann Harney, Jessica Kramer

Indexer: Claudia Bourbeau

John Wiley & Sons Canada, Ltd

Bill Zerter, Chief Operating Officer

Jennifer Smith, Publisher, Professional & Trade Division

Alison MacLean, Managing Editor, Professional & Trade Division

Karen Bryan, Vice-President, Publishing Services

Publishing and Editorial for Consumer Dummies

Diane Graves Steele, Vice President and Publisher, Consumer Dummies

Kristin Ferguson-Wagstaffe, Product Development Director, Consumer Dummies

Ensley Eikenburg, Associate Publisher, Travel

Kelly Regan, Editorial Director, Travel

Composition Services

Debbie Stailey, Director of Composition Services

Contents at a Glance

Table of Contents

Introduction

Trading used to be the purview of institutional and corporate entities that had direct access to closed securities trading systems. Recent technical advances have levelled the playing field, making securities trading much more accessible to individuals. After Canada's Bre-X Minerals scandal of 1997 and the general stock market crash of 2000, when many people lost large sums of money because professional advisers or mutual fund managers didn't protect their portfolio principal, investors chose between two options — getting out of the market altogether and seeking safety, or finding out more about how to manage their own portfolios. Many who came back into the market ran from it again in late 2008 when the market saw its worst year since the Great Depression.

The concept of buying and holding forever died after that 2000 stock crash; it saw some revival from 2004 to 2007, but then suffered another death in 2008. Despite Canada's decent recovery in 2009, people are now looking for new ways to invest and trade. Although investors still practise careful portfolio balancing using a buy and hold strategy, they look much more critically at what they are holding and are more likely to change their holdings now than they were before the crash. Others have gotten out of the stock market completely.

Still others have moved on to the world of trading. Many kinds of traders ply their skills in the markets. The ones who like to take on the most risk and want to trade as a full-time business look to day trading. They seldom hold a position in a security overnight. Swing traders hold their positions a bit longer, sometimes for a few weeks or even a few months.

But we're not focusing on the riskier types of trading in this book; instead, we focus on position trading, which involves executing trades in and out of positions and holding positions for a few weeks or months and maybe even a year or more, depending on trends that are evident in the economy, the marketplace, the commodity prices for Canada's natural resources, and ultimately, individual stocks.

About This Book

Many people have misconceptions about trading and its risks. Most people think of the riskiest type of trading — day trading — when they hear the word *trader*. We're definitely not trying to show you how to day trade. We're not going to show you how to trade penny stocks. Instead, we want to introduce you to the world of position trading, which is much safer, less risky, and yet a great way to build a significant portfolio.

Don't get the wrong idea: trading in securities always carries risks. Never trade with money you can't risk losing. That means aggressive trading with your children's Registered Education Savings Plan isn't a good idea. If you want to trade, set aside a portion of your savings that isn't earmarked for any specific use and that you believe you can put at risk without ruining your lifestyle.

Obviously, we plan to show you ways to minimize risk, but we can't promise that you won't take a loss. Even the most experienced traders, the ones who put together the best trading systems, don't have a crystal ball and periodically get hit by a market shock and accompanying loss. By using the basics of fundamental and technical analyses, we show you how to minimize your risk, how to recognize when the market is ripe for a trade, when specific sectors in the market are the right places to be, how to figure out which phases economic and market cycles are in, and how to make the best use of all that knowledge. We guide you through Canada's many ways to invest with before-tax dollars rather than after-tax dollars.

Foolish Assumptions

We've made a number of assumptions about your basic knowledge and stock-trading abilities. We assume you're not completely new to the world of investing in stocks and that you're familiar with the stock market and its basic language. We review many key terms and phrases as we explore the basics of trading.

We also assume you know how to operate a computer and use the Internet. If you don't have high-speed access to the Internet now, be sure you do have it before trying to trade. Many of the resources we recommend in this book are available online, but you'll need high-speed access to be able to work with these valuable tools.

How the Book Is Organized

We've broken this book down into six logical parts. Well, we tried anyway. The first focuses on tools, and then we explore the basics of fundamental analysis right before delving into technical analysis. After getting the basics out of the way, we discuss how you can use your newly discovered tools to develop and begin building your own strategies and trading system. Just in case you want to move on to riskier types of trading, we include some basic information about day trading, swing trading, and trading derivatives and foreign currency. We also include the basics of option trading, which was pioneered in Canada. That said, we highly recommend you seek additional training before trying any of the riskier forms of trading.

Part I: So You Want to Be a Trader: Gathering Your Tools

Trading is a business, and just like any other business, you need to put together a good set of tools to be successful. In Part I, we talk about the basics of trading, introduce the markets and the exchanges, discuss various alternatives for finding a discount broker or investment adviser and setting up your investment account, and describe the minimum computer hardware and software necessities you need to succeed as a trader. We also discuss your Internet needs and point you to some good basic resources on the Internet that can help get you started. All of Canada's tax shelters are featured, namely the RRSP, RRIF, RESP, IPP, and TFSA.

Part II: Reading the Fundamentals: Fundamental Analysis

Many traders don't use fundamental analysis. They believe technical analysis is the only thing you need to understand. We don't agree. You can gather plenty of valuable information about the economy, markets, sectors, and individual stocks that can help you excel as a trader. We start you out with the economy, the basics of the business cycle, sector rotation, and various economic indicators because they can help you make your calls. Next we show you how to delve into financial statements to find the crucial information you need to pick the companies whose stocks you want to trade. Finally, we talk about analysts and what information you can get and use from them and what you shouldn't use. We also explain how you can listen in on analysts' calls to get the most current information about a company and how executives perceive their company numbers.

Part III: Reading the Charts: Technical Analysis

You can't even begin to think about trading if you don't understand technical analysis and how to build and read charts so you can pick entry and exit points when buying and selling stocks. We take you step by step through the process of building a chart, and we describe how to identify trends and distinguish between transitions from one trend to another. In this part, you find out how to recognize bull and bear patterns and how to differentiate between a stock that is range bound and one that is trending. We also introduce you to some of our favourite tools and give you several examples of how to use them.

Part IV: Developing Strategies for When to Buy and Sell Stocks

After finding out how to use the tools of fundamental and technical analyses, you're ready to develop strategies for your own trading. First you need to explore good money discipline to avoid taking major losses and be around to trade for another day. You also need to determine when to stay in a position and when to trade out of it. You certainly want to take your profits at the right time, but you also want to avoid standing idly by as a profit turns into a loss. Next we talk about how you can gather key information through fundamental analysis and then add the results of your technical analysis to build an optimum trading strategy. And we talk about the mechanics of trading before finally exploring how you can build your own trading system.

Part V: Risk-Taker's Paradise

You may want to try the riskier forms of trading, such as swing trading, day trading, or trading in derivatives and foreign currency. We definitely won't be sharing any strategies for actually participating in these types of trading, but we will introduce you to the basics and warn you about what you need to become familiar with before entering these wilder forms of trading. Be careful out there and don't get caught up in any of the many frauds and scams that are common with these types of trading.

Part VI: The Part of Tens

The final part of the book is a hallmark of the *For Dummies* series — the Part of Tens. In it, we highlight ten huge trading mistakes and ways you can avoid them, and we review the top ten basics you'll need to remember for surviving in the world of trading.

Icons Used in This Book

For Dummies books use little pictures, called icons, to flag certain chunks of text. Here's what they actually mean:

Watch for these little flags to get ideas on how to improve your trading skills or where to find other useful resources.

If something is particularly important for you to remember, we mark it with this icon.

The trading world is fraught with dangers and perils. A minor mistake can cost you a bunch of money, so we use this icon to point out particularly perilous areas.

When you see this icon, know that we're discussing higher-end, more technical material for the experienced trader.

Where to Go from Here

You're ready to enter the exciting world of trading. You can start anywhere in the book; each chapter is self-contained. But if you're totally new to trading, starting with Chapter 1 is the best way to understand the basics. If you already know the basics, understand everything about the various markets and exchanges that you care to know, have an adviser picked out, and have all the tools you'll need, you may want to start with fundamental analysis in Part II. Remember, though, to have fun and enjoy your trip through the exciting world of trading.

Part I

So You Want to Be a Trader: Gathering Your Tools

The 5th Wave   By Rich Tennant

I told Julian to take our money to Rappenship's and put it into a good company.

You want to mail your life savings to Procter and Gamble?!

RAPPENSHIP BROKERAGE

Nick's NEWS

WRAP 'N SHIP

In this part . . .

Want to discover how you can be a successful trader and why you should get involved in trading? That's what you get in Part I. You'll explore the nuances of the various markets and trading exchanges on which you place your trades, and find out about the investment advisers and discount brokers and the types of investment dealers and online trading frequently used by traders. In addition, we describe what computer hardware and software and Internet access you'll need, and provide several useful Internet resources to get you started.

Chapter 1

The Ups and Downs of Trading Stocks

Making lots of money is the obvious goal of most people who decide to enter the world of trading. How successful you become as a trader depends on how well you use the tools, gather the needed information, and interpret what you've got. You need to develop the discipline to apply all that you know about trading toward developing a winning trading strategy.

Discovering how to avoid getting caught up in the emotional aspects of trading — the highs of a win and the lows of a loss — is key to developing a profitable trading style. Trading is a business and needs to be approached with the same logic you'd apply in your approach to any other business decision. Setting goals, researching your options, planning and implementing your strategies, and assessing your success are just as important for trading as they are for any other business venture.

In this book we help you traverse these hurdles, and at the same time we introduce you to the world of trading. In this chapter, we give you an overview of trading and an introduction to the tools you need, the research skills you must use, and the basics of developing all this information into a successful trading strategy.

Trading versus Investing

First, we need to discuss how trading differs from investing. Investors buy stocks and hold them for a long time — often too long, riding a stock all the way down and possibly even buying more along the way. Traders, on the other hand, hold stocks for as little as a few minutes or as long as several months, and sometimes possibly even a year or more. The specific amount of time depends on the type of trader you want to become.

Investors want to carefully balance an investment portfolio among growth stocks, value stocks, domestic stocks, and foreign stocks, along with long-, short-, and intermediate-term bonds. A well-balanced Canadian portfolio generally offers the investor a steady return of between 5 percent and 8 percent, depending on the type of investments and amount of risk he or she is willing to take.

An aggressive, well-balanced portfolio with a mix of 80 percent invested in stocks and 20 percent in bonds can average as high as a 12 percent annual return for investors during a 20-year period; in some years the portfolio will be down, and in others it will go through periods of high growth. The opposite, a conservative portfolio with 20 percent invested in stocks and 80 percent in bonds, is likely to provide a yield on the lower end of the spectrum, closer to 5 percent. The volatility and risk associated with the latter portfolio, however, would be considerably less. Investors who have 10 or more years before they need to use their investment money tend to put together more aggressive portfolios. Those who need to live off the money tend to put together less aggressive portfolios that give them regular cash flows, which is what you get from a portfolio invested mostly in bonds.

As a trader, you look for the best position for your money and then set a goal of exceeding what an investor can otherwise expect from an aggressive portfolio. During certain times within the market cycle, your best option may be to sit on the sidelines and not even be active in the market. In this book, we show you how to read the signals to decide when you need to be in the market, and how to find the best sectors in which to play the market and the best stocks within those sectors.

Why Trade?

Improving their potential profit from stock transactions is obviously the key reason why most people decide to trade. People who want to grow their portfolios rather than merely maintain them hope that the way they invest does better than the market averages. Regardless of whether traders invest through mutual funds or stocks, they hope the portfolio of securities they select gives them superior returns — and they're willing to work at it.

People who decide to trade make a conscious decision to take a more active role in increasing their profit potential. Rather than just riding the market up and down, they search for opportunities to find the best times and places to be in the market based on economic conditions and market cycles.

Traders who successfully watched the technical signals before the stock crash of 2000 either shorted stocks or moved into cash positions before stocks tumbled and then carefully jumped back in as they saw opportunities for profits. Some position traders simply stayed on the sidelines, waiting for the right time to jump back in. Even though they were waiting, they also carefully researched their opportunities, selected stocks for their watch lists, and then let technical signals from the charts they kept tell them when to get in or out of a position.

Successful Trading Characteristics

To succeed at trading, you have to be hard on yourself and, more than likely, work against your natural tendencies, fighting the urge to prove yourself right and accepting the fact that you're going to make mistakes. As a trader, you must develop separate strategies for when you want to make a trade to enter a position and for when you want to make a trade and exit that position, all the while not allowing emotional considerations to affect the decisions you make on the basis of the successful trading strategy you've designed.

You want to manage your money, but in doing so you don't have to prove whether your particular buying or selling decision was right or wrong. Setting up stop-loss points for every position you establish and adhering to them is the right course of action, even though you may later have to admit that you were wrong. Your portfolio will survive, and you can always reenter a position whenever trends indicate the time is right again.

You need to make stock trends your master, ignoring any emotional ties that you have to any stocks. Although you may indeed miss the lowest entry price or the highest exit price, you nevertheless will be able to sleep at night, knowing that your money is safe and your trading business is alive and well.

Traders find out how to ride a trend and when to get off the train before it jumps the tracks and heads toward monetary disaster. Enjoy the ride, but know which stop you're getting off at so you don't turn profits into losses.

Tools of the Trade

The first step you need to take in becoming a trader is gathering all the right tools so you can open and operate your business successfully. Your computer needs to meet the hardware requirements and other computer specifics we describe in Chapter 4, including processor speed, memory storage, and screen size. You may even want more than one screen, depending on your trading style. High-speed Internet access is a must; without it, you may as well never open up shop.

We also introduce you to the various types of software in Chapter 4, showing you what can help your trading business ride the wave to success. We evaluate traders' charting favourites, such as MetaStock and TradeStation, along with Internet-based charting and data-feed services. We also talk about the various trading platforms that are available and how to work with investment dealers and online brokers.

After you have all the hardware and software in place, you need to hone your analytical skills. Many traders advocate using only technical analysis, but we show you how using both technical and fundamental analyses can help you excel as a trader.

Taking Time to Trade More Than Just Stocks

The ways traders trade are varied. Some are position traders, while others are swing traders and day traders. Although many of the tools they use are the same or similar, each variety of trader works within differing time frames to reach goals specific to the type of trades they're making.

Position trading

Position traders use technical analysis to find the most promising stock trends and enter and exit positions in the market based on those trends. They can hold positions for just a few days, a few months, or possibly as long as a year or more. Position trading is the type of trading that we discuss the most in this book. After introducing you to the stock markets, the types of advisers and brokers and market makers with whom you'll be dealing, and the tools you need, we discuss the basics of fundamental analysis and technical analysis to help you become a better position trader.

Weathering a bear market

Housing stocks crumbled in the housing crunch. Financials were crushed in the credit crisis. We can't claim any special foresight or knowledge to know when a stock is about to take a big plunge or a company in the United States is going to be taken over by the American government. We don't have a crystal ball.

But we are able to keep most of our money safe from the ravages of a down market. By using strategies that we discuss throughout this book, we can exit positions before giving back most of our accumulated profits — while many others unfortunately do just that.

An impending pullback is not illuminated with flashing beacons. No instant indicator tells that it's time to sell everything. Instead, we close individual positions as each stock's technical conditions deteriorate. The tools we describe in this book enable us to recognize when risk levels have changed, when few stocks are attractive, and when simply leaving most of our trading capital in cash is the best course of action.

We have no idea how long the current credit crunch will affect the market. In fact, it's already gone on longer and been much more brutal than we had guessed. Nevertheless, adhering to the techniques featured in this book has kept us from committing the bulk of our trading capital to failing stocks. We will weather this market with the majority of our trading capital intact and even make a little money by shorting a few stocks or buying some short or double-short exchange-traded funds. Thanks to the tools we show you in this book, we will be ready to trade aggressively when the technical condition of stocks begins improving.

Short-term swing trading

Swing traders work within much shorter time frames than position traders, rarely holding stocks for more than a few days and looking for sharp moves that technical analysis uncovers. Even though we don't show you the specifics of how to become a swing trader, we nevertheless discuss the basics of swing trading and its strategies in Chapter 16. You can also read about the basics of technical analysis and money management strategies, both of which are useful topics to check out if you plan to become a swing trader. However, you definitely need to seek additional training before deciding to pursue this style of trading — reading *Swing Trading For Dummies* by Omar Bassal (Wiley) would be a good start.

Day trading

Day traders never leave their money in stocks overnight. They always cash out. They can trade into and out of a stock position in a matter of hours, minutes, or even seconds. Many outsiders watch day traders in action and describe it as more like playing a video game than trading stocks. We discuss this high-risk type of trading in Chapter 17, but we won't be showing you the specifics of how to do it. If day trading is your goal, this book will take you only part of the way there. You'll discover the basics of technical analysis, but you need to seek out additional training before engaging in this risky trading style — check out *Day Trading For Dummies* by Ann C. Logue (Wiley).

Going Long or Short

Before you start trading, you absolutely have to know what stocks you want to buy and hold for a while — called *going long,* or holding a long stock position. You likewise have to know at what point holding that stock is no longer worthwhile. Similarly, you need to know at what price you want to *enter* or trade into a position and at what price you want to *exit* or trade out of a position. You may be surprised to find out that you can even profit by selling a stock without ever owning it, in a process called *shorting.* We discuss these vital trading strategies in Chapter 13.

You can even make money buying and selling options on stocks to simulate long or short stock positions. Buying an option known as a *call* enables you to simulate a long stock position, in much the same way that buying an option known as a *put* enables you to simulate a short stock position. You make money on a call when the option-related stock rises in price, and you make money on a put when the option-related stock falls in price.

When placing orders for puts and calls you're never guaranteed to make money, even when you're right about the direction a stock will take. The values of options are affected by how volatile stock prices are in relationship to the overall direction (up or down) in which they're headed. We discuss options and how they work in greater detail in Chapter 18.

Managing Your Money

Managing your trades so that you don't lose a bunch of money is critical. Although we can't guarantee that you'll never lose money, we can provide you with useful strategies for minimizing your losses and getting out before your stock portfolio takes a huge hit. The key is knowing when to hold 'em and when to fold 'em, and we cover that in great detail in Chapter 12.

One thing we can't emphasize enough is that you must think of your trading as a business and the stocks you hold as its inventory. You can't allow yourself to fall in love and thereby hang on to a stock out of loyalty. You'll find it especially hard to admit you've made a mistake; nevertheless, you have to bite the bullet and exit the position before you take a huge hit. You'll discover that housecleaning and developing successful strategies for keeping your inventory current are important parts of managing a trading portfolio.

Setting a target price for exiting a position before ever trading into it is the best way to protect your business from major losses. Stick with those predetermined exit prices and you'll avoid a major pitfall that many traders face — holding a position too long and losing everything. You obviously don't want to turn a profit into a loss, so as your position in a stock produces a profit, you can periodically raise your target exit price while continuing to hold the position to ensure you keep most of that profit.

Understanding your risks — market risks, investment risks, and trading risks — helps you to make better trading decisions. We review the different kinds of risks as they relate to specific situations at several points throughout the book.

Understanding Fundamental Analysis

You've probably heard the phrase, "It's the economy, stupid." Well that's true, and we show you how understanding the basics of the business cycle can help you improve your trading successes. In Chapter 5, you find out how to identify periods of economic growth and recession and how these differing periods impact bull and bear stock markets. We also explore sector rotation and how to use it to pick the right sectors for your trading activities.

You can also discover plenty of information about how money supply, inflation rates, deflation, unemployment, and consumer confidence impact the mood of the market and stock prices and how the economy can be driven by how confidently (or not) political and monetary leaders speak out about it. We discuss the roles of the Bank of Canada (BoC) and the American Federal Reserve (Fed) and how when the Governor of the BoC or the Chairman of the Fed speaks, the markets listen.

Understanding how the economy works isn't the only fundamental analysis tool that's important to you. You also need to read financial statements to understand the financial status of the companies you want to buy. We delve into financial statements in Chapter 6.

A company's income statements, on the other hand, give you a look at the results for the most recent period and provide a basis for comparison with prior years and periods. You can use these statements to look at whether revenues are growing, and if they are, by what percentage. You also can see how much profit the company is keeping from the revenue it generates. The cash flow statement shows you how efficiently a company is using its cash and whether it's having problems meeting its current obligations. The balance sheet gives you a snapshot of a company's assets and liabilities and shareholders' equity.

You can use this information to develop your own estimate of a company's growth and profit potential. In Chapter 6, we show you how to do a few basic ratio calculations that you can use to compare similar stocks and then choose the one with the best potential.

Analysts use this information to project a company's financial growth and profits. Never depend entirely on what analysts say, but do your own research and collect the opinions of numerous analysts. One of the best ways to find out what analysts are saying and what aspects of the financial statements may raise a red flag is by looking at the analyst call. In Chapter 7, we explain how you can listen in on some of these calls and understand the unique language used in them to make better choices when selecting stocks. We also discuss the pros and cons of using analyst reports.

Getting a Grip on Technical Analysis

You use fundamental analysis to determine what part of the business cycle the economy is in and what industries offer the best growth potential. Then you use that information to select the best target companies and identify prices at which you'd want to buy their stocks.

After choosing your targets, you then use technical analysis to follow trends in the prices of the target stocks, so you can find the right time to get in and ultimately to get out of a stock position. These targets become part of your stock-watch list. After you've established that list, you then use the tools of technical analysis to make your trades.

In Chapter 8, we introduce you to the basics of technical analysis, how it works, and how it needs to be used. Although some people think of technical analysis as no more than fortune-telling, others believe it yields significant information that can help you make successful trades. We obviously believe that technical analysis provides you with extensive tools for your trading success, and we show you how to use those tools to be profitable.

Your first step in technical analysis is finding out how to create a chart. We focus on the most popular type — bar charting. In Chapter 9, you discover the art of deciphering simple visual stock patterns and how to distinguish between trends and trading ranges, all so you're able to spot when a stock moves from a trading range into either an upward or downward trend and know when you need to act.

In Chapter 10, we show you how to use your newfound skill of identifying trends to locate areas of support and resistance within a trend that ultimately help you find the right times to make your move. You find out how to read the patterns in the charts to identify trading signals and what to do when you've acted on a failed trading signal.

Chapter 11 fills you in on moving averages and how to use them to identify trends. You also find out about oscillators and other indicators that traders use for recognizing trading signals. As a rookie trader, you'll probably find that your greatest risk is paralysis by analysis — you may find you're having so much fun reading the charts or are just so confused about which chart has the right signal that you feel paralyzed by the variety of choices. We show you how to create and use a tiny subset of tools available in today's charting software packages to simplify your life and make your choices easier. You'll likewise discover how to use such odd-sounding but critical tools as an MACD indicator or a stochastic oscillator, and we help you take advantage of the powerful concept of relative strength.

Putting Trading Strategy into Practice

After you get used to using the tools, it's time to put your new skills into practice making money. In Chapter 13, we show you how to put together your newfound affinities for fundamental analysis and technical analysis to develop and build your trading strategy. Using fundamental analysis, you can

- ✔ Determine which part of the economic cycle is driving the market.
- ✔ Determine which sector makes the most sense for stock trading.
- ✔ Figure out which sectors are in the best positions to go up.
- ✔ Find out which stocks are leading in the ascending sectors.
- ✔ Evaluate where the BoC and the Fed stand on the economy and which of their potential moves can impact the strength of the market.
- ✔ Evaluate and hopefully anticipate potential shocks to the market. Although doing so may seem like gazing into a crystal ball, you really can pick up some signs by checking out the key economic indicators. We show you what they are.

After you complete your fundamental analysis, we show you how to use your new technical analysis skills successfully to

- ✔ Trade within the overall technical conditions.
- ✔ Confirm which economic cycle a market is in by using index charts.
- ✔ Determine whether an ascending sector is stuck in a range or ready to enter a new upward trend.
- ✔ Determine whether leading stocks are stuck in ranges or ready to break out in upward trends.

Finally, we show you how to use your newfound skills to manage risk, set up a stop-loss position, and choose your time frame for trading.

After honing your skills, you're ready to start trading. So in Chapter 14 we focus on the actual mechanics of trading by

- ✒ Discussing how to enter or trade into a position
- ✒ Explaining bid and ask prices
- ✒ Discussing the risks of market orders
- ✒ Explaining how to use limit and stop orders

We also explore how to exit or trade out of a position and still stay unattached emotionally, when to take your profits, and how to minimize your losses, in addition to discussing potential tax hits and how to minimize them.

Now that you know how to research the fundamentals, effectively use the technical tools, and mechanically carry out a trade, the next step is developing and managing your own trading system. We explore the basic steps to developing the system, which include

1. Designing and keeping a trading log.

2. Identifying reliable trading patterns.

3. Developing an exit strategy.

4. Determining whether you'll use discretionary trading methods or mechanical trading. We explore the pros and cons of each.

5. Deciding whether to develop your own trading system or buy one of the ones available off the shelf.

6. Testing your trading systems and understanding their limitations before making a major financial commitment to your new system.

We also discuss assessing your results and fixing any problems.

After you've designed, built, and tested your system, you're ready to jump in with both feet. The key to getting started: Make sure you begin with a small sum of money, examining your system and then increasing your trading activity as you gain experience and develop confidence with the system that you develop.

Trading at Higher Risk

Some traders decide they want to take on a greater level of risk by practising methods of swing trading or day trading or by delving into the areas of trading derivatives or foreign currency. Although all of these alternatives are valid trading options, we steer clear of explaining even the basics of how to use these high-risk trading alternatives; instead, we provide you with a general understanding of the ways these trading alternatives work and the risks that are unique to each of them.

If you decide, however, that you want to take on these additional risks, don't depend on the information in this book to get started. Use the general information we offer here to determine what additional training you need to feel confident before moving into these trading arenas.

Remember: Have Fun!

Although you are without question considering the work of a trader for the money you can make, you need to enjoy the game of trading. If you find you're having trouble sleeping at night because of the risks you're taking, then trading may not be worth all the heartache. You may need to put off your decision to enter the world of trading until you're more comfortable with the risks or until you've designed a system that better accommodates your risk tolerance.

You may find that you need to take a slower approach by putting less money into your trades. You don't need to make huge profits with your early trades. Just trading into and out of a position without losing any money may be a good goal for you when you're just starting out. If you notice your position turning toward the losing side, knowing you can trade your way out of it before you take a big loss may help you build greater confidence in your abilities.

Remember, making a losing trade doesn't mean that you're a loser. Even the most experienced traders must at times face losses. The key to successful trading is knowing when to get out before your portfolio takes a serious hit. On the other side of that coin, you also need to know how to get out when you're in a winning or profitable position. When you're trying to ride a trend all the way to the top, it sometimes starts bottoming out so fast that you lose some or possibly even all of your profits, causing you to end up in a losing position.

Trading is a skill that takes a long time to develop and is perfected only after you make mistakes and celebrate successes. Enjoy the rollercoaster ride!

Chapter 2

Exploring the Markets and the Stock Exchanges

*B*illions of shares trade in Canada and the United States every day, and each trader is looking to get his or her small piece of that action. Before moving into the specifics of how to trade, we first want to introduce you not only to the world of stock trading, but also to trading in other key markets — futures, options, and bonds. In this chapter, we also explain differences and similarities among key stock exchanges and how those factors impact your trading options. After providing you with a good overview of the markets, we delve into the different types of orders you can place with each of the key exchanges.

Introducing the Broad Markets

You may think the foundation of the Canadian economy resides at the Royal Canadian Mint in Winnipeg, where the country manufactures billions of loonies and toonies, or that the foundation of the United States economy resides inside Fort Knox where the country holds its billions of dollars in gold. Nope. The continent's true economic centres are Bay Street and Wall Street, where billions of dollars change hands each and every day, thousands of companies are traded, and millions of people's lives are affected.

Stocks are not the only things sold in the broad financial markets. Every day, futures, options, and bonds also are traded. Although we focus on stock exchanges in this chapter, we first need to briefly explain each type of market.

Stock markets

The stocks of almost every major Canadian and U.S. corporation and many major foreign corporations are traded on stock exchanges in Canada and the United States each day, and none of the money involved in these trades goes directly into the companies being traded. Today numerous local and international stock exchanges trade stocks in publicly held corporations; moreover, the only major corporations not traded are those held privately — usually by families or original founding partners that choose not to sell shares on the public market. Canada's top private companies include Jimmy Pattison Industries, A&W Food Services, and Custom House Global Foreign Exchange. *Forbes* magazine's top privately held American corporations are Cargill, Koch Industries, PricewaterhouseCoopers, and Mars. Many of the large private corporations that are not traded publicly do have provisions for employee ownership of stock and must report earnings to the American SEC, so they straddle the line of public versus private corporations.

A *share* is actually a portion of ownership in a given company. Few shareholders own large enough stakes in a company to play a major decision-making role. Instead, shareholders purchase stocks, hoping that their investments rise in price, so that those stocks can be sold at a profit some time in the future.

For the majority of this chapter, we focus on the four top stock exchanges in North America:

- The Toronto Stock Exchange (TSX),
- The New York Stock Exchange (NYSE),
- Nasdaq (the National Association of Securities Dealers Automated Quotation system), and
- The American Stock Exchange (Amex).

We also introduce you to the evolving world of electronic communication networks (ECNs) on which you can trade stocks directly, thus bypassing brokers.

Futures markets

Futures trading actually started in Japan in the 18th century to trade rice and silk. This trading instrument was first used in North America in the 1850s for trading grains and other agricultural entities. Basically, futures trading means establishing a financial contract in which you try to predict the future value of a commodity that must be delivered at a specific time in the future. (Yup, a working crystal ball would be very useful here.) This type of trading is done on a commodities exchange. The largest such exchange in North America today is the Chicago Mercantile Exchange. Commodities include any product that can be bought and sold. Oil, cotton, and minerals are just a few of the products sold on a commodities exchange.

Futures contracts must have a seller (usually the person producing the commodity — a farmer or oil refinery, for example) and a buyer (usually a company that actually uses the commodity). You also can speculate on either side of the contract, basically meaning:

✔ When you buy a futures contract, you're agreeing to buy a commodity that is not yet ready for sale or hasn't yet been produced at a set price at a specific time in the future.

✔ When you sell a futures contract, you're agreeing to provide a commodity that is not yet ready for sale or hasn't yet been produced at a set price at a specific time in the future.

The futures contract states the price at which you agree to pay for or sell a certain amount of this future product when it's delivered at a specific future date. Although most futures contracts are based on a physical commodity, the highest-volume futures contracts are based on the future value of stock indexes and other financially related futures.

Unless you're a commercial consumer who plans to use the commodity, you won't actually take delivery of or provide the commodity for which you're trading a futures contract. You'll more than likely sell the futures contract you bought before you actually have to accept the commodity from a commercial customer. Futures contracts are used as financial instruments by producers, consumers, and speculators. We cover those players and futures contracts in much greater depth in Chapter 18.

Bond markets

Bonds are actually loan instruments. Companies sell bonds to borrow cash. If you buy a bond, you're essentially holding a company's debt or the debt of a government entity. The company or government that issues the bond agrees to pay you a certain amount of interest for a specific period of time in exchange for the use of your money. The big difference between stocks and bonds is that bonds are *debt obligations* and stocks are *equity*. Shareholders actually own a share of the corporation. Bondholders lend money to the company with no right of ownership. Bonds, however, are considered safer, because if a company files bankruptcy, bondholders are paid before shareholders. Bonds are a safety net and not actually a part of the trading world for individual position traders, swing traders, and day traders. While a greater dollar volume of bonds is traded each day, the primary traders for this venue are large institutional traders. Many individuals will use short-term bonds and treasury bills as a safe place to park their cash while waiting to enter a trading position. We want to mention them here but don't discuss them further in this book.

Options markets

An *option* is a contract that gives the buyer the right, but not the obligation, either to buy or to sell the underlying asset upon which the option is based at a specified price on or before a specified date. Sometime before the option period expires, a purchaser of an option must decide whether to exercise the option and buy (or sell) the asset (most commonly stocks) at the target price. Options also are called *derivatives*. We talk more about this investment alternative in Chapter 18.

Reviewing Stock Exchanges

Most of this book covers stock trading, so we obviously concentrate on how the key exchanges — TSX, NYSE, Nasdaq, and Amex — operate and how these operations impact your trading activity.

Toronto Stock Exchange (TSX) and other Canadian exchanges

Most securities in Canada trade on the Toronto Stock Exchange (TSX), which was established in 1852. The TSX is owned by the TMX Group, which also operates the TSX Venture Exchange for small new companies as well as the Montreal Exchange for derivatives trading. Fixed-income bonds, natural gas, crude oil, and electricity contracts also trade through the TMX Group. TSX is the eighth largest in the world by market capitalization.

A handful of electronic exchanges have taken some blue-chip stock trading business from the TSX because of improved technology and lower fees. Rivals include Alpha and Chi-X Canada, which operate as alternate trading systems (ATS). Pure trading is another ATS that is connected to the Canadian National Stock Exchange (CNSX), where shares of emerging companies are traded.

New York Stock Exchange (NYSE)

The U.S. stock market dates back to May 17, 1792, when 24 brokers signed an agreement under a buttonwood tree at what today is 58 Wall Street. The 24 brokers specifically agreed to sell shares of companies among themselves, charging a commission or fee to buy and sell shares for others who wanted to invest in a company. Yup, the first American stockbrokers were born that day.

A formalized exchange didn't come into existence until March 8, 1817, when the brokers adopted a formal constitution and named their new entity the New York Stock & Exchange Board. Brokers actually worked outdoors until 1860, when operations finally were moved inside. The first stock ticker was introduced in 1867, but it wasn't until 1869 that the NYSE started requiring the registration of securities for companies that wanted to have their stock traded on the exchange. Registration began as a means of preventing the over-issuance (selling too many shares) of a company's stock.

From these meagre beginnings, the NYSE built itself into the largest stock exchange in the world with many of the largest companies listed on the exchange. Trading occurs on the floor of the exchange, with specialists and floor traders running the show. Today these specialists and floor traders work electronically, which first became possible when the exchange introduced electronic capabilities for trading in 2004. For traders, the new electronic trading capabilities are a more popular tool than working with specialists and floor traders. Electronic trading capabilities were enhanced when the NYSE merged with Archipelago Holdings in 2006. The exchange expanded its global trading capabilities after a merger with Euronext in 2007, which made trading in European stocks much easier. Some European companies, such as German insurer Allianz, have delisted from the NYSE due to the American regulatory burden of Sarbanes-Oxley legislation. The federal law of 2002 seeks to promote corporate accountability.

You may not realize just how much the concept of supply and demand influences the trading price of a stock. Price swings of a stock frequently are caused by shifts in the supply of shares available for sale and the demand created by the number of buyers wanting to purchase available shares.

The specialist

Specialists — whose title soon may change to *designated market makers* — buffer dramatic swings when news about a company breaks. If news that has a major impact on a stock's price breaks, specialists buy shares or sell the ones they hold in a company to make the trend toward a higher or lower stock price more orderly. For example, if good news breaks, creating more demand for the stock and overwhelming existing supply, the specialist becomes a seller of the stock to minimize the impact of a major price increase by increasing supply. The same is true when bad news strikes, creating a situation in which having more sellers than buyers drives the stock price down. In that situation, the specialist becomes a buyer of the stock, easing the impact of the drop in price.

The floor trader

The guys you see on the floor of the stock exchange, waving their hands wildly to make trades, are the *floor traders*. They're actually members of the NYSE who trade exclusively for their own accounts. Floor traders also can act as a floor broker for others and sell their services.

The specialist's book

You may wonder how a specialist keeps track of all this information. That one's easy: The specialist records all trades and quotation changes in the specialist's order book. Any questions that arise about trading activities can be researched using this book.

Open outcry

The NYSE still uses what's becoming an outdated method of trading called *open outcry*, in which stocks are sold like a public auction with verbal bids and offers shouted at the trading post. These trading posts are centred on the specialist's location for particular stocks. Other exchanges exclusively use computer-based network systems for trading.

The NYSE is the last big stock exchange to use open outcry, but even here it's taking a backseat to automated execution. Only a tiny fraction of trades are handled through open outcry. Except for a small group of very high-priced stocks, almost everything is handled immediately by electronic execution.

NYSE Hybrid Market

The New York Stock Exchange uses the Hybrid Market program to integrate the best aspects of the open outcry or auction market with electronic trading. Most NYSE trades are now handled electronically, but brokers can still choose to route customer orders to the floor for open-outcry trading.

Nasdaq

Nasdaq, which used to stand for National Association of Securities Dealers Automated Quotations but now is just like any other proper name, is the fastest-growing stock market today. The market was formed after an SEC study in the early 1960s concluded that the sale of over-the-counter (OTC) securities — in other words, securities that aren't traded on the existing stock exchanges — was fragmented and obscure. The report called for the automation of the OTC market and gave the responsibility for implementing that system to the National Association of Securities Dealers (NASD).

The NASD began construction of the Nasdaq system in 1968, and its first trades were made beginning February 8, 1971, when Nasdaq became the world's first electronic stock market. Nasdaq continues to be the world leader in volume trading per hour.

Market makers

Unlike the specialist structure of the NYSE, in which one specialist represents a particular stock, Nasdaq market makers compete with each other to buy and sell the stocks they choose to represent. More than 500 member firms act as market makers for Nasdaq. All market makers are members of the NASD. Each uses its own capital, research, and system resources to represent a stock and compete with other market makers.

Market makers compete for customers' orders by displaying buy and sell quotations on an electronic exchange for a guaranteed number of shares at a specific price. After market makers receive orders, they immediately purchase or sell stock from their own inventories or seek out the other side of the trades so they can be executed, usually in a matter of seconds. The four types of market makers are

- ✔ **Retail market makers:** Serve institutional and individual investors through brokerage networks that provide a continuous flow of orders and sales opportunities.

- ✔ **Wholesale market makers:** Serve primarily institutional clients and other brokers or dealers who aren't registered market makers in a particular company's stock but who need to execute orders for their customers.

- ✔ **Institutional market makers:** Execute large block orders for institutional investors, such as pension funds, mutual funds, insurance companies, and asset management companies.

- ✔ **Regional market makers:** Serve companies and individuals of a particular region. By focusing regionally, these market makers offer their customers more extensive coverage of the stocks and investors in a particular area of the country.

Nasdaq continues to be the leader in electronic trading. Its system, called the Nasdaq Crossing Network, enables fully anonymous trade execution to minimize the market impact of trading.

Over-the-counter and bulletin-board stocks

Stocks that do not meet the minimum requirements to be listed on Nasdaq are traded as *over-the-counter* or *bulletin-board* stocks (OTCBB). The OTCBB is a regulated quotation service that displays real-time quotes, last-sale prices, and volume information for the stocks traded OTCBB. These stocks generally don't meet the listing qualifications for Nasdaq or other national securities exchanges, and fewer than two (and sometimes zero) market makers trade in these stocks, making buying and selling them more difficult.

Over-the-counter stocks are also traded on what is quaintly called the Pink Sheets — harkening back to a time when stock quotes were printed on pink coloured paper. Effectively little or no regulatory power exists over companies whose shares trade on the OTCBB or the Pink Sheets. Sadly, this is where many fraudulent penny stocks and their promoters have migrated from what used to be the Vancouver Stock Exchange, complete with its "penny dreadfuls." Five words of advice: Buyers beware; sellers be quick.

Listing requirements

Nasdaq has the easiest minimum listing requirements of all the broad-market exchanges, followed by the NYSE Alternext US (formerly Amex). The New York Stock Exchange (NYSE) has the toughest requirements to meet for companies to be listed. In addition to listing requirements, companies on the exchanges must conform to certain rules, including publishing quarterly reports, soliciting proxies, and publicly announcing developments that may affect the value of the securities.

Amex

When the NYSE moved indoors, some stocks still weren't good enough to be sold on the exchange. Those stocks were called *curb traders* and ultimately made up what became known as the American Stock Exchange (Amex), which moved indoors in 1921. Amex lists stocks that are smaller in size than those on the NYSE yet still have a national following. Many firms that first list on Amex work to meet the listing requirements of the NYSE and then switch over.

The Amex trading system was integrated into the NYSE trading system after the merger with the NYSE was completed in 2008. It is now called the NYSE Alternext US, and trades small-company stocks.

Electronic communications networks (ECNs)

Many traders look for ways to get around dealing with a traditional broker. Instead they access trades using a *direct-access broker*. We talk more about the differences in Chapter 3. A new system of electronic trading that is developing is called the *electronic communications network* (ECN).

ECNs enable buyers and sellers to meet electronically to execute trades. The trades are entered into the ECN systems by market makers at one of the exchanges or by an OTC market maker. Transactions are completed without a broker-dealer, saving users the cost of commissions normally charged for more traditional forms of trading.

Subscribers to ECNs include retail investors, institutional investors, market makers, and broker-dealers. ECNs are accessed through a custom terminal or by direct Internet connection. Orders are posted by the ECN for subscribers to view. The ECN then matches orders for execution. In most cases, buyers and sellers maintain their anonymity and do not list identifiable information in their buy or sell orders.

In the last few years ECNs have gone through consolidation, and only two independent ECNs are left. The two independent ECNs, Nomura's Instinet and Bloomberg Tradebook, primarily service the institutional marketplace. Archipelago now operates under the HYSE umbrella as HYSE Arca Options.

Understanding Order Types

Buying a stock can be as easy as calling a broker and saying you want to buy such and such a stock — but you can place an order in a number of other ways that give you better protections. Most orders are placed as day orders, but you can choose to place them as good 'til cancelled orders. The four basic types of orders you can place are market orders, limit orders, stop orders, and stop-limit orders.

Understanding the language and using it to protect your assets and the way you trade are critical to your success as a trader. The next few sections explain the nuances of placing orders so you don't make a potentially costly mistake by placing a market order when you intended to place a limit order. Putting a stop-limit order in place may sound like the safest way to go; however, doing so may not help you in a rapidly changing market.

Market order

When you place a *market order,* you're essentially telling advisers to buy or sell a stock at the current market price. A market order is the way your adviser normally places an order unless you give him or her different instructions. The advantage of a market order is that you're almost always guaranteed that your order is executed as long as willing buyers and sellers are in the marketplace. Generally speaking, buy orders are filled at the ask price and sell orders are filled at the bid price. If, however, you're working with a dealer who has a smart-order routing system, which looks for the best bid/ask prices, you sometimes can get a better price on the Nasdaq or NYSE Alternext US exchanges. In most investment dealers, market orders are the cheapest to place with the lowest commission level.

The disadvantage of a market order is that you're stuck paying the price when the order is executed — possibly not at the price you expected when you placed the order. Investment dealers and real-time quote services quote you prices, but because the markets move fast, with deals taking place in seconds, you'll probably find that the price you're quoted rarely is the same as the execution price. Whenever you place a market order, especially if you're seeking a large number of shares, the probability is even greater that you'll receive different prices for parts of the order — 100 shares at $25 and 100 shares at $25.05, for example.

Limit order

If you want to avoid buying or selling stock at a price higher or lower than you intend, you must place a *limit order* instead of a market order. When placing a limit order, you specify the price at which you'll buy or sell. You can place either a buy limit order or a sell limit order. Buy limit orders can be executed only when a seller is willing to sell the stock you're buying at the limit price or lower. A sell limit order can be executed only when a buyer is willing to pay your limit price or higher. In other words, you set the parameters for the price you'll accept. You can't do that with a market order.

The risk you take when placing a limit order is that the order may never be filled. For example, a hot stock piques your interest when it's selling for $10, so you decide to place a limit order to buy the stock at $10.50. By the time you call your broker or input the order into your trading system, the price already has moved above $10.50 and never drops back to that level; thus, your order won't be filled. On the good side, if the stock is so hot that its price skyrockets to $75, you also won't be stuck as the owner of the stock after purchasing near the $75 high. That high will likely be a temporary top that quickly drops back to reality, forcing you to sell the stock at a significant loss at some point in the future.

Most firms charge more for executing a limit order than they do for a market order. Be sure you understand the fee and commission structures if you intend to use limit orders.

Stop order

You may also consider placing your order as a *stop order,* which means that whenever the stock reaches a price that you specify, it automatically becomes a market order. Investors who buy using a stop order usually do so to limit potential losses or protect a profit. Buy stop orders are always entered at a stop price that is above the current market price.

When placing a sell stop order, you do so to avoid further losses or to protect a profit that exists in case the stock continues on a downward trend. The stop price is always placed below the current market price. For example, when you have a stock that you bought for $10 that now is selling for $25, you can decide to protect most of that profit by placing a sell stop order that specifies that stock be sold when the market price falls to $20, thus cementing a $10 gain.

You don't have to watch the stock market every second; instead, when the market price drops to $20, your stop order automatically switches to a market order and is executed.

The big disadvantage of a stop order is that if for some reason the stock market gets a shock during the news day that affects all stocks, it can temporarily send prices lower, activating your stop price. If it turns out that the downturn is actually merely a short-term fluctuation and not an indication that the stock you hold is a bad choice or that you risk losing your profit, your stock may sell before you ever have time to react.

The bottom can fall out of your stock's pricing. After your stop price is reached, a stop order automatically becomes a market order and the price that you actually receive can differ greatly from your stop price, especially in a rapidly fluctuating market. You can avoid this problem by placing a stop-limit order, which we discuss in the next section.

Stop orders are not officially supported on Nasdaq. However, most dealers offer a service to simulate a stop order. If you want to enter a stop order for a Nasdaq stock, your adviser must watch the market and enter the market or limit order you designate as a stop when the stock reaches your specified sale price. Some investment dealers won't accept a stop order on some securities and almost never accept a stop order for OTC stocks. If you intend to use stop orders, make sure that you

- ✔ Check with the dealers you're planning to use to ensure they accept stop orders.
- ✔ Find out what your dealers charge for stop orders.
- ✔ Review how your dealers' stop orders work, so you don't run into surprises.

After all, you don't want to execute a stop order and end up selling a stock that you didn't intend to sell or at a price you find unacceptable.

Stop-limit order

You can protect yourself from any buying or selling surprises by placing a *stop-limit order*. This type of order combines the features of both a stop order and a limit order. When your stop price is reached, the stop order becomes a limit order rather than a market order.

A stop-limit order gives you the most control over the price at which you will trade your stock. You can avoid a purchase or sale of your stock at a price that differs significantly from what you intend. But you do risk the possibility that the stop-limit order may never be executed, which can happen in fast-moving markets where prices fluctuate wildly.

For example, you may find that deploying stop-limit orders is particularly dangerous to your portfolio, especially when bad news breaks about a stock you're holding and its price drops rapidly. Although you have a stop-limit order in place, and the stop price is met, the movement in the market may happen so rapidly that the price limit you set can be missed. In this case, the limit side of the order actually prevents the sale of the stock and you risk riding it all the way down until you change your order. For example, say you purchased a stock at $8 near its peak. On the day the company's CEO and CFO were fired, the stock dropped to $4.05. You may have had a stop-limit order in place to sell at $5, but on the day of the firing, the price dropped so rapidly after the company announced the firing that your stop-limit order could not be filled at your limit price.

Stop-limit orders, like stop orders, are more commonly used when trading on an exchange than in an OTC market. Investment dealers likewise can limit the securities on which stop-limit orders can be placed. If you want to use stop-limit orders, be sure to review the rules with your broker before trying to execute them.

Good 'til cancelled orders

You can avoid having to replace an order time and again by using a good 'til cancelled (GTC) order. GTC orders are placed at a limit price and last until the order actually is executed or you decide to cancel it. A GTC order won't be executed until the limit price is reached, regardless of how many days or weeks it takes.

You can choose to use this type of order whenever you want to set a limit price that differs significantly from the current market price. Many brokerage firms limit how much time a GTC can remain in place, such as 90 days, and most of them charge more for executing this type of order.

Other order types

Less commonly used order methods include contingent, all-or-none, and fill-or-kill orders. *Contingent orders* are placed on the contingency that another one of your stock holdings is sold before the buy order is placed. An *all-or-none order* specifies that all the shares be bought according to the terms indicated or none of the stock should be purchased. A *fill-or-kill order* must be filled immediately upon placement or killed.

Chapter 3

Going for Broke(r): Discovering Your Investment Options

As an individual, you can't trade stocks — or bonds, or options, or futures — unless you have an investment adviser or a discount broker. That doesn't mean, however, that you have to work with a human being to trade stocks. Online or discount brokers and direct-access brokers enable you to make trades electronically, so you never have to speak with a human being unless you're having a technical problem.

The differences are based on prices, services, and special capabilities. High-volume swing traders and day traders typically require the services of a direct-access broker, while position traders can and do trade successfully with more traditional discount, online, and full-service investment advisers. In this chapter, we help you understand the options that are available, the types of accounts you can establish, and the basic trading rules you must follow.

Why You Need a Discount Broker or Investment Adviser

Unless you plan to get your designation as a Registered Representative through your provincial securities commission and set up shop yourself (which is hard — and expensive — to do), you need to work with an investment adviser or a discount broker to be able to buy and sell stocks. How you choose is based on the level of individual services you want. The more services you want, the more you pay for your ability to trade. We cover the many levels of brokers and investment advisers in greater detail when we talk about licensing in Chapter 20.

On one end of the spectrum is the full-service adviser, who does a lot of hand-holding and offers stock research and advice and other human-based services. When using a full-service adviser, you pay a negotiated commission for each stock trade. In the middle are online discount brokers, who offer fewer services but charge less per trade. On the opposite end are direct-access brokers, who offer few human-based services and instead provide extensive trading platforms so you can trade electronically and access the stock exchange systems directly on a real-time basis.

Exploring Types of Brokers and Investment Services

Before you can pick the type of professional that best fulfills your needs, you have to understand the kinds of services that each provides. After you have acquired an understanding of your options and have selected the types of services you want, carefully research each broker or adviser that matches your needs. Within each classification are good and bad professionals. We give you the tools for researching investment firms in the sections that follow.

Just a word or two on the titles we use for the professionals who are there to help you in your trading. In the bad ol' days there were stockbrokers, who worked with fixed commissions. Other titles alongside stockbrokers were investment executives, account managers, financial planners, money managers, account executives, and investment advisers. The formal title of those licensed through their provincial governments to assist with your trading was Registered Representative, although very few stockbrokers ever put that name on their business card.

Then the Internet arrived, thank goodness, and commissions virtually disappeared thanks to the arrival of online or discount brokers. Throughout the _For Canadians For Dummies_ financial books we try to cut through the confusion of all these titles for professionals who help with your trading — we use two titles: investment advisers and discount brokers. Of course this is a generalization, and of course some overlap exists between the two areas of investment practice.

We try to standardize the names for the companies that employ those two types of professionals into the two camps of investment dealers and online brokers, rather than referring to all of them as brokerage houses.

Full-service investment advisers

If you want someone to assist you with making and implementing buying decisions, check out the full-service advisers. They offer extensive research and other services. Usually, they call you with trading ideas — all you need to do is say yes or no. You pay a negotiated commission percentage based on dollar volume, or you pay a monthly fee so you can trade at will. You can invest in treasury bills, exchange-traded funds, stocks, futures, options, bonds, mutual funds, money market funds, and variable annuities. You can work with a full-service adviser by telephone, mail, fax, or Internet. Most have Web sites you can access for information, and many allow you to enter your own trades.

All investment advisers offer financial planning advice so that more of your trading profits go into your pocket (rather than the tax man's pocket). Investment advisers are happy to undertake a review of your estate planning, and can give advice on how to enhance your credit rating. Most investment advisers are social creatures who like to meet face to face. Some traders enjoy this personal interaction, others are put off. Take your pick.

To illustrate, the following mini table shows the transaction fee schedule for one of the better-known full-service investment advisers (others can be as much as twice as high):

Transaction Size	Commission Rate
$0–$2,499	$40 plus 1.7% of principal
$2,500–$6,249	$65 plus 0.66% of principal
$6,250–$19,999	$85 plus 0.34% of principal
$20,000–$49,999	$115 plus 0.33% of principal
$50,000–$499,999	$170 plus 0.11% of principal
$500,000+	$270 plus 0.09% of principal

Alternatively, some full-service advisers do permit you to make all the trades you want per year for a fee of 0.30 percent to 2.5 percent of the total assets in your account. Using language common to traders, that's 30 to 250 basis points. You have to have more than $1 million in an account to get the lowest fee. Traders with less than $100,000 pay closer to the 2.5 percent of assets to access the unlimited trading features.

Just because you choose to use a full-service adviser doesn't mean you can simply sit back and watch your money grow after placing it into an account. Advisers make money on commissions for trading stocks. If they have no transactions during a given month, they don't get paid. Unscrupulous advisers recommend trades to their customers to generate new commissions even when those decisions are not necessarily the best investment advice for their clients.

The Ontario Securities Commission (OSC) has led the crusade across the country in resolving the conflicts of interest between the work done by research analysts and their investment banking partners. See Chapter 7 for an explanation of the research disclosures imposed in Canada today.

In the United States, even the research arms of many American full-service brokerage houses have come under scrutiny from the U.S. Securities and Exchange Commission (SEC) in the past few years, primarily because their analysts didn't accurately reflect the values of stocks in companies that used the firms' investment-banking capabilities. Analysts tend to see their firms' clients through rose-coloured glasses when providing research reports, especially when their firms make a lot of money by providing investment-banking services to those companies.

Just because you choose to work through a full-service adviser doesn't mean you can sidestep doing your own research. You always need to perform due diligence, independently researching your stock purchases. Although you certainly can use the research arm of your investment firm, it shouldn't be your sole source of research on any stock you're thinking about buying or that you already hold.

If you're planning to be a trader, do your own research and implement your own trading strategies. Why pay for the services of a full-service adviser? We really don't recommend that you spend your money on the additional costs of maintaining a full-service investment account or paying the high transaction fees and commissions after you have the tools and the confidence to go it alone. If you're lucky enough to find a full-service investment adviser who will offer you discounts on your trading commissions, then you have the best of both worlds. Well done!

Discount brokers

Many discount brokers offer the same services as full-service investment advisers, including research. The big exception is that you won't get individual attention or unsolicited advice on what to buy or sell. Some discount brokers send out monthly newsletters with stock recommendations; most don't trade futures or sell variable annuities. You can access a discount broker by telephone, mail, fax, or using an Internet connection. To get the lowest fees, you need to do your own trades by accessing the broker's Web site.

The big difference to you, as an individual trader, is that you can save a lot of money on trading costs, provided you know what you're doing and you understand the language of stock trading. Transaction fees for online trades can range from as low as $5 up to about $30 with a discount broker. If you want special services requiring a broker's assistance, you can work with a human being. Depending on the discount broker and the level of service required, fees can range from $25 to $50 per trade. Some discount brokers provide broker-assisted trades using a commission rate schedule similar to the ones offered by full-service advisers, but for lower fees per trade. If you get involved in more complicated trading transactions that require human assistance, costs can rise significantly. Whenever you're planning to use a broker's assistance, be sure you understand any additional costs that may be charged to your account for that assistance.

Direct-access brokers

If you want to bypass the traditional brokers and trade directly through an exchange or market maker, you need to open your account with a direct-access broker so you can use one or more of the electronic communications networks (ECNs) to make your trades. Traders usually download software onto their PCs so they can access the ECN directly using their Internet connection.

Traders using direct-access brokers typically get real-time Nasdaq Level I quotes, which show the latest bid and ask prices, quote size, the last trade, and volume.

Direct-access brokers also offer Nasdaq Level II. Nasdaq fees are higher for Level II, and the brokerage may also charge a fee for this type of access. In addition to what you see in a Level I quote, you also find the number of market makers participating in the market for any one stock.

A Nasdaq Level II quote screen shows the best bid price and the best ask price for specific stocks from participating market makers. All the bid and ask prices are ranked from best to worst. Some direct-access brokers combine Nasdaq Level II information and ECN book data to show the complete market depth for a specific stock. The ECN book is not a printed book like you would expect to find on a bookstore shelf. It's a compilation of all the trades and the bid and ask quotes available on all the electronic networks. We show you some examples of Level I and Level II quote screens in Chapter 14.

Traders can review the quotes and select which market maker or ECN to use for each transaction. Most full-service and discount brokers make that choice for you when you're working with them. A few discount brokers are providing access to ECNs.

When working with direct-access brokers, one key difference is that the software you use may reside on your own computer and not on your broker's server, which greatly accelerates the speed at which you can trade. Again, some discount brokers provide software to enable you to receive direct raw data on your home computer, but their software is not as sophisticated as what direct-access brokers have to offer. We cover software issues in detail in Chapter 4.

We often talk about how you can miss trading at the prices you want, especially in fast-moving markets. Well, having direct access doesn't guarantee you won't miss a price, but your chances of catching those prices are better, because you won't have to wait for pages to download from your broker's server. Of course, to work this advantage you must have high-speed Internet access (through DSL, cable, or satellite).

Working with a direct-access broker gives you a steady stream of raw financial data — the actual trades, current bid and ask prices, trading volume, and market statistics. The depth of the bids and offers — that is, what bids are behind the highest bid and what offers are behind the lowest offer — is very useful information. The trading software you load onto your computer determines how these data are organized and presented on your computer monitor. Providing better access is how direct-access brokers distinguish their services from other brokers.

Software prices and access fees vary greatly and can cost you as much as $300 per month. The broker sometimes will waive the fees, especially if your trading volume is high enough — typically about 50 or more trades per month. As you can see, you have to make regular trades for a direct-access broker to be more cost effective than a discount broker. That said, even some discount brokers offer limited direct access using less-sophisticated software.

Futures brokers

Unless you're working with a full-service investment firm, you may have to open a separate account with a futures trader if you want to trade commodities or other types of futures. Many direct-access brokers provide futures trading services, but you will not always find them at a discount broker. We talk more about licensing in Chapter 20 and about trading futures in Chapter 18.

Services to Consider When Choosing Your Broker/Adviser

Don't even think about choosing your professional purely on the basis of price. You need to know what types of services are offered that enable you to make the types of trades you want to make. Check out the types of orders they support, whether they can offer you a data feed, what types of charts they provide, and, if you want to make your own trades electronically, whether they can give you ECN access.

Types of orders

As we mention in Chapter 2, not all brokers provide stop orders for OTC and Nasdaq trades. The Nasdaq has no facility for handling stop orders, so the broker must monitor your stop prices and enter either market or limit orders when your price is triggered. Although monitoring stop prices usually is done automatically, not all brokers offer the service — if you know you'll be using stops with many of your trades, find a broker who does. Some discount brokers will, provided you're willing to pay.

As such, you also need to compare not only prices but also the respective brokers' reputations for effectively and efficiently providing those services. And if you want to place contingent orders (see Chapter 2), you may discover that few discount brokers offer that service, even for a price.

Steer clear of brokers who accept *payment for order flow,* a practice in which some exchanges or market makers pay brokerage firms for routing orders to them. Firms can make a penny or more per share, but the regulators require the firm to inform you whether it receives payment for order flow when you first open an account and thereafter on an annual basis. Each time a firm receives a payment for order flow, it must disclose that information on the trade confirmation. If you see an indication on one of your trades that your broker received this type of payment, you have the right to request notification in writing about the source and type of payment related to that transaction. These payments may encourage unethical brokers to steer orders away from the best prices and toward the market maker offering such payments.

Data feed

The type of data to which you want to have access is crucial. Most brokers provide basic stock quotes, usually in real time, and some may even offer market data providing a much deeper look at the market that includes not only current but previous sales information. If you want access to a higher level of data, be certain you open your account with a firm that provides the level of data you need, or you may buy it from a third party. Again, pricing for differing data feeds can vary among firms. Firms that offer ways for you to get the data feed through your home computer (as opposed to accessing it from their servers) charge more, but keep in mind that you'll receive the information quicker. The faster your Internet connection, the more quickly and reliably you'll receive the information. We cover data feeds in greater detail in Chapter 4.

Charts

Data fed into your home computer are raw stock market data. How this information is formatted on your computer and the kind of charts you're able to build from it depends on the software provided by your dealer. Charting software can be critical to your ability to make trading decisions. Your dealer may charge you to use the software, but will usually discount or waive the fee based on the size of your portfolio or your volume of trading activity. Many free charting alternatives are also available online, including StockCharts. com, which we used to produce the charts for this book. We talk about charting capabilities in Chapter 4.

ECN access

If direct access to stock exchanges and market makers is important to you, then you need to find a broker that provides ECN access. You don't have to open an account through a direct-access broker; some discount brokers do provide ECN access. Be sure to check out the section on "Choosing the Right Broker/Adviser for You," later in this chapter.

Understanding the Types of Investment Accounts

You can open your investment accounts in a couple different ways — as a cash account or a margin account. You also may open separate accounts for retirement or education savings. Because retirement accounts have more restrictions, your trading alternatives are more limited in those accounts, but that isn't necessarily a bad thing. You shouldn't be risking your retirement or education funds on speculative trading anyway.

Cash accounts

The traditional investment account is a *cash account*. With a cash account, you must deposit the full cost of any purchases by the settlement date of the transaction. Most dealers require that funds to buy stocks be in your cash account before you can place an order. The amount of cash you need to have on deposit varies; some let you open an account for as little as $100 or $1,000, but others require as much as $10,000 or more to open a new cash account.

Margin accounts

You don't have to have as much cash on hand to buy stock when you open a *margin account*. This type of account enables you to borrow certain amounts of money using cash or securities already in the account as collateral. Because using a margin account essentially is buying stocks, bonds, or commodities on credit, each respective firm has its own screening procedure to determine whether you qualify for the loan and can buy on margin.

A $2,000 minimum deposit usually is required to open a margin account. You can borrow on margin to 50 percent of the initial purchase price. Not all stocks can be bought on margin. Some firms enforce even stricter margin rules, especially if you choose to invest in volatile stocks valued at less than $5. When buying stocks on margin you pay an interest rate on the margin loans, but most firms charge relatively low rates to encourage the transaction business. Be sure to check out the "Margin requirements" section later in this chapter.

When opening a margin account, the firm requires you to sign what's called a *margin agreement,* which stipulates regulations for the account and permits the broker to have a lien on your account whenever the balance falls below the minimum maintenance margin (more about that in a moment). The agreement also enables your firm to loan your shares to short sellers. That's where shorted stock comes from. We talk more about short selling and the mechanics of margin trading in Chapter 14.

You're taking a risk by purchasing shares with borrowed money and using shares you own as collateral. If your stock holdings fall in value below the minimum maintenance margin requirement, your dealer can force you to sell stock you don't want to sell and use other assets you may not want to use to cover the outstanding loan. The risks and regulations for using a margin account are described more fully in the section on margin requirements later in this chapter.

Options

If you want to trade options, your dealer will require you to sign a special options agreement acknowledging that you understand the risks associated with trading options or derivative instruments. This practice became common after dealers were sued by some clients because they suffered huge losses when trading options and claimed they were unaware of the risks. The agreement protects the dealer from being sued if you lose a lot of money, so you need to know what you're doing when dealing with derivatives (see Chapter 18).

Although you may be able to find a firm that allows you to trade using options — long puts and calls, which are a type of option (see Chapter 18) — you need to know exactly what you're doing and the cost of doing it. Only about 25 percent of the 30,000 people approved to work in stock markets in Canada are licensed to trade options.

Registered Retirement Savings Plans (RRSPs)

RRSP accounts in which you're saving for retirement do not allow you to trade on margin at all. These limitations are for your protection to avoid risking major losses in your long-term investments that never should be put at such high levels of risk. The amount you can contribute each year to all retirement accounts is limited by the *Income Tax Act,* so you must be careful with this money.

Because these accounts are tax-deferred, you can't write off any losses in them against any gains from investments held outside of them — that is, in other taxable accounts. In other words, you don't have the same tax-planning choices with registered retirement accounts to offset gains and losses. All money taken out of an RRSP at retirement is taxed at your current income tax rate. This differs from stocks held outside an RRSP. For these stocks, you can use stock losses to minimize the tax you might have to pay on stock gains. Here are some additional trading limitations of registered retirement accounts:

- ✔ **Margin is not allowed:** Using funds within a retirement account as collateral for trading on margin is not permitted. It's against the law. You won't find a firm in Canada that will approve margin in a registered retirement account.

- ✔ **Short positions are prohibited:** Speculative trading using short positions, which is a common trading strategy for futures contracts and widely used by experienced stock and bond traders, requires a margin account. When someone shorts a stock, he or she borrows the stock and sells it in the hope of buying it back later for less. Selling short requires the use of margin, and is therefore not permitted in a registered retirement account. We talk more about short selling in Chapter 14.

✔ **Trading policies are more stringent:** All firms have more stringent trading policies for registered retirement accounts. Before you open a registered retirement account, check with your firm about its trading limitations to be sure they match your intentions for the account.

✔ **Certain options trading may be permitted:** If you're an experienced trader, you can find some firms that allow options trading in your registered retirement account. Not all types of options, however, can be traded in a retirement account. The ones that you can trade are short covered calls, long calls, and put positions. We talk more about puts and calls in Chapter 18.

Registered Retirement Income Funds (RRIFs)

These accounts are basically RRSPs in reverse. Rather than making big contributions early, which is the RRSP motto, the best plan here is to make small withdrawals as late as possible. The annual compulsory RRIF withdrawals are added to your taxable income. That's why you must shelter your investments inside your RRIF for as long as possible.

If you're trading successfully in your RRSP, then converting to your RRIF at age 71 requires only that your account number changes. Nothing else in your portfolio needs to change. Do not be bullied.

Individual Pension Plans (IPPs)

An individual pension plan (IPP) is a benefit plan for individual participants providing benefits permitted under the *Income Tax Act* to maximize tax-sheltered retirement savings. Larger tax-sheltered contributions than an RRSP are allowed for high-paid employees.

IPPs are attractive because contributions increase while the maximum RRSP contributions are set by law, and IPP assets are creditor-proof. You'll be happy to know that when you establish an IPP to use as your trading account you have the ability to increase future contributions if your return on investments is not sufficient to meet the defined benefits. If you're eligible, you'll need the help of an accountant or an actuary to open and operate one of these plans due to their complex nature. The effort can be worth every penny, because much larger contributions allow you to accumulate bigger amounts of tax-deferred capital. Don't do this at home alone.

Registered Education Savings Plans (RESPs)

The federal government wants our children and grandchildren to do something useful after finishing high school. Registered Education Savings Plans have been set up to encourage savings to cover the costs of post-secondary tuition and other expenses. The magic of RESPs lies in what is called the Canada Education Savings Grant (CESG). To us, this is free money. If you contribute $2,500 to an RESP, you will get $500 as a gift in the form of the CESG. Your annual $2,500 contribution to an RESP for your (grand) children is matched by a $500 contribution from the government . . . that's $500 every year for free! Start early, do not mess with the money, and do not take risks that will not pay off unless absolutely certain. The free matching of government grant money means your return is guaranteed to be at least 20 percent on your contributions.

Because the stock market in Canada has averaged less than 10 percent since the Second World War, no need exists for taking any risk at all. Doing nothing other than buying bonds or treasury bills will give you more than twice what the smartest money is making.

Avoid the temptation to dabble with this money by trading unless you have great confidence in your success. Just because you can trade in an RESP doesn't mean you should.

Tax-Free Savings Accounts (TFSAs)

Beginning in 2009 Canadians were lucky enough to be permitted what are effectively miniature Swiss bank accounts, where you can wheel and deal to your heart's content and pay no taxes. You can make $5,000 in deposits every year, and you can put back what you've taken out. When your trading has developed some sure-fire winners, this is the place to do it. Be careful, though, because this is very precious money.

We call this money precious because it's in the only account where your profits are totally tax-free. Your interest income earned is tax-free. Your dividends received are tax-free. Your capital gains are tax-free. Other accounts such as RRSPs, RRIFs, and RESPs are tax-*deferred*. TFSAs are tax-free. That's why they're precious. That's why we call them miniature Swiss bank accounts. That's why you use your TFSA for trading only your sure-fire winners. You cannot offset your losses against your gains, and you cannot put more than $5,000 per year of new money into your TFSA.

Choosing the Right Broker/Adviser for You

Before beginning a search for the right broker or adviser, you must first decide what type of trader you want to be and what services you need. If you want to be a position trader, or one who trades infrequently, your best bet is either a full-service investment adviser or a discount broker. The choice depends upon how independently you want to operate as a trader. If you want advice on your stock investing plans, you need to seek out a full-service adviser, but we don't always recommend this expensive option. Before risking your money on trading, however, you need to be comfortable enough with the language and mechanics of trading and how to conduct your own research. If you don't need the services of a direct-access broker, your best bet is to select a discount broker.

Considering more than price

Your choice should be based on much more than who can offer you the cheapest price. Although price definitely is a factor in your selection, it's one of many factors you need to consider. The most important factors are the services your broker offers and how effective and efficient the broker is in carrying out those promised services. Look for brokers that offer smart and quick order routing capabilities, but steer clear of the ones that accept payment for order flow (see the "Types of orders" section earlier in this chapter).

You may find an online broker that provides all the bells and whistles at the cheapest price, but if its systems break down at a critical trading moment and you're not able to implement your trades when you want to, those bells and whistles mean nothing, and not being able to rely on them can result in huge losses. Look for brokers that allow you to test drive a demo version of their order entry systems.

Doing a little research

If you expect to become an active and successful trader and want full access so you can trade electronically through the exchanges, you more than likely need to research direct-access brokers. If, however, you believe that your volume of trades per month will be lower than 50, you may want to consider a discount broker that offers access to ECNs. Basically, your choice comes down to the types of services and accounts you need and which broker offers the best mix for what you want to do and pay.

Your first step is to make lists of your financial objectives, the types of trading you want to do, and the services you know you're going to need. Talk with other traders you know and be sure to find out what their experiences have been with various brokers.

You can also research and compare ratings of brokers on the Internet. Try to find the annual rankings of online brokers done by *The Globe and Mail* every autumn. This survey has been published in the *Report On Business* section in September or October since at least 2001.

The most recent survey ranked 13 online brokers in terms of their costs, tools, trading, customer satisfaction, account information, and Web sites. Be aware that 11 of the 13 discount brokers are owned by banks and credit unions. Due to this connection, you might consider using your own bank or credit union's online service for your trading. You might be able to drive a better bargain if you do your chequing, mortgage, line of credit, retirement savings, and credit cards at the same place you do your trading. Stay close to home until you're confident you know what you're doing, then seek the best service for your particular trading. The same banks and credit unions also have full-service investment advisers who are able to assist in your trading as well as your overall money management. You can also find a few independent investment firms in Canada that take pride in their independence and unbiased advice.

Norman Rothery has operated the Stingy Investor Web site since 1995, where he summarizes the choices in finding a good broker. As he points out it's often the qualitative aspects of the broker–client relationship that matter most (see www.stingyinvestor.com).

You can find another review of discount brokers at Surviscor (www.surviscor.com), where sites are ranked by passive, serious, and active investors.

After narrowing down your choices, check out the disciplinary histories of the firms you're considering. You can do that by going to the Web site of the Canadian Securities Administrators (www.securities-administrators.ca) to find out what disciplinary actions (if any) have been taken by securities regulators. You might call your provincial regulator to be sure the specific dealer you're thinking about working with is licensed to do business in your province. This information can be crucial. If you work with an unlicensed dealer who goes out of business, you may not have any way of recovering lost funds even if an arbitrator or court rules in your favour.

Understanding how you'll be paying

After conducting your initial research into investment dealers firms and narrowing down your choices, be sure you understand how the they are paid by

- Reviewing each firm's fee and commission schedule. The schedules should include the fees or charges you're required to pay when opening the account and what you pay to maintain and close the account.

- Finding out how your adviser is compensated if you're planning to work with a human being rather than trade online. Many advisers receive higher compensation when they sell their firm's own products, so they may try to steer you toward them rather than another product that may be a better match for your trading objectives. Rarely are dealer products good trading vehicles.

One other level of protection that you need to check on is the dealer's membership in the Canadian Investor Protection Fund (CIPF). Although CIPF membership won't insure you against losses caused by market declines, the CIPF does give you some protection if your firm faces insolvency. You can find out more about the CIPF at www.cipf.ca. If you can't find your discount broker or investment adviser on the CIPF's current member list, then look elsewhere to do your trading.

Getting to Know the Rules

After you pick your dealer, you must be sure you know the trading rules. Although provincial law mandates margin requirements, sets trade settlement rules, and bans free riding (nope, we're not talking about horseback riding here), dealers sometimes have even more stringent rules for their clients. We review the provincial requirements here, but check with your dealer to find out any additional rules your chosen firm imposes.

Rules for stock trading fall under the jurisdiction of the provincial Securities Acts, and encompass margin accounts, securities transactions, credit extended based on securities, and other factors related to securities markets. We don't review all the specifics here, but instead home in on three key areas that impact your trading choices — margin requirements, settling trades, and free riding.

Margin requirements

The provincial Securities Acts specify how much you can borrow when you use a margin account to purchase new shares of stocks on margin. This *initial margin requirement* permits you to borrow up to 50 percent of the cost of shares trading over $5. For example, if you open a new margin account with a $10,000 cash deposit, you can buy up to $20,000 worth of stock. After your $20,000 purchase, your account will have a cash balance of $0, an equity balance of $10,000, and a margin balance of $10,000. At this time, all your equity is committed to this trade, so you cannot enter any new positions unless you deposit additional funds or securities. Some investment firms allow you to borrow 70 percent of the value of shares trading above $5, but only 20 percent of shares between $1.50 and $1.74 — it's a sliding scale for the cost of your loan to offset the risk of cheap shares.

If the stock price increases, your equity balance increases. If the stock price decreases, your equity balance decreases. In either case, your margin balance remains the same, $10,000. The only way to reduce the outstanding margin balance is to deposit extra cash or securities into your account or sell the shares.

When your stock price increases, your equity balance increases and you may use the increased equity as collateral to borrow additional money to buy additional shares. You may borrow up to the value of the increased equity balance. This will increase your margin balance.

However, if your equity balance decreases, so does the minimum equity position permitted in your account. Currently, the minimum is 25 percent of the total value of all margined securities. Some brokers may require more.

In the single-stock example earlier in this chapter, if the total value of the stock falls below $13,332, then the equity balance in your portfolio will be less than 25 percent of the total value. The math is simple: 25 percent of $13,332 is $3,333. Your cash balance is still $0 and your margin balance is still $10,000. Subtract $10,000 from $13,332 to determine your equity balance, which is $3,332. Your equity balance is less than 25 percent of your total account balance.

When this occurs, your broker will call and demand additional collateral to support the outstanding margin loan. This is a *margin call.* You may meet your margin call requirements by depositing more cash, or you may deposit fully paid, unmargined securities from another account. If you do not deposit additional collateral, your dealer is permitted to sell up to four times the amount of stock required to meet your margin call, and may sell any of the securities in your portfolio.

If you have more than a few positions, margin calculations become complex. It helps to think about it like this: When initiating a new position, you can never borrow more than half of the value of the position. To maintain sufficient collateral, your dealer will insist that the value of your stocks be more than enough to cover the loan. Therefore, if your equity balance falls below 25 percent of the total portfolio value, your adviser will ask for additional collateral in the form of a margin call.

As a trader, you should seldom satisfy a margin call. Instead, close the offending position(s). It's possible that an extraordinary event may cause the value of your stocks to fall below the amount owned on your outstanding margin loan. If this happens, your dealer will close your positions, but you must still repay the debt. Unlike a cash account, you can lose more than 100 percent of the money you deposit into a margin account.

Not all stocks can be bought on margin, and neither can all stocks be used as collateral. If you want to trade on margin, be sure you understand the margin requirements imposed by your dealer. Some investment dealers require even stiffer requirements to maintain a margin account, especially if you trade low-priced volatile or lightly traded stocks.

Settling trades

When you place an order to buy a stock, you must settle that transaction in three business days. This *settlement cycle* is known as *T + 3*. The firm must receive your payment for any securities you buy no later than three days after the trade is executed. If you're selling a stock, it's probably being held in your account and will be taken out of that account on the day of settlement. Options and government securities trade on a *T + 1* settlement cycle, which means these transactions settle the next trading day.

Free riding

No, we're not talking about hopping a train on the sly. *Free riding* in the stock-trading world can get you in a bunch of trouble, so keep reading. Basically it means that you must pay for a stock before you can sell it, and because it takes three days to settle a stock transaction, that means, in theory, you can buy a stock and then place an order to sell it before the stock purchase actually settles.

This is a cash account problem. Although many swing and day traders do turn around stock purchases and sales that quickly, they typically trade in a margin account and are able to sidestep the problem. Margin traders use the unsettled proceeds of a trade as collateral to borrow money until the trade is settled. Still, swing traders and day traders must have enough cash or buying power in their accounts to cover all purchases of stock.

Formally, in a cash account, a dealer may buy a security on your behalf — or sell a security — when either of the following applies:

✔ You have sufficient funds in the account.

✔ The firm accepts in good faith your agreement to make a full-cash payment for the security before you sell it.

If you do ever buy and sell a security before the settlement cycle (T + 3) is complete — or even on the same day — and without sufficient cash in your account, an investment firm can make what is called an *intraday extension of credit* (a loan), but that exposes the firm to increased risks — especially the risk that you may overextend your financial resources and be unable to settle your trades. Most firms require active traders who buy and then sell securities within the settlement cycle to conduct those activities within a margin account.

If you take a free ride and haven't made some type of credit arrangement with your firm, it's likely to freeze your account for 90 days. During that 90-day period, the firm requires you to pay for any purchase on the date that you make the trade. In other words, you lose the option of settling your trades within three days. Some firms require you to have enough cash in your account to complete the transaction before you make the trade so you thus avoid even the risk of free riding.

We talk more about these rapid forms of trading (swing trading and day trading) in Chapters 16 and 17.

Chapter 4

Putting Your Computer to Work: Your Key Business Tool

*B*ack in the old days, you'd call your investment adviser to enter an order and then wait for him or her to phone back and report the fill price. Active traders? They'd hang out in the investment dealer's lobby, watching the ticker, boasting over winning trades, commiserating over losing trades, and shooting the breeze. In the bad old days, there were no discount brokers.

If you kept charts, you either made them yourself or had them delivered by postal carrier in book form. They arrived at the end of each week. If you couldn't afford that extravagance, you'd buy monthly summaries and update them yourself.

Every retail investor bought and sold stocks the same way. The pros had the advantage, but it was more or less a level playing field for the rest of us.

Today, you'd be hard pressed to find a ticker-tape machine in any discount brokerage or investment dealer's office. The Internet has changed everything. You can still buy chart books, but now they're delivered via the Internet, and so are stock prices, real-time intraday charts, and research reports. You can enter orders online, have your orders filled within seconds, and receive notification showing the order's price almost as quickly.

Online discount brokers and full-service investment advisers provide a vast array of research and trading tools for their clients. Real-time streaming quotes, proprietary and third-party research, sophisticated charts, and extensive order-entry capabilities make today's traders better informed and better equipped than ever before.

If you're anything like us, you're going to spend many hours with your trading platform. So it pays to spend a little time now thinking about what information you need, how you'll use it, and what you may need in the future. With just a little foresight, you can set up your trading platform so that it's effective today and upgradeable in the future without completely disrupting your day-to-day activities.

In this chapter, we review the basic computer hardware you need to access all that's on offer for traders, explore the software options you'll want to consider for managing your trading activities, and discuss various trading platforms and data-feed alternatives. Finally, we give you a road map to the options available on the Internet.

Making Use of Your Computer

Although tracking the market and charting stock prices by hand is an excellent learning exercise — it gives you a feel for the market that you can't get by reviewing computer-generated charts — we doubt you want to travel to the local library or your investment adviser's office to research the stocks that interest you. (Most online discount brokers don't have an office for you to visit even if you want to!) The wealth of online information that can help you improve your trading results is simply remarkable. In this section we list some of the things you can do with your computer.

Identifying trading candidates

With your computer, you can do all of the following:

- ✔ Display and interpret price charts
- ✔ Research stocks, bonds, IPOs, options, and futures
- ✔ Read analyst reports and company reports
- ✔ Screen stocks for technical or fundamental constraints
- ✔ Monitor economic reports, earnings reports, and business news
- ✔ Monitor market indexes, sectors, and trading statistics

Managing your account

Managing your account can involve some or all of the following:

- ✔ Entering and executing trades, and monitoring open orders
- ✔ Controlling and tracking order routing
- ✔ Receiving almost instant fill reports
- ✔ Monitoring and analyzing your portfolio and all open positions
- ✔ Tracking profits and losses
- ✔ Analyzing your trading history
- ✔ Preparing your income tax returns

Improving your trades

You can become a better trader by doing the following:

- ✔ Evaluating trading systems and testing trading ideas
- ✔ Keeping trading logs to audit your trading performance
- ✔ Monitoring the tax consequences of your trades
- ✔ Staying in touch with other traders

Finding Price Charts

Price charts show the history of a stock's price over time. These charts conceal useful trading information that is revealed with careful analysis. Chapters 8 through 11 describe how to read, interpret, and understand what you see in a price chart.

Fortunately, price charts are easy to find. If your broker or adviser doesn't provide an adequate charting package, you can find excellent charting tools on dozens of online sites. If you have to go outside your broker's environment, you may have to put up with Internet banner ads. Most of the charts on free Web sites display 20-minute delayed prices. You may have to pay for Internet charts that update in real time (prices range from $9.95 to $34.95 a month — we provide some examples in the next section).

At a minimum, you need control over the time frame and the types of charts displayed. For example, you probably want 1-minute, 5-minute, 15-minute, and 60-minute charts to go with daily, weekly, and monthly charts. Other features to look for include:

- ✔ Trading volume. (It's critical.)

- ✔ Moving averages, to show average prices over time. You'll want at least two types, simple moving averages and exponential moving averages, and you'll want control over the period being averaged. Moving averages are discussed in Chapter 11.

- ✔ Indicators and oscillators, to help evaluate a stock's direction and momentum. We use the MACD (moving average convergence divergence) indicator and the stochastic oscillator. We discuss indicators and oscillators in Chapter 11.

- ✔ A variety of chart styles, including bar charts and candlestick charts. Bar charts are the most popular stock charts, and they're the ones we use throughout this book. We describe how to read and interpret them in Chapter 9. Candlestick charts display the price data using a slightly different format that is preferred by some traders. The analysis techniques in this book work for both styles.

- ✔ Ability to display data in a log or semi-log format. This allows equal percentage price changes to appear the same on the price chart, which is helpful for comparing the price movements of two differently priced stocks. For example, if a $10 stock rises to $20, that's a 100 percent price change. If a $50 stock rises to $100, that's also a 100 percent price increase, but it will look like a much larger price increase on a standard price chart. Use a log or semi-log format to show similar percentage changes so they look the same on the chart.

- ✔ Ability to group charts together so you can quickly scan open positions or trade candidates.

- ✔ Ability to show support and resistance levels, draw trend lines, and make annotations.

Two kinds of online charts exist: real-time charts and delayed-price charts. Although the charts may be identical, the prices shown in the charts are not. Real-time charts display current price data updated within a few seconds of the trade. Delayed-price charts do not show the most current trades. Instead, the prices shown on the chart are at least 15 to 20 minutes old.

Although many excellent online charting alternatives are out there, they typically aren't as flexible or configurable as the ones offered in stand-alone charting packages or integrated trading platforms. And you probably won't have access to trading-system development and testing software that is required to create and test your own trading system. We discuss the advantages and disadvantages of online charts, stand-alone charting packages, and integrated trading platforms in the following sections. We cover methods for developing and testing personalized trading systems in Chapter 15.

Internet charts, delayed prices

Although real-time charts are desirable, they're a necessity only for extremely active short-term traders. Analyzing the market and developing your trading plan are best done before the market in which you plan to make your trades opens, or after it closes. Delayed-price charts are more than adequate for these planning and analysis activities.

You can use delayed-price charts to identify support and resistance levels, display moving averages, find emerging trends, and select possible entry and exit points for tomorrow's trading day.

Here are a few sources for online charts:

- ✔ **Globe Investor Stock Charts (www.globeinvestor.com/static/hubs/charts.html):** *The Globe and Mail* provides this excellent resource for stock charts and other pertinent financial information regarding publically traded companies.

- ✔ **BigCharts (www.bigcharts.com):** BigCharts is part of the CBS MarketWatch family. The site is free and offers an excellent charting package with plenty of options, including interactive charts, industry analysis, and stock screeners. You can define a list of favourite charts for quick review. You'll also find news and market commentary.

- ✔ **Investor's Business Daily (www.investors.com):** *Investor's Business Daily* (IBD) publishes its proprietary ranking system online and in its daily paper. Using the stock-picking methodology developed by publisher William O'Neil, the site provides charts and rankings by relative strength and earnings growth. Available by subscription.

- ✔ **Decision Point (www.decisionpoint.com):** Decision Point is another subscription charting site but it takes a different approach, providing chart books, hundreds of unique charts, and market commentary based primarily on technical analysis. If you're looking for a quick way to scan a large group of stocks, this site provides excellent tools. You may find that Decision Point is a nice complement to a more traditional charting site or charting software package.

Internet charts, real-time prices

Although most online brokers provide support for real-time prices, not all provide real-time charting capabilities. If your broker doesn't offer what you need, and you find delayed prices are just too frustrating, you can find a number of sites that offer real-time price charts. Real-time, browser-based Internet charts usually aren't free. You will generally find them priced between $9.95 and $34.95 per month.

Getting analysis from online newspapers

If you're managing money in Canada — either your own or other people's — get into the daily habit of reading at least the headline of every article in the business section of the two national newspapers. The *Financial Post* comes with the *National Post,* and the *Report On Business* accompanies *The Globe and Mail.*

Both of these newspapers have a variety of columnists and guest writers from Bay Street, many of whom are comfortable with both technical and fundamental analysis.

- ✔ **The Financial Post (www.financial post.com):** This Canadian investment paper was first published weekly in 1907 and moved to a daily edition during 1988. Ten years later it became a complete section of the *National Post.* Traders enjoy the coverage provided by Don Vialoux, chartered market technician, current director and past president of the Canadian Society of Technical Analysts (www.csta.org). He is the author of a free daily report on equity markets, sectors, commodities, equities, and ETFs (see www.timing themarket.ca.)

- ✔ **Report On Business (www.globeand mail.com):** The business section of Canada's traditional newspaper often includes Skot Kortje, who has been analyzing stock market trends for more than 15 years using trend analysis. His Stock Trends indicators have been published by *The Globe and Mail* since 1995. (For more go to www.stocktrends.ca.)

Sites offering real-time charts include the following:

- ✔ **StockCharts (www.stockcharts.com):** Chip Anderson started StockCharts early in Internet history. He's one of the few independents still around, and for good reason – the site is excellent. We use charts from this Web site throughout the book. StockCharts offers many excellent free charting tools, but the best parts are available by subscription. Advanced features include real-time, intraday pricing, and the ability to create and store chart annotations, create large lists of your favourite charts, define custom chart settings, and create custom scans based on technical indicators.

- ✔ **FreeRealTime.com (www.freerealtime.com):** The free capabilities of the site are fairly limited, and you'll have to put up with banner ads and the occasional full-page ad that display before the page you actually want appears. The free portion of this site uses data from electronic communications networks (ECNs), not data from the major stock exchanges. Unfortunately, ECNs do not trade all stocks, so real-time charts and quotes may not always be available. And ECN prices may not always match prices on the major exchanges, but they'll be very close. If you can put up with these limitations, the charts and price quotes are in real time. And they're free.

Charting software

Before taking a step up toward a stand-alone charting application, make sure you explore the tools provided by your broker and other brokers and by Web sites offering Internet charts. Some of these online tools are powerful and may be more cost-effective than a stand-alone package.

Stand-alone charting software, however, often provides capabilities beyond what you can find online. For example, charting software packages offer system testing but rarely are they part of a Web site's tool set.

Several packages are available; two examples are

- ✔ **MetaStock (www.metastock.ca):** MetaStock comes in two flavours, a standard end-of-day trading package, and a professional version for intraday charts with real-time data provided by Reuters, which is now owned by Canada's Thomson Corporation. Each offers a variety of analysis tools, technical indicators, system development and testing capabilities, and access to fundamental stock data. MetaStock's operation in Canada is run from Edmonton.

- ✔ **TradeStation (www.tradestation.com):** TradeStation is the gold standard of charting software. It is powerful, flexible, and configurable, and it's designed to work the same way institutional trading platforms do. You can fully automate your trading system by programming your strategies into the system and then having TradeStation execute them in real time. (Whether you should do so, however, is open for discussion.) It also supports direct access to all ECNs and stock exchanges.

Many other charting packages are available, but these two packages are widely used and give you a good basis for comparing all the other available products.

The drawback to stand-alone charting software is the expense. In addition to the price of the software, you need a data provider to deliver end-of-day or intraday market prices. When selecting a charting software package, make sure it supports the data service you plan to use. They must work together.

Finding Fundamental Information

Fundamental data — corporate information such as revenue, earnings, and cash flow — aren't as perishable as price data or trading statistics, but the ability to access these numbers directly from your trading platform as they're updated is a nice feature. We discuss analysis of fundamental data in Chapters 5, 6, and 7. Many brokers provide access to at least some fundamental data, but if you'd like to run the numbers yourself check out these online sources, many of which can review the raw financial data:

- ✔ **SEDAR (www.sedar.com):** SEDAR (short for System for Electronic Document Analysis and Retrieval) is used for filing most securities-related information with the Canadian Securities regulatory authorities. SEDAR filing started in 1997 and is now mandatory for public companies in Canada.

- ✔ *The Wall Street Journal* **(www.wsj.com):** *The Wall Street Journal* is available online by subscription. It provides access to a wide variety of information including stock quotes, stock valuation indexes, fundamental ratios, industry comparisons, insider transactions, earnings estimates, and stock analysis reports. Delayed-price charts also are available.

- ✔ **EDGAR (www.sec.gov/edgar.shtml):** All publicly traded companies are required to file electronically with the Securities and Exchange Commission (SEC) through its Electronic Data Gathering Analysis and Retrieval System (EDGAR). These reports are available online to everyone at no charge.

Finding Analyst Reports

Sometimes you can find these research reports at your local library, especially for big outfits like Standard & Poor's and Value Line. Many analysts sell research in the form of investment newsletter subscriptions. We've used several of the following subscription services through the years, with varying degrees of success:

- ✔ **Standard & Poor's (www.standardandpoors.com):** Registration is required, but access is free. You cannot access the full reports and recommendations on this site, but *BusinessWeek* magazine's Web site (www.businessweek.com/investor) offers several complete S&P reports, stock screens, and industry reports at no charge.

- ✔ **Value Line (www.valueline.com):** The Value Line Investment Survey has been around for a long time. It profiles many major corporations and provides a variety of stock screens based on proprietary models. It also offers opinions on current economic and market climates. Some reports and updates are available on the site at no charge, but a subscription is required to access the complete site.

- ✔ **Briefing.com (www.briefing.com):** This site has free and subscription components. Advanced features include access to analysts' upgrades and downgrades as they're released, access to updated earnings guidance, an IPO calendar, notification of changes in stock indexes, and quite a bit more.

> ✔ **Morningstar (www.morningstar.ca):** Morningstar probably is best known for its analysis of mutual funds, but it also provides extensive stock analysis, editorial commentary, a stock-screening tool, and a thorough snapshot tool that shows financial performance, fund ownership, and recent fund transactions. You need a subscription to access the premium content.

Selecting a Trading Platform

You'll find as many different approaches to trading as you'll find traders. Fortunately, almost as many alternatives for setting up your trading environment also exist.

As technology develops and expands, online brokers are providing increasingly powerful trading tools for their clients. These tools include market research, charting capabilities, streaming prices, and news services. If your broker doesn't offer a specific service, you probably can find it offered on the Internet.

When selecting a trading platform, look for the capabilities you need today with an eye toward future expandability. You may want to consider the features in the three lists that follow.

Trading tools to look for include the following:

- ✔ Stock trading

- ✔ Support of sophisticated option trading strategies

- ✔ Futures trading, especially single-stock and index futures

- ✔ Nasdaq Level II access

- ✔ Direct-access trading and ECN book data

- ✔ Watch lists

- ✔ Automatic e-mail or text message notification when a stock hits your price point

Analysis tools to shop for include these:

- ✔ Sector analysis

- ✔ Proprietary and third-party analysts' reports

- ✔ News feeds (Dow Jones, Reuters, and so on)

- ✔ Real-time charting capabilities

- ✔ Time and volume sales reports

Account management tools you may need include the following:

- ✔ Real-time account balances
- ✔ Real-time updates of buying power and margin exposure
- ✔ Portfolio management tools
- ✔ Open-order status
- ✔ Ability to transfer funds electronically to/from your account

Before putting your computer to work as a trading platform, you need to understand the two primary techniques for delivering trading tools and services. The first uses your Internet browser to enter orders and deliver all information. The other approach uses a stand-alone software program, called an *integrated trading platform,* to interact with your discount broker and your investment account.

The approach that suits you best depends somewhat on your trading style, cost considerations, and your computer's configuration. You may find that the level of service your dealer offers depends on the size of your account or your trading volume. You have to balance your cost with your actual information needs.

Integrated trading platforms typically are direct-access systems. We discuss both direct-access brokers and traditional online brokers in Chapter 3. Although direct-access systems are offered in browser-based configurations, active swing traders and day traders may require a completely integrated, direct-access trading platform.

Browser-based trading environment

For most new traders, trading volume starts out relatively small, perhaps five or fewer trades each month. Your time frame for holding a position probably is measured in days to weeks or weeks to months or months to years. You probably won't be making many intraday trades, except to automatically exit a position after a stop price is hit. In that case, a browser-based trading environment certainly is good enough to get you started and may be all you'll ever need.

These systems can be tightly integrated or somewhat disjointed, depending on the way the dealer implements them. Some dealers, for example, automatically fill in order-entry screens with as much data as it can glean from your account. Others make you type all your data into the order screen, which can be cumbersome and time-consuming. Some dealers provide pop-up order confirmation and fill reports, and others make you continually press the Enter or Refresh key while waiting for a trade execution to show in your account.

Mike's hybrid trading platform

Mike here: My trading horizon is relatively long, and I don't execute enough trades each month to justify the cost of an integrated direct-access trading environment. My trading strategies don't depend on having access to Nasdaq Level II data or direct electronic communications network (ECN) access.

However, I prefer working with a charting package versus evaluating charts by using a browser. I've used several popular packages, and a couple of homegrown applications. (Yes, I'll admit that I'm sort of a geek.)

My solution was to implement a hybrid approach that uses browser-based tools for account management and order entry alongside a software-based charting application. This approach provides me with access to more market data than I ever had when I worked as a broker, gives me tremendous flexibility, and minimizes my trading costs.

And it suits my trading style. For some reason, the world looks different when I'm sitting in front of a computer. I feel rushed, somehow, and I don't make my best decisions. That's one of the reasons I don't day trade. The pace works against me; I get caught up in the moment and end up making mistakes.

I think and plan better when I'm sitting by myself, in a quiet corner of my home, with a pen in my hand. I'll print the reports and charts that interest me, sit in a comfy chair, mark up my reports, and deliberately chart my trading course.

Only then am I ready to enter orders online.

Pros

For the most part, almost any Internet-ready computer can support a browser-based trading platform. Although Windows is most often used for trading platforms, even Apple Macintosh or Linux systems can be used for most browser-based applications.

Much of the browser-based information offered by your dealer is available to all clients, regardless of account size or trading volume. If your dealer doesn't offer something you want, you usually can find it elsewhere on the Internet, either free or for a modest fee.

Cons

When compared to an integrated software solution, browser-based trading is relatively slow, requiring you to open many browser windows and manually update account information. Depending on how well your dealer implements these systems, a bit more typing may be necessary to enter and execute your orders.

On some browser-based trading platforms, your Internet session may be disconnected whenever your screen is inactive for an extended period of time. This kind of interruption can be frustrating at best. Similarly, to operate correctly some configurations require that you use a specific browser, or that you download and install a special browser plug-in.

Integrated trading platforms

For very active traders, especially swing traders and day traders, and for traders looking to develop personalized trading systems, an integrated trading platform that doesn't rely on your Internet browser can be a better solution. You typically download these software programs, install them on your computer, and then use them to access your investment account and trading tools. They range from rudimentary text-based applications with modest graphing capabilities to sophisticated technical-analysis programs that enable you to design and implement custom trading systems.

The most sophisticated of these platforms provide an institutional-level trading experience. Some, for example, permit trading baskets that enable you to simultaneously enter orders for a number of different stocks. Others help you to define hot keys for fast order entry.

You'll also find that integrated trading platforms provide support for sophisticated strategies. The most flexible among them give you the ability to enter contingent orders, where, for example, a stock's price may trigger an option order, or the execution of one order automatically cancels another. Several dealers will notify you by e-mail or text message when a stock hits a price you've specified or an indicator reaches a preset level. One dealer even gives you the ability to automatically execute trades based on recommendations from well-known and reputable advisory services.

Pros

These trading platforms typically are faster and easier to use and to customize than browser-based applications. The best among them have system-testing tools that help you fine-tune your personal trading strategies.

Cons

Integrated trading platforms can be expensive. Unless you have a large account balance, your dealer may charge you either a monthly fee or base the access on your making a minimum number of monthly trades.

Furthermore, these platforms often require up-to-date computer equipment with a fast processor and plenty of storage to run well. Older equipment will not run this software satisfactorily. And it's likely you'll need to use the Windows operating system.

Determining Computer Requirements

Few new traders actually need a fully integrated direct-access trading platform to begin trading or to trade profitably. But if you're considering a new computer system, you may find the hardware and software requirements for these high-powered platforms to be of benefit. Otherwise, you may be unable to upgrade your new computer to run these applications.

Decisions, decisions . . .

Most trading platforms are designed for Windows, but die-hard Mac and Linux fans aren't completely locked out. If you're starting with a browser-based approach, almost any modern, Internet-ready computer can handle the task. Browser-based Internet tools usually work equally well on any hardware or operating system. Some sites require functions provided by a specific browser, but that is becoming increasingly rare.

If you're planning to buy new computer hardware for trading, we recommend that you avoid Mac hardware or Unix/Linux operating systems. Although Mac and Linux support browser-based applications at least as well as Windows, you may be unable to upgrade if ever you want a more integrated trading platform. We don't know of any commercially available trading platforms for independent traders (as opposed to institutional traders) that run on Linux or either Mac OS 9 or OS X.

Configuring your computer system

Regardless whether you decide to employ a browser-based approach or an integrated trading platform, you're going to need a reliable computer with sufficient horsepower, memory, and storage space.

Some of today's high-powered, integrated trading software requires equally high-powered computer systems. We give you general hardware guidelines in this section, but if you decide you want a computer that can be upgraded to handle a high-performance integrated trading platform check with specific software vendors to identify any special hardware requirements. Make certain your hardware supports your software!

Software vendors often claim that their products can run on relatively modest hardware configurations; however, you'll probably be disappointed and frustrated with system performance under such conditions. These software packages run much better on a computer that surpasses the system requirements. Trading platforms — especially testing applications and multichart, multiwindow, multimonitor displays — consume considerable system resources and can make many computers run unbearably slow.

The following minimum configurations easily support browser-based solutions. Upgraded configurations, however, may be required to adequately support fully integrated trading environments.

- **Central processing unit (CPU):** At a minimum, you need a 1 GHz processor. Ideally, something much faster works better. Trading applications tend to rely on making many mathematical calculations, so you want to avoid the value-priced CPU chip sets. Look instead for systems that are primarily designed for graphics or gaming applications. Ideally, select a dual-core processor.

  The slowest machines being sold today are rated in gigahertz multiples, and most modern machines have enough CPU horsepower to run charting application programs. However, high-end programs like TradeStation take advantage of specialty hardware such as multi-CPU and hyperthreading configurations. Check with software manufacturers for specific details.

- **RAM memory:** 1GB of RAM is the absolute minimum, but you probably want more. Memory is inexpensive compared with other hardware upgrades, and having too much of it is next to impossible. Error-correcting memory may buy only extra peace of mind, but it doesn't cost much more than standard memory.

- **Available disk space:** 1GB of free disk space should be enough to start out, but you'll need much more for long-term storage of real-time price data, which will be useful for developing and testing your own trading system. Chapter 15 discusses methods to personalize a trading system.

- **Operating system:** If you're running a Windows environment, you need at least Windows XP or Vista. Although browsers and software applications will run on older versions of Windows, XP and Vista give you more stability and reliability than earlier versions. For trading applications, you want the most reliable system you can find and afford. Windows XP and Vista may not be bulletproof, but they're so much better than their predecessors that you definitely want to upgrade if you haven't already. (At the time of publication, we were unable to test any applications on Windows 7.)

- **Video card:** Although you may be able to squeak by using a shared-memory video system (it shares some of your RAM), you'll be better off with a stand-alone video card that relies on its own video memory. A minimum configuration for a single monitor requires at least 128MB of video memory, but 256MB of video RAM is better. You may even want 1GB whenever you opt for a single video card that supports dual monitors.

- **Monitor size:** Modern high-resolution LCD monitors are excellent and inexpensive. A 17-inch monitor probably is the smallest you should consider. Bigger is better. Even more important than size is the monitor's resolution. Anything less than 1024×768 resolution is useless for reading chart detail, but you will want more. If you're going with a single monitor setup, consider a 20- or 22-inch monitor with resolution up to 1920×1200.

- **Dual-monitor configurations:** Some traders swear by the dual-monitor configuration. The idea is to pull up your charts on one monitor and everything else on the other. Many video cards support dual monitors.

- **Network interface:** You need some way of accessing a high-speed Internet connection (see the next section). Many computers now come with either a built-in Ethernet port or an extra Ethernet Interface Card. Either works fine.

- **Power supply:** We recommend you use an uninterruptible power supply (UPS). A UPS is relatively inexpensive and provides an extra measure of security. Some protect against lightning strikes. If you live in an area where power fluctuations are common, a UPS is a must.

Accessing the Internet

You must have reliable Internet access, and that means a high-speed connection — either DSL or cable Internet will work fine. Some very active day traders will spring for a fractional T1 or dedicated T1 line for an additional measure of reliability, but either approach is expensive. A backup connection is a good idea. Consider a wireless laptop card or even a second high-speed Internet connection.

A dial-up connection is not fast enough or reliable enough for trading. If dial-up is your only alternative, you may be able to temporarily squeak by with it, but look for an alternative as soon as possible.

Connecting to the Internet

Depending on where you live, you may have several good high-speed alternatives for reliably connecting to the Internet. Cable and DSL connections usually work well.

Because of security concerns, avoid wireless networks unless you're absolutely certain you know how to configure the network to keep prying eyes from seeing your private trading and account information.

Picking a browser

Any modern browser probably will do. Although it's possible you might stumble across a site that uses some browser-specific functions, that scenario is becoming increasingly rare. Microsoft's Internet Explorer is bundled with the Windows operating system at no additional charge. It will serve your needs well enough. Mozilla Firefox (www.mozilla.org) is another excellent — and free — choice.

Securing your computer

The Internet is a dangerous place. You must protect your computer system and its data against attacks by vandals, hackers, and thieves. Make sure you have modern virus-scanning software, and keep your virus definitions up to date.

Norton's AntiVirus program gets good reviews and seems to do the job just fine. It can automatically update its virus definitions. You can get more information about Norton's program at www.symantec.com. McAfee Security's VirusScan also gets high marks from those in the know. Additional information is available on the Web at www.mcafee.com.

We also recommend that you use a firewall. The Windows Vista firewall is sufficient. Third-party firewalls like the free Zone Alarm firewall from Check Point Software Technologies (www.zonealarm.com) also work well. Zone Alarm monitors your connection to the Internet and is able to detect trojans and worms that are trying to call home. This is an increasingly critical requirement. In addition, consider installing a hardware firewall to provide an additional layer of security. Most routers include a hardware firewall, and allow you to share your Internet connection with multiple computers.

Finally, keeping up to date with your operating system's security patches, especially when you're running Windows, is important. More viruses are written for Windows than for any other operating system.

You can configure Windows to automatically check for system updates. To do so, go to Security in the Vista Control Panel, or System Properties, under Performance and Maintenance, in the Windows XP Control Panel. Select the Automatic Updates tab and check the appropriate settings to keep your Windows system up to date. You can also go to the Windows Update site (windowsupdate.microsoft.com) to make sure all your system patches have been applied.

Part II
Reading the Fundamentals: Fundamental Analysis

The 5th Wave   By Rich Tennant

EARLY INVESTORS TRACKING A STOCK

In this part . . .

We show you what you need to know to analyze the fundamental health of stocks and the markets. You'll need that information, because this part is where you discover how the economy and the business cycle affect your trading activities and how you can dig into the financial statements of a company to unearth good trading candidates. We also explain the roles played by stock analysts and how you can leverage their efforts as you trade.

Chapter 5

Fundamentals 101: Observing Market Behaviour

*Y*ou hear plenty about recession and inflation. You know both can signal bad economic news, but do you really understand what they mean and why they happen? Regardless of what the economic gurus do, the economy cycles between periods of economic growth and recession. If growth becomes overheated, periods of inflation are likely. Inflation can also be caused when the value of the currency falls. For example, when the value of the dollar falls, that causes an increase in the price of imports and commodities like oil. That in turn impacts the price of just about every other good sold.

The Board of Directors of the Bank of Canada (BoC) and the Board of Governors of the American Federal Reserve (Fed) oversee moves that are made in monetary policy, and the legislative and executive branches of government are responsible for tax changes and other fiscal policy moves. The actions of the BoC and the Fed and the governments can minimize the impact of inflation or recession and spur economic growth, but nothing can be done to erase economic cycles. Markets and traders try to anticipate these cyclical moves with an eye toward recording gains. This chapter will help you understand which economic indicators tend to lead these cycles and how you can use them to understand the current state of the markets and the economy.

The Basics of the Business Cycle

The old adage "What goes up must come down" is as true for the economy as it is for any physical object. When a business cycle reaches its peak, nothing is wrong in the economic world; businesses and investors are making plenty of money and everyone is happy. Unfortunately, the economy can't exist at its peak forever. In the same way that gravity eventually makes a rising object fall, a revved-up economy eventually reaches its high and begins to tumble.

The peak is only one of the four distinct parts of every business cycle — peak, recession, trough, and expansion/recovery (see Figure 5-1). Although none of these parts is designated as the beginning of a business cycle, here are the portions of the business cycle that each represents:

- ✔ **Peak:** During a *peak,* the economy is humming along at full speed, with the gross domestic product (GDP — more about that later in the chapter) near its maximum output and employment levels near their all-time highs. Income and prices are increasing, and the risk of inflation is great, if it hasn't already set in. Businesses and investors are prospering and very happy.

- ✔ **Recession/contraction:** As the old adage goes, "All good things must come to an end." As the economy falls from its peak, employment levels begin to decline, production and output eventually decline, and wages and prices level off, but more than likely won't actually fall unless the recession is a long one.

- ✔ **Trough:** When a recession bottoms out, the economy levels out into a period called the *trough.* If this period is prolonged it can become a depression, which is a severe and prolonged recession. The most recent depression in North America was in the late 1920s and early 1930s. Output and employment stagnate, waiting for the next expansion.

- ✔ **Expansion/recovery:** After the economy starts growing again, employment and output pick up. This period of expansion and recovery pulls the economy off the floor of the trough and points it back toward its next peak. During this period, employment, production, and output all see increases, and the economic situation again looks promising.

How do we know which part of the business cycle the economy is in? Officially, we don't usually find out until months after that part of the cycle has either started or ended.

Figure 5-1:
The basic
business
cycle.

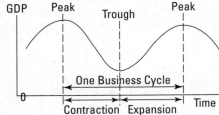

The underlying process of the business cycle is of interest to analysts and traders. Statistics Canada's foray into this area has been well received by analysts over the years. Although no other organization has undertaken the work, it's worth noting that Statistics Canada is not providing "official" reference cycle dates in the sense that the results are beyond dispute or that StatsCan has a legislated requirement to do so.

In identifying the economy's ups and downs by determining the cyclical turning points, StatsCan allows a better understanding for policymakers and traders alike.

In America, the National Bureau of Economic Research (NBER) officially declares the peaks and troughs. The NBER is responsible for formally announcing the ends of peaks and troughs and signalling when a recession (end of a peak) or expansion (end of a trough) starts. You can see a table explaining the peaks and troughs since 1857 at `www.nber.org/cycles/cyclesmain.html`. The NBER identified December 2007 as the peak of the most recent economic expansion, but did not make that pronouncement until December 2008. By the time the peak was declared, the market had been in a downtrend for 15 months, including the sharp selloff in September 2008.

As you can see, the time lag between events and when the NBER makes its announcements can be lengthy. But it can get worse. For example, the NBER declared on November 26, 2001, that the peak of the current business cycle was reached March 21, 2001. That was eight months later. But then, in January 2004 the NBER revised its position by announcing that the peak may have actually occurred as early as November 2000. The end of the trough for this cycle, November 2001, wasn't announced until July 17, 2003. In other words, the economy was in a period of expansion/recovery for 20 months before the NBER made it official.

Unfortunately for all concerned, information that the NBER needs to make its official announcements isn't always immediately available. The process of collecting economic data and revised preliminary estimates of economic activity takes time. Estimates and data don't become available immediately after a particular part of any business cycle ends. As a result, before drawing any conclusions the NBER must wait until it sees a clear picture of what's happening with the economy. Although many economists identify recessions and expansions based on at least two quarters (six months) of economic data, NBER uses its own models. Still, a growth spurt that lasts one full quarter won't indicate the start of an expansion; nor will a decline that lasts a quarter indicate the start of a recession. Bearing that in mind, a time lag of at least six months is typically required before the NBER even considers declaring a recession or a recovery, which effectively renders the official announcement useless for traders.

The peak of a business cycle occurs during the last month before some key economic indicators begin to fall. These indicators include employment, output, and new housing starts. We talk more about economic indicators and which of them are critical for traders to watch in the "Understanding Economic Indicators" section later in the chapter. However, because neither a recession nor a recovery can be declared until enough data are accumulated, finding a way around the time lag in official information is impossible.

Signals that the economy was weakening became clear to the markets as early as October 2007, when the major indexes hit their peaks. Looking at an earlier business cycle, you can see the whole process. Just as in October 2007, clear signs the economy was headed toward a recession were seen as early as the spring of 2000, which is when the Nasdaq index hit its peak and began its downward spiral. The effects of the recession took a bit longer to hit the other major exchanges, but they started a downward trend by the summer of 2000. Just like in 2008, job losses had started mounting by mid-2000, and many economists already were sending alarms that the economy was headed into a recession.

Even though the NBER announced the official beginning of that recession as March 21, 2001, and the official end of the trough and beginning of the recovery as November 2001, no significant recovery was seen in the markets until October 2002. Job growth remained anemic as of early 2004. The first sign of job growth was seen during the fourth quarter of 2003, after nearly three years of job losses. That economic expansion finally picked up steam, and ultimately lasted through 2007.

Identifying periods of economic growth and recession

Considering the type of lag time between events and official pronouncements from the NBER, we're sure you're wondering how you can determine which part of the cycle the economy is in and how you can use this information as a trader. Most economists attribute changing business cycles to disturbances in the economy. Growth spurts, for example, result from surges in private or public spending. One way public spending can surge is the building or upgrading of infrastructure, when government spending increases and companies in industries related to the construction effort prosper. They often need to increase hiring to fulfill government orders. Employees at these companies usually receive increases in their take-home pay and start spending that extra money. As consumer optimism increases, other companies must fulfill consumers' wants and needs, so production and output also increase in companies that are unrelated to the building of highways, schools, hospitals, hockey rinks, bridges, and other infrastructure projects.

When these same factors work in reverse, the start of a recession is sure to follow. For example, a cut in government spending will likely result in layoffs at related industrial plants, reduced take-home pay, and finally declines in output and production to cope with reduced spending.

In addition to government spending, a decision by the BoC and the Fed to either raise or lower interest rates is another major disturbance to the economy. When interest rates rise, spending slows, and that can lead to a recession. When interest rates are cut, spending usually goes up, and that can aid in spurring an economic recovery.

Another school of economic thought disagrees with the notion that government policy or spending is responsible for changes in the business cycle. This second group of theorists believes that differences in productivity levels and consumer tastes are the primary forces driving the business cycle. From this point of view, only businesses and consumers can drive changes in the economic cycle. These economists don't believe that governmentally driven monetary or policy changes impact the cycle.

Which camp you believe is not critical; the key is picking up the signs of when the economy is in a recession and when it's in an expansion. Peaks and troughs are flat periods (periods where the high or low stays primarily even before moving in the opposite direction) and are impossible to identify until months after they end. As a trader, you can identify shifts in buying and spending behaviour by watching various economic indicators. By doing so, you can discover when the economy is in the early stages of a recovery or recession or if it's fully into a recession or recovery.

It's not very often that the economies of Canada and the United States are out of sync. At the time this book was published, Canada's companies did not warrant any American-style bailouts — well, except for the American automobile manufacturers in Ontario and the usual favours so often extended to Air Canada in Quebec. In fact, Canada's economy was so admired by foreign investors that our dollar almost reached parity with the U.S. dollar again while our interest rates were at all-time lows. The escalating value of our dollar can lead to deflation, but our international purchasing power is enhanced and we do not import as much inflation.

Relating bull markets and bear markets to the economy

You've probably heard the terms *bull market* and *bear market*. To understand what they mean, you first need to know how economic cycles affect the stock market. *Bulls* are people who believe that all is right with the world and the stock market is heading for an increase. They definitely think the economy is expanding. *Bears* are people who believe the economy is heading for a downturn, and stocks will either stagnate or go down. A *bull market* is a market in which a majority of stocks are increasing in value, and a *bear market* is a market in which a majority of stocks are decreasing. Bears definitely believe the economy is either in a recession or headed that way.

You can make money as a trader regardless of whether the bulls or the bears are right. The key: Identify the way the market is headed and then buy or sell into that trend. During a bear market, traders make their money by selling short, or taking advantage of falling prices (more about that in Chapter 14). Traders sell short by borrowing stock from their broker and then selling it with the hope of making a profit when the price falls.

Even during a bear market, some stocks offer opportunities for traders to make money, including oil and gas stocks and real estate investment trusts (REITs). Some petroleum stocks and REITs pay higher dividends and, therefore, are most attractive when the rest of the market is falling or showing no growth potential. During a bull market, riding a stock through recovery but getting out before a fall is key. We talk more about trends and what they mean in Chapter 10.

Sector Rotation

In general, the markets are divided into sectors, and at any given time some of those sectors will be expanding, even during a bear market. Some traders are adept at rotating their investments from one sector to another that is more likely to benefit from the part of the business cycle that is driving the economy. This basic trading strategy is called *sector rotation*.

The American guru of traders who want to take advantage of sector rotation is Sam Stovall, chief investment strategist for Standard & Poor's, who wrote *Sector Investing* — the classic work on sector rotation — in 1996. Stovall developed the Sector Rotation Model shown in Figure 5-2. As you can see, he found that market cycles tend to lead business cycles. Markets tend to bottom out just before the rest of the economy is in a full recession. The start of a bull market, on the other hand, can be seen just before the rest of the economy starts its climb toward recovery. Markets reach their tops first and enter a bear market before the general economic indicators show a peak.

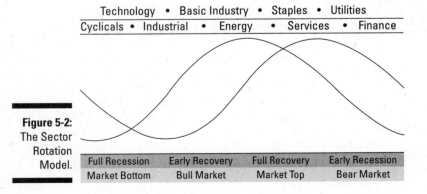

Figure 5-2:
The Sector
Rotation
Model.

Technology • Basic Industry • Staples • Utilities
Cyclicals • Industrial • Energy • Services • Finance

Full Recession	Early Recovery	Full Recovery	Early Recession
Market Bottom	Bull Market	Market Top	Bear Market

As a trader, you can take advantage of this knowledge by knowing which sectors are more likely to rise during the various parts of a market cycle. You need to buy into the sectors with stock prices that are likely to rise, or you can sell short the sectors in which prices are expected to fall. (We discuss short selling in Chapter 14.)

Early recovery

You can spot an early recovery when consumer expectations and industrial production are beginning to rise while interest rates are bottoming out. That scenario was evident during a recent economic cycle discovered during the fall and early winter months of 2003. During the early stages of recovery, Stovall found that industrial, basic industry, and energy sectors tend to take the lead.

Full recovery

When the economy has fully recovered, we start seeing signs that consumer expectations are falling and productivity levels and interest rates are flattening out. These factors were seen during the economy's recent period of full recovery leading up to the economic peak in December 2007. During that period, companies in the consumer staples and services sectors exhibited a tendency to take the lead, and interest rates had actually started to fall. As knowledgeable investors know, when that happens it's only a matter of time before a recession follows. The staples of life are needed even in times of recession, so the stocks of those companies tend to benefit.

Early recession

When the economy reaches the earliest part of a recession, consumer expectations fall more sharply and productivity levels start to drop. Interest rates also begin to drop. Most of the 217,200 Canadian job losses during the 2001 economic downturn occurred during late 2001 and early 2002. During 2001, the Bank of Canada cut interest rates nine times to try to ease the concerns about the upcoming recession. The BoC started to raise rates in 2002, but then lowered them in 2003 and again in 2008 during the mortgage crisis. At the time of this writing, the BoC's bank rate (the interest rate the BoC charges to banks) was 0.50 percent. Another key recession sign was the mounting job losses in 2008 and early 2009.

Dissecting sector rotation

Some wag once said that the stock market predicted 15 of the last 8 recessions. And although it's true that the market isn't a terribly precise economic prognosticator, that's sort of beside the point. Economic indicators can help you understand the big picture, which, in turn, can help you make better trading decisions.

Of all the economic tools available, sector rotation analysis is probably the most valuable. Even if the Sector Rotation Model can't help you identify an economic cycle, it can identify sectors and stocks that are ripe for further study.

When we trade, we want the strongest stocks in the strongest sectors, which is why we monitor sector performance carefully. Knowing the sectors that are performing best enables you to anticipate which sectors are likely to begin outperforming and which are likely to fade. Using those projections, you can start monitoring stocks in those up-and-coming sectors. For a sector to outperform, the stocks within it must also outperform. You need to be monitoring those stocks before they begin their runs.

Plenty of data are available to help you separate the strongest sectors from the underperformers. *Investor's Business Daily,* for example, ranks nearly 200 industry groups by price performance. StockCharts.com provides a similar capability with its Performance Charts (`stockcharts.com/charts/performance`). You can also monitor sectors by following exchange-traded funds (ETFs), such as the Select Sector SPDRs (Standard & Poor's Depository Receipts) at `www.spdrindex.com`.

Utilities and finance-sector stocks are the most likely to see rising prices during the first part of a recession, because under those circumstances investors seek stocks that provide some safety (because owning them involves less risk) and pay higher dividends. Gold and other valuable mineral stocks also look good to investors seeking safety. Though the financial sector did not follow this pattern in the 2008 recession, it is still typical to see banks, insurance companies, and investment firms perform well during the early parts of a recession.

Full recession

Although it may not make much sense intuitively, during a full recession is when we first start seeing indications that consumer expectations are improving, which is shown by increased spending. However, industrial productivity remains flat, and businesses won't increase their production levels until they believe consumers actually are ready to spend again. Additionally, interest rates continue to drop, because both business and consumer spending are slow, so demand for the money weakens while competition for new credit customers grows among banks and other financial institutions. During a full recession, cyclical and technology stocks tend to lead the way. Investors look to safety during a recession, so companies that satisfy that need tend to do best.

Understanding Economic Indicators

The key to knowing where, as a trader, you are during the business cycle is watching the economic indicators. Every day you open your newspaper, you see at least one story about how the economy is doing based on various economic indicators. Popular indicators track employment, money supply, interest rates, housing starts, housing sales, production levels, purchasing statistics, consumer confidence, shipping, and many other factors that indicate how the economy is doing.

Economic indicators are useful to your trading. Some are definitely more useful than others. We don't have the space here to describe each of the indicators; instead, we focus on the ones that can provide you with the most help in making your trading decisions.

BoC and Fed watch: Understanding how interest rates affect markets

Watching the Governor of the Bank of Canada and the Federal Open Market Committee (FOMC) of the Federal Reserve (which includes the seven members of the Board of Governors, the president of the New York Federal Reserve Bank, and presidents of 4 of the other 11 Federal Reserve Banks) and tracking what it may or may not do to interest rates is almost a daily spectator sport in the business press. Although members of the FOMC meet only eight times per year, discussions about whether the Bank of Canada and the Federal Reserve will raise or lower interest rates serves as fodder for stories published on at least a weekly, if not daily, basis. Every time BoC Governor Mark Carney or Fed Chairman Ben Bernanke speaks, people look for indications of what the BoC or the Fed may be thinking. Speeches by other members of the BoC staff or the Fed likewise are carefully dissected between FOMC meetings. Most press coverage will shortcut all this by saying the BoC or the Fed may raise or lower interest rates.

The Canadian and U.S. economies tend to move in lock step, so the perception is for monetary policy in both countries to go in the same direction. However, that has been less true since late 2000, when the Bank of Canada established eight pre-set dates per year to announce its key interest rate policy. This schedule is referred to as the BoC's fixed announcement dates, or fixed dates. In setting interest rates, Canada has recently tended to focus more closely on the inflation rate than the United States, which tends to be concerned with employment.

Because the Canadian economy is inextricably linked with the U.S., our manufacturing costs and output are structured around a Canadian dollar valued at a discount against the U.S. currency. The Canadian dollar is often perceived as a petro-currency by international investors: it fluctuates with oil and gas commodity prices. When the interest rate policy also starts to attract investors to Canada, the effect of a strong loonie is a struggle for our exporters. Higher interest rates and high energy prices causing a high currency exchange rate further increase the cost of our exports.

Therefore, Canadian interest rate policy is crafted with an eye to U.S. rate policy. Canada must be aware of U.S. interest rates in order to stay competitive with the potential of expanding exports to the United States. So that we are not totally dependent on our southern neighbour, we undertake regular trade missions to the growing markets across the Pacific.

The key reason for you to be concerned is that a change in interest rates can have a major impact on the economy and thus on how you make trades. An increase in rates is likely to slow down spending, which can lead to an overall economic slowdown. For the most part, when the BoC or the Fed raises interest rates, it's because the board believes the economy is overheated, which can fuel the risk of inflation. An increase in interest rates can reduce spending and thus ease overheating. If, on the other hand, the BoC or the Fed fears an economic downturn or is trying to fuel growth during a recession, the board frequently decides to cut interest rates to spur spending and growth.

The Bank of Canada's policies and strategies can be gleaned from its quarterly *Monetary Policy Report*. The current economic state of the nation and implications for inflation are covered at length. The information at www.bankofcanada.ca dates back to 1995.

Speeches by the BoC Governor and Deputy Governor are also listed at this informative Web site. The speeches often are made at the press conferences that accompany the *Monetary Policy Report* or an opening statement to a Standing Committee of the Senate or House of Commons.

For the American perspective, you can get a good hint about what the Fed is thinking by reading the Beige Book, which is a report compiled by the 12 federal reserve banks. Summaries about current economic conditions in each of the 12 districts are circulated to Federal Reserve Board members two weeks prior to the FOMC meeting, at which monetary policy, including interest rates, is set. The summaries are developed through interviews with key business leaders, economists, market experts, and others familiar with each individual district. You can read the Beige Book online at www.federal reserve.gov/FOMC/BeigeBook/2008/. Find out about past FOMC statements at www.federalreserve.gov/fomc. These links give you access not only to current issues of the Beige Book and FOMC statements but also to information from those two sources dating back as far as 1996. They can provide an excellent overview of economic trends and possible shifts in Federal Reserve monetary policy.

Money supply

The money supply is a key number to watch, because growth in money supply can be a leading indicator of inflation in situations when the money supply is greater than the supply of goods. When more money than goods is around, prices are likely to rise. Commodities and money traders will want to keep close watch over these three aggregates — money supply, inflation, and goods and services.

The Bank of Canada and the Fed track two monetary aggregates: M1 and M2. M1 includes money used for payments, such as currency in circulation plus chequing accounts in banks, trust companies, credit unions, and *caisses populaires*. The Canadian monetary aggregates can be tracked at www.bankofcanada.ca (see Weekly Financial Statistics) and at www.statcan.gc.ca (see Economic and Financial Data). Currency sitting in bank vaults and bank deposits at the central banks are not part of M1, but instead are part of the monetary base. M2 includes M1 money plus retail nontransaction deposits, which is money sitting in retail savings accounts and money market accounts. You can follow the American money stock measures for M1 and M2 at www.federalreserve.gov/releases/h6/Current. When you total the money base, M1 and M2, you can track the total amount of money sitting in someone's account or circulating in the economy.

The Bank of Canada attempts to manage money growth through short-term interest rates, or through the reserves provided to deposit-taking institutions. When short-term rates change, they affect mortgage and lending rates at banks and credit unions. When interest rates rise, consumers and businesses pay off existing loans. The result is slow growth of M1+ and other monetary aggregates. The BoC monitors several indicators to achieve its inflation target. The growth of M1+ provides useful information on the future economy and is a leading indicator of the rate of inflation. The Bank of Canada's monetary policy supports a level of spending on goods and services consistent with keeping inflation within its target range. By monitoring the supply of money and credit, the BoC ensures that total spending in the economy is consistent with controlling inflation.

The Fed decided in July 2000 that it no longer would set target ranges for growth rates of the monetary aggregates. In the late 1970s, money supply drove the Fed's decision-making process. As money supply grew to what was considered out of hand, the Fed kept raising interest rates until they were so high that many believe the Fed's moves actually caused the recession in the early 1980s. After that time, managing interest rates became a higher priority than managing money aggregates. The Fed didn't kill the idea of target ranges for the money supply until it was certain that managing interest rates alone would help stem inflation. Now that the Fed has proved interest-rate management works, it decided it no longer needed to set a target for monetary aggregates.

Inflation rate

Several key economic indicators point us toward ways of identifying the risk of inflation. The primary overall indicator is GDP: a country's gross domestic product. (GDP is released quarterly by Statistics Canada; in the United States, the Department of Commerce's Bureau of Economic Analysis (BEA) tracks GDP.) You can also follow monthly trends by keeping your eye out for the Consumer Price Index, the Industrial Product Price Index, the Producer Price Index, and the Retail Trade Survey, as described in the list that follows.

- ✔ **Gross domestic product (GDP)** represents the monetary value of goods produced during a specific period in the economy. GDP is released quarterly in three different versions. The first version, which includes advance data, is released at 8:30 a.m. on the last business day of January, April, July, and October for the previous quarter. Preliminary data are released a month later, and the final numbers are released a month after that. GDP is important to traders because it indicates the pace at which the economy is growing. In the GDP, you'll find numbers for consumer spending, private domestic investment, government or public spending, and net exports. Essentially, it includes all information about labour and property involving business activities inside the confines of Canada and the United States. If GDP fails to meet expectations set by the analysts or exceeds market expectations, stock prices will be affected at least temporarily. For a glimpse of what may be in store for the future, pay attention to the rate that inventories are increasing. It can be a leading indicator that growth is slowing or consumer demand is changing. Even though the final official numbers are released quarterly, the advance reports and preliminary reports give you a good indication of what to expect in the final numbers. Canadian GDP reports can be found at www40.statcan.gc.ca/l01/cst01/gdps04a-eng.htm. You can get full details about the American GDP reports at http://bea.doc.gov/national/index.htm#gdp. You can track the release schedule for the GDP reports, as well as other government statistical reports, at http://bea.doc.gov/national/index.htm. Often the report is posted at the Bureau of Economic Analysis early in the morning before the actual release and embargoed until the official release time, so as a trader you may be able to get a heads up before the news is actually reported by the press.

- ✔ **Consumer Price Index (CPI)** measures the cost of a representative basket of goods and services, including food, energy, housing, clothing, transportation, medical care, entertainment, and education. Each type of cost is weighted. For example, medical costs are weighted more highly in recent years, because they are rising at a faster pace, especially as the current population ages. In addition to the broad CPI, a core rate is issued that excludes food, mortgage interest, and energy, which are considered more volatile. The core rate is an indicator you can watch for general price shifts. The financial markets, in general, look for a rate of increase in the range of 1 percent to 2 percent; anything higher may be a sign of inflation and can cause at least a temporary shock to stock prices. Any shock to stock prices obviously can be an opportunity for traders. CPI statistics are released in Canada by Statistics Canada at 7 a.m. ET around the 18th of each month. You can find CPI data at either www.statcan.gc.ca or www.bankofcanada.ca. This cost of living measure uses a shopping basket of about 600 goods and services used by most households. The American CPI is released by the U.S. Labor Department at 8:30 a.m. ET around the 15th of each month and reflects data from the previous month. You can track the U.S. CPI at the Web site of the U.S. Department of Labor's Bureau of Labor Statistics at www.bls.gov/cpi/home.htm.

✔ **Industrial Product Price Index (IPPI)** measures price changes for major commodities sold by manufacturers in Canada. The prices collected are for goods sold at the factory gate. As a result, the prices covered by the IPPI refer not to what a purchaser pays but to what the producer receives. They exclude all indirect taxes, such as sales tax and tariffs, because this money does not go to the factors of production (such as labour, capital, or profit). They also exclude any transportation service performed by a common carrier beyond the factory gate and any distribution services performed by the retail or wholesale trade industries (www.statcan.gc.ca).

✔ **Producer Price Index (PPI)** is an American basket full of other indexes that affect domestic producers, including goods manufacturing, finishing, and agricultural and other commodities. The U.S. Labor Department collects more than 100,000 prices each month from 30,000 production and manufacturing firms to calculate this basket. The markets pay close attention to the index, because even though it isn't as powerful an inflation index as the CPI, it gives traders clues about what to expect in the next CPI release. The PPI is released a couple of days before the CPI, at 8:30 a.m. ET usually around the 13th of each month, and it reflects data from the previous month. You can track PPI data at www.bls.gov/ppi.

✔ **The Retail Trade Survey** is a monthly collection of sales by province and territory from a sample of retailers. Sales estimates are a key indicator of consumer purchasing patterns in Canada. Furthermore, retail sales are an important component of the GDP. The Bank of Canada relies partly on monthly retail sales when determining interest rate policy. Retail sales don't include door-to-door selling or vending machines. Internet sales are included only when conducted through the same retail establishment. Canada excludes restaurant food sales, whereas the U.S. does include these food sales in its Retail Sales Data. Statistics Canada reports Retail Trade at www40.statcan.gc.ca/l01/cst01/media01-eng.htm.

✔ **Retail Sales Data** tracks information in the United States about (you guessed it) retail sales by large corporations and by small mom-and-pop retail outlets. The U.S. Census Bureau, which is a part of the Department of Commerce, surveys hundreds of firms each month using a random sampling of retail outlets that make federal insurance contributions to collect the data, which is particularly important whenever you're trading stocks in the retail sector. The survey looks at changes in retail numbers from month to month — a negative number means sales levels decreased from the previous month. This type of negative news can be a shock to stock prices, especially for companies in the retail sector. The data are released about two weeks after they are collected, or at 8:30 a.m. ET about the 12th of each month. You can track the retail sales data online at www.census.gov/marts/www/marts.html.

Deflation

In addition to watching the economic indicators for inflation discussed in the previous section, traders also need to watch the numbers for signs of deflation. Serious concern about the possibility of deflation takes centre stage when prices start falling. *Deflation* occurs when a sustained period of falling prices takes place. The Great Depression of the 1930s was a classic period of deflation. Many economists believe that printing more money cures deflation, because (as mentioned in the "Money supply" section) increases in the money supply normally lead to increases in prices when more money is around than goods to be purchased.

During periods of deflation, increasing the money supply isn't necessarily the answer. Some economists believe injecting more money into the economy is risky, especially when production capacity is in excess, and producers continue to produce goods even though prices are falling. In other economic situations, producers commonly stop producing when prices fall.

In early 2004, Japan faced a continuing period of deflation even though its central bank had lowered rates to an effective negative interest rate and continued printing money in attempts to prop up its sagging pricing structure, and yet prices were continuing to drop. Some economists believe the Japanese experienced a liquidity trap. No matter how much money Japan printed, prices continued downward in a deflationary spiral.

With housing prices, commodity prices, and stock prices falling, some are concerned that Canada and the United States could be headed in a similar direction. In fact, while we were writing this chapter in 2009, one of the arguments in favour of the stimulus bill was to ward off a deflationary spiral.

Jobless claims

The Labour Force Survey, another report from Statistics Canada (www.
statscan.gc.ca), is one of the most important leading indicators to watch.
This report is the first critical economic indicator released every month
and frequently sets the expectations for the rest of the month's reports. For
example, signs of a weak labour market reported in the Labour Force Survey
usually are a strong indication of poor retail sales and other possible negative reports later in the month. The summary also breaks down data by
industry, such as construction and manufacturing. For example, a significant
drop in employment numbers for the construction sector is a strong sign that
the housing starts report also will be negative.

This report can send shockwaves through the financial markets, especially
if the numbers that are released vary greatly from expectations. Stock prices
often fall whenever the report doesn't meet expectations or employment statistics show signs of weakness. On the other hand, stock prices can rise dramatically whenever the report indicates better than expected numbers. As
is true with any shock to the market, changes in prices are temporary unless
other indicators also exhibit the same trend or tendency.

The employment report can drive markets so strongly because its data are
only a few days old. Because it is so timely, this report is widely recognized as
the best indicator of unemployment and wage pressure. Rising unemployment
can be an early sign of recession, while increased pressure on wages can be an
early sign of inflation. The report also is a broad-based snapshot of the entire
labour market, covering 50,000 Canadian households and every major industry.

Statistics Canada releases the report at 8:30 a.m. ET on the first Friday of
each month with data for the previous month. The two key parts of the
report that traders need to watch are

- Unemployment and new jobs created
- Average weekly hours worked and average earnings

In the United States, the Bureau of Labor Statistics (BLS) (www.bls.gov)
produces the quaintly named Employment Situation Summary.

Another employment indicator traders like to watch is the Employment
Cost Index (ECI). It's especially relevant during actual times of inflation or
when fear exists that an inflationary period may be imminent. The ECI is a
quarterly survey of employer payrolls that tracks movement in the cost of
labour, including wages, benefits, and bonuses. Wages and benefits make up
75 percent of the index. The BLS surveys more than 3,000 private-sector firms
and 500 local governments in the United States to develop the index. The ECI,
which reports data from the previous quarter, is released on the last business day in January, April, July, and October.

Consumer confidence

The Conference Board of Canada's survey of Canadian households has been ongoing since 1980. It measures consumers' level of optimism regarding current economic conditions. This index of consumer confidence is a crucial indicator of near-term sales for companies in the consumer product sector. It is constructed from responses to four attitudinal questions posed to random samples of Canadian households. Those surveyed are asked to give their views about their household's current and expected financial position and their short-term employment outlook. They are also asked to assess whether now is a good or a bad time to make a major purchase such as a house, car, or other big-ticket item. The Conference Board of Canada has revived the Help Wanted Index. Rather than major newspapers, the index tracks 79 job-posting Web sites throughout Canada. This leading indicator of employment level was abandoned by Statistics Canada during early 2003 as it was deemed to have lost its predictive power. The index is published monthly at www.222.conferenceboard.ca.

Keeping an eye on consumer confidence in the United States is another way of casting a glance into the future of the market. When confidence is high, consumers are more likely to spend. The best overall index for monitoring American consumer confidence is the Consumer Confidence Index (CCI), which is put out by the Conference Board. This index is compiled through a sampling of 5,000 households and is widely respected as the most accurate indicator of consumer confidence.

Although minor changes in the CCI are not strongly indicative of a problem, major shifts can be a sign of choppy waters ahead. Most people who watch the CCI look for three- to six-month trends. The Fed, as an example, looks closely at consumer confidence when determining interest rate policy, which as you know can greatly affect stock prices. When confidence is trending lower, the Fed is more likely to lower interest rates. Stock markets love to hear about the Fed lowering interest rates. Confidence levels that are trending higher can be a warning of a pending inflationary period. A rapidly rising trend in consumer confidence can lead the Fed to raise interest rates to cut off inflation; moreover, a rise in interest rates can send stock prices lower.

The Conference Board releases the CCI at 10 a.m. ET the last Tuesday of each month. The biggest weakness of this index is that it isn't based on actual spending data. Instead, it's a survey of planned spending. You can track the CCI online at www.conference-board.org/economics/consumer confidence.cfm.

Business activity

A number of key economic indicators can give you a good idea of what business is doing and how that information may impact the stock markets. Key business indicators to watch include

- **The Ivey Purchasing Managers Index:** This index, sponsored by the Richard Ivey School of Business (University of Western Ontario) and the Purchasing Management Association of Canada (PMAC), shows month-to-month variation in economic activity.

  The Ivey Purchasing Managers Index measures monthly changes in purchases as indicated by a panel of purchasing managers from across Canada. The 175 participants have been selected geographically and by sector to match the Canadian economy as a whole. The index includes both the public and private sectors. Index panel members indicate whether activity is higher than, the same as, or lower than the previous month across five categories: purchases, employment, inventories, supplier deliveries, and prices. The index is released at 10 a.m. ET on the third or fourth working day of each month at `http://iveypmi.uwo.ca`.

- **The American Purchasing Managers Index (PMI):** One of the first economic indicators released each month is the American Manufacturing Report on Business, which surveys purchasing managers and provides reviews of new orders, production, deliveries, and inventories. This report is released at 10 a.m. ET the first business day of each month and reflects data compiled from the previous month. You can track this report online at the Institute for Supply Management `www.ism.ws`.

- **Durable Goods Orders:** The American Commerce Department releases another critical economic indicator of business activity in the area of Durable Goods Orders. This indicator measures the dollar volume of orders, shipments, and unfilled orders of durable goods, or types of merchandise that have a life span of three years or more. This report serves as a leading indicator of manufacturing activity and can move the stock market, especially when its numbers vary from expectations. You can track the Durable Goods Orders online at `www.census.gov/indicator/www/m3/index.html`.

- **The Building Permits Survey for Canada:** This survey covers 2,400 municipalities representing 95 percent of the population. It provides an early indication of building activity. In addition to data on the number and value of building permits issued by Canadian municipalities, this publication provides information on the average value of dwellings, the number and value of mobile homes, and permits issued for building renovation. The value of planned construction activities shown in this release excludes engineering projects (such as waterworks, sewers, or culverts) and land. The Building Permits Survey is released by Statistics Canada on the fourth business day of each month at 8:30 a.m. ET and can be found at `www.statcan.gc.ca`.

✔ **Housing Starts and Building Permits:** The American report is another that's released by the Commerce Department. It can be a leading indicator of the direction the economy will take. When the number of permits rises, a positive economic indicator results. About 25 percent of investment dollars are plowed into housing starts, and that makes up about 5 percent of the overall economy. The report is broken down by regions — Northeast, Midwest, South, and West — so you can also get a strong indication of the strength of the economy on a regional basis. You can track this indicator online at `www.census.gov/const/www/C40/table2.html`.

✔ **Manufacturing Surveys:** The Canadian Monthly Survey of Manufacturing covers 21 industry groups that produce goods for both industrial and consumer use. The manufacturing sector's activity is monitored monthly and annually, as it accounts for a large part of Canada's gross domestic product. It's released by Statistics Canada around the 16th of each month at 8:30 a.m. ET and can be found at `www.statcan.gc.ca`.

Each Federal Reserve Bank district in the United States compiles data from regional manufacturing surveys that can help you find a score of indicators including new orders, production, employment, inventories, delivery times, prices, and export and import orders. Positive reports indicate an expanding economy. Negative reports indicate a contracting economy. The two most closely watched are the Philadelphia survey at `www.phil.frb.org/econ/bos/bosschedule.html` and the Chicago survey at `www.chicagofed.org/economic_research_and_data/cfmmi.cfm`. If you're trading in regional stocks, following the manufacturing surveys from the Federal Reserve Banks in key regions that you follow can help you determine the direction of the economy for the areas most relevant to the stocks you're trading.

Using the Data

You can see that plenty of data are available, but not all are relevant to the types of stocks you want to trade. Organizing your data collection and tracking the trends can make choosing economic signs and analyzing which part of the business cycle is driving the markets easier for you. We offer a few steps that can make this task much easier:

1. **Maintain a calendar of the release dates for the key economic indicators you decide to follow.**

The markets may move in anticipation of this data, so if you know that a key economic indicator is about to be released, be sure to watch stock price trends for the possible impact the anticipated release may be having on the market.

2. **Know the parts of the economy that are most impacted by the economic indicators you're following.**

   For example, the GDP strongly suggests the path of economic growth, but PPI and CPI are strong measures of inflation.

3. **Know which economic indicators are most important to the market.**

   For example, in times of inflation, economic indicators that reveal key data regarding inflation are the biggest market movers. If the markets are worried about growth, the growth components of GDP and other indicators will have the greatest potential for moving the markets.

4. **Know what the market is expecting to see in the numbers.**

   The actual number is not as critical as whether that number was expected by the markets. Surprises are what move the markets.

5. **Know what parts of the economic indicator are important.**

   Newspapers may write headlines for shock value, but the parts of the index they cover may not be what are critical to your decision making. For example, traders know that food and energy components of the CPI are volatile, so the more important number to watch is the core CPI, which doesn't include food and energy. The news media may focus only on the more volatile number.

6. **Don't overreact to a newly announced economic indicator that didn't meet market expectations.**

   Indicators frequently are revised after they're initially issued. The difference may merely be related to a revision and not an indication of a shift in the business cycle. However, be sure to check information about revisions to the previous month and how those revisions have impacted the current month's trend.

7. **Monitor the trends.**

   On your calendar, keep track of key components of each economic indicator that you watch. Follow the trends of the most important data components to get a good idea of where the business cycle is headed.

Keeping a tight watch on economic indicators is the best way for you to determine at what point the economy is in a new business cycle. Waiting for official pronouncements is much too late. By the time they're released, that phase of the cycle may be over and a new cycle may be driving the markets.

Chapter 6

Digging Into the Critical Parts of Fundamental Analysis

Most traders don't worry about the fundamentals. These numbers include the general economic and market conditions that impact a stock, as well as the financial information known about a company's activities and its financial successes and failures. Instead, traders tend to focus entirely on technical analysis and trends that can be seen using that type of analysis.

Taking the time to analyze the fundamentals of a stock puts you one step ahead of the trading crowd. Using fundamental analysis, you can determine how a stock's price compares with those of similar companies based on earnings growth and other key factors, including business conditions. This chapter helps you understand critical parts of fundamental analysis and how you can use the information gathered from it to make better trading decisions.

When starting a fundamental analysis, select an industry or business sector that interests you for possible stock purchases. Sometimes, a particular company piques your fancy, and you start your research by looking at the major players in that company's sector or by turning to the sector's fundamentals. Regardless of how you start, you need to narrow down your list of the companies you want to compare to the ones that are in similar businesses within the sector, so you can find the best opportunity. You also want to be sure the stock trades well by looking at its daily volume of trades. Stocks with low trading volume can be hard to get into and out of, making them riskier stocks.

Most of the tools used in fundamental analysis require you to compare at least two companies operating in similar business environments to understand the meaning of the information. For the purposes of discussion in this chapter, we look at two big players in the home improvement retail sector: Home Depot and Lowe's. If you've followed the business conditions in this sector, you know that both faced a severe downturn after the housing bubble burst in 2007. Although in 2008 they were still building new stores, they slowed down their expansions waiting for a better market environment.

The destruction of value that recently took place in the American housing market did not affect Canada as much because our lenders are more prudent. Also, our mortgage expenses are not tax deductible so our real estate loans tend to be smaller. Home Depot and Lowe's had much more pleasant corporate conditions in Canada during 2008 and 2009, but our market is too small to compensate for the sad state in the States.

Before discovering the tools of fundamental analysis, you first must understand how to read key financial statements, including the critical parts of the income statement, cash-flow statements, and the balance sheet.

Checking Out the Income Statement

The *income statement* is where a company periodically reports its revenues, costs, and net earnings or profit. It's basically a snapshot of how much a company is earning from its operations and any extraordinary earnings that may have impacted its bottom line during a specific period of time. From the income statement, you'll be able to determine the impact of taxes, interest, and depreciation on a company's earnings and to forecast earnings potential.

Every income statement has three key sections: revenue, expenses, and income. The revenue section includes all money taken into the company by selling its products or services minus any costs directly related to the sale of those products or services (called cost of goods sold). The expenses section includes all operating expenses for the company not directly related to sales, as well as expenses for depreciation (writing off the use of equipment and buildings — tangible assets), amortization (writing off the use of patents, copyrights, and other intellectual property or intangible assets such as goodwill), taxes, and interest.

The income section includes various calculations of income. Usually you'll find one calculation that shows income after operating expenses and before interest, taxes, depreciation, and amortization, called EBITDA. This will be followed by net income, which is the bottom line showing how much a company earned after all its costs and expenses were deducted. Public companies must file financial reports with the OSC and the SEC on a quarterly and annual basis. You can read any public company's financial reports at

Canada's System for Electronic Document Analysis and Retrieval (SEDAR) (`www.sedar.com`) and at the EDGAR Web site (`www.sec.gov/edgar.shtml`) for American issuers.

A year's worth of figures won't show you much, so you need to look at the trends throughout a number of years to be able to forecast growth potential or assess how well a company is doing compared with its competitors. We discuss a number of good sources for finding fundamental information in Chapter 4.

Both quarterly and annual reports are important. Comparing a company's results on a quarter-to-quarter basis gives the trader an idea of how well the company is meeting analysts' expectations as well as the company's projections. Also, looking at, for example, results for the first quarter of 2008 versus the first quarter of 2009 you can see whether a company's earnings are increasing or decreasing in a similar market environment. While for some types of companies the first quarter is generally productive, other types of companies, such as retail stores, are dependent mostly on fourth-quarter holiday results, so you need to know what is expected in earnings for the various quarters. Quarterly results allow you to monitor results from similar time periods.

Annual statements give you a summary for the year. You can also compare current-year results to the results over a number of years to see at what rate the company is growing.

Revenues

The first line of any income statement includes the company's sales revenues. This number reflects all the sales that have been generated by the company before any costs are subtracted. Rather than go to all the trouble of showing their math — gross sales — any sales discounts, adjustments for returns, or other allowances = *net sales*. Most companies show only net sales on their income statements. From these figures, you want to see obvious signs of steady growth in revenues. A decrease in revenues from year to year is a red flag that indicates problems — it's probably not a good potential trading choice unless you're considering shorting the stock.

Cost of goods sold

The *cost of goods sold* (also known as cost of merchandise sold or cost of services sold, depending on the type of business) is an amount that shows the total costs directly related to selling a company's products or services. The costs included in this part of the revenue section include purchases, purchase discounts, and freight charges or other costs directly related to selling a product or service.

Gross margins

The gross margin or gross profit is the net result of subtracting the cost of goods sold from net sales. This figure shows you how much money a company is making directly from sales before considering other operating costs. The gross profit is the dollar figure calculated by subtracting costs of goods sold from net revenue. The gross margin is a ratio calculated by dividing gross profit by net revenue. Watching year-to-year trends in gross margins gives you a good idea of a company's profit growth potential from its key revenue sources.

You can calculate a gross margin ratio by dividing a company's gross profit by its net sales:

Gross margin ratio = Gross profit ÷ Net sales

The *gross margin ratio,* expressed as a percentage, considers revenue from sales minus the costs directly involved in making those sales and is a good indicator of how well a company uses its production, purchasing, and distribution resources to earn a profit. The higher the percentage, the more efficient a company is at making its profit.

By comparing gross margin ratios among various companies within the same industry or business sector, you can get an idea of how efficient each company is at generating profits. Investors favour companies that are more efficient.

To give you an idea of how to use this ratio and others in this chapter, we compare figures from two of the leaders in the home improvement retail sector — Home Depot and Lowe's. Tables 6-1 and 6-2 present the gross profits section from the past three annual income statements (information taken from Yahoo! Finance) for each respective company. Table 6-3 compares the gross margin ratios for the two companies.

Table 6-1   Home Depot Gross Profits (all numbers in thousands)

Fiscal Year Ending	Feb 3, 2008	Jan 28, 2007	Jan 29, 2006
Net Revenue	77,349,000	90,837,000	81,511,000
Cost of Goods Sold	51,352,000	61,054,000	54,191,000
Gross Profit	25,997,000	29,783,000	27,320,000

Table 6-2	Lowe's Gross Profits (all numbers in thousands)		
Fiscal Year Ending	**Feb 1, 2008**	**Feb 2, 2007**	**Feb 3, 2006**
Net Revenue	48,283,000	46,927,000	43,243,000
Cost of Goods Sold	31,556,000	30,729,000	28,453,000
Gross Profit	16,727,000	16,198,000	14,790,000

Table 6-3	Comparing Gross Margin Ratios by Year		
Fiscal Year	**2008**	**2007**	**2006**
Home Depot	33.6%	32.7%	33.5%
Lowe's	34.6%	34.5%	34.2%

You can see that Lowe's is slightly more efficient at using its production, purchasing, and distribution resources than Home Depot, because Lowe's has consistently higher gross margin ratios. Both corporations, however, show a trend toward improvement. The advantage of using this ratio rather than the actual revenue and profit numbers for comparison is that it makes comparing large companies with small companies within the same business or industry sector much easier. Even though Home Depot's sale volume is considerably higher, the ratio enables you to compare how efficiently each company uses its resources.

Expenses

The next section of the income statement shows the expenses of operating the business, including the sales costs and administrative costs of business operations. When comparing a company's year-to-year results, watch for signs of whether expenses are increasing faster than a company's gross profits — this can be an indication that a company is having a problem controlling its costs and won't bode well for future profit growth potential.

When you see expenses drop from one year to the next, while gross margins increase, that's usually a good sign and means a company likely has a good cost control program in place. The potential for growth in future profit margins is good.

Gross profits and expenses that rise at about the same rate are neither a significant positive nor negative sign. When that happens, the best way to get a reading on how a company is controlling its expenses is to compare its expenses with the expenses of other companies in similar businesses.

Interest payments

The interest payments portion of the expense section of an income statement gives you a view of a company's short-term financial health. Payments shown here include interest paid during the year on short- and long-term liabilities (more about those in the "Looking at debt" section later in the chapter). These payments are tax-deductible expenses, which help reduce a company's tax burden.

To determine a company's fiscal health, use the *interest expense number* and the earnings before interest and taxes (EBIT) number, which is usually shown on the income statement. If not, you can calculate it by subtracting interest and tax expenses from operating income (which will be gross profit minus expenses, also usually shown on the income statement). You can use this figure to determine whether the company is generating sufficient income to cover its interest payments using the interest coverage ratio. You can calculate the company's *interest coverage ratio* (expressed as a percentage, this ratio provides a clear-cut indicator of company's solvency) using this formula:

Interest coverage ratio = EBIT ÷ Interest expenses

Companies with high interest coverage ratios won't have any problems meeting their interest obligations, and their risk of insolvency (going belly up) is low. On the other hand, a low interest coverage ratio is a clear sign that a company has a problem and may face bankruptcy. Whether an interest coverage ratio tends to run high or low depends a great deal on the type of industry or business a company is in. Comparing the interest coverage ratios of several companies in the same industry or business is the best way to judge the value of the ratios.

Table 6-4 shows annual EBITs and interest expenses from three successive annual income statements for Home Depot, and Table 6-5 shows the corresponding numbers for Lowe's. Table 6-6 shows the respective interest coverage ratios for Home Depot and Lowe's.

Table 6-4	Home Depot Interest Payments (all numbers in thousands)		
Fiscal Year Ending	*Feb 3, 2008*	*Jan 28, 2007*	*Jan 29, 2006*
EBIT	7,316,000	9,700,000	9,425,000
Interest	696,000	392,000	143,000

Table 6-5	Lowe's Interest Payments (all numbers in thousands)		
Fiscal Year Ending	*Feb 1, 2008*	*Feb 2, 2007*	*Feb 3, 2006*
EBIT	4,750,000	5,152,000	4,654,000
Interest	239,000	154,000	158,000

Table 6-6	Comparing Interest Coverage Ratios		
Fiscal Year	*2008*	*2007*	*2006*
Home Depot	10.5%	24.7%	65.9%
Lowe's	19.9%	33.5%	29.5%

Lowe's is in a stronger position to make its interest payments, but neither company is in trouble. Lowe's has almost 20 times more income than it needs to make its interest payments and Home Depot has 10.5 times more income than it needs. Home Depot has taken on a lot more debt since 2006, when it had almost 66 times more income than it needed. Analysts generally consider a company in trouble whenever its interest coverage ratio falls below 3.

Tax payments

Corporations are always looking to avoid taxes, just like you. The *income tax expense* figure on the income statement shows the total amount that a company paid in taxes. A corporation pays between 15 percent and 38 percent of its income in taxes, depending on its respective size; however, corporations have many more write-offs they can use to reduce their tax burdens than you have as an individual taxpayer. Most large corporations have teams of tax specialists who spend their days looking for ways to minimize taxes. When you're looking at tax payments, it's important to review how well the company you're interested in manages its tax burden compared with other similar companies.

Dividend payments

Companies sometimes pay a *dividend,* hopefully part of the company profits, for each share of common stock that an investor holds. This dividend is distributed to shareholders usually once every quarter after the company's board of directors reviews company profits and determines whether to pay and how much the dividend will be. Paying dividends is not a tax-deductible expense for companies that pay them. In the past, traders have preferred growth stocks that do not pay dividends. However, the way dividends are taxed in Canada may have altered the way traders view dividend-paying stocks. Dividends are more attractive, because the tax on dividends is reduced by the dividend tax credit applied to dividends received from Canadian companies.

Testing profitability

You now can use the income statement to quickly check your company's profitability by using one or both of two ratios — the operating margin and net profit margin. The *operating margin* looks at profits from operations before interest and tax expenses, and the *net profit margin* considers earnings after the payment of those expenses.

We calculate operating margin using this formula:

Operating margin = Operating income ÷ Gross profit or net sales

We calculate net profit margin using this formula:

Net profit margin = Earnings after taxes ÷ Gross profit or net sales

Table 6-7 shows the gross profits, operating incomes, and earnings after taxes from three successive annual income statements for Home Depot; Table 6-8 shows the corresponding numbers for Lowe's. Table 6-9 compares the respective profitability margins for Home Depot and Lowe's.

Table 6-7   Home Depot Profitability (all numbers in thousands)

Fiscal Year Ending	Feb 3, 2008	Jan 28, 2007	Jan 29, 2006
Gross Profit	25,997,000	29,783,000	27,320,000
Operating Income	7,242,000	9,673,000	9,363,000
Earnings After Taxes	4,210,000	5,761,000	5,838,000

Table 6-8   Lowe's Profitability (all numbers in thousands)

Fiscal Year Ending	Feb 1, 2008	Feb 2, 2007	Feb 3, 2006
Gross Profit	16,727,000	16,198,000	14,790,000
Operating Income	4,705,000	5,152,000	4,654,000
Earnings After Taxes	2,809,000	3,105,000	2,765,000

Table 6-9   Comparing Profitability Margins

Fiscal Year	2008	2007	2006
Operating Margin			
Home Depot	27.9%	32.5%	34.3%
Lowe's	28.1%	31.8%	31.5%
Net Profit Margin			
Home Depot	16.2%	19.3%	21.4%
Lowe's	16.8%	19.2%	18.7%

You can see from the numbers in Table 6-9 that Lowe's did slightly better than Home Depot in the year ending February 2008. The mortgage mess of 2007 definitely had a strong impact on both stores. Home Depot's operating margin dropped by 4.6 percent from its year ending January 28, 2007 to its year ending February 3, 2008. Lowe's saw a downturn as well from 2007 to 2008, but slightly less at 3.7 percent. The drop in income for Home Depot after taxes are figured in was 3.1 percent between 2007 and 2008. Lowe's drop in income was 2.4 percent. Checking operating and net profit ratios is a good idea because doing so shows you the impact of taxes and interest on a company's profits.

Looking at Cash Flow

When you review income statements, you're looking at information based on accrual accounting. In *accrual accounting*, sales can be included when they're first contracted, even before revenue from them is collected. Sales made on credit are shown even if the company still needs to collect from the customer. Expenses are recorded as they're incurred and not necessarily as they're paid. However, the income statement definitely does not show a company's cash position. A company that's booking a high level of sales can have a stellar income statement but nevertheless be having trouble collecting from its customers, which may put that company in a cash-poor situation. That's why cash-flow statements are so important.

You can get an idea of your favourite company's actual cash flows from the adjustments shown on its *cash-flow statement.* The three sections to this statement are operating activities, investment activities, and financial activities. Cash-flow statements are filed with the OSC and the SEC along with income statements on a quarterly and annual basis.

Operating activities

Looking at cash flow from *operating activities* gives you a good picture of the cash that's available from a company's core business operations, including net income, depreciation and amortization, changes in accounts receivable, changes in inventory, and changes in other current liabilities and current assets. We talk more about these accounts in the "Scouring the Balance Sheet" section later on.

Calculating cash flow from operating activities includes adjustments to net income made by adding back items that were not actually cash expenditures but rather were required for reporting purposes. Depreciation is one such item. Similarly, expenses or income items that were reported for accrual purposes are subtracted out. For example, changes in accounts receivable are subtracted out, because they represent cash that has not been received. Conversely, changes in accounts payable represent payments that have not yet been made, so the cash still is on hand.

The bottom line: This section of a company's cash-flow statement shows actual *net cash from operations.* Table 6-10 compares three successive years of cash flow from operating activities at Home Depot and Lowe's.

Table 6-10	Total Cash Flow from Operating Activities (all numbers in thousands)		
Fiscal Year	*2008*	*2007*	*2006*
Home Depot	5,727,000	7,661,000	6,484,000
Lowe's	4,247,000	4,502,000	3,842,000

Looking at the numbers in Table 6-10, you can see both Lowe's and Home Depot's cash position dropped from 2007 to 2008. Home Depot's drop was more significant at $1.9 billion. If you're thinking about purchasing Home Depot stock, you'd certainly want to look more closely at cash-flow changes in operating activities to find out why it dropped so significantly in 2008. No doubt the economic climate was tough, but Home Depot faced a much more significant drop than Lowe's.

Depreciation

For all companies, one of the largest adjustments to cash flow is depreciation. Depreciation reflects the dollar value placed on the annual use of an asset. For example, if a company's truck will be a useable asset for five years, then the cost of that truck is depreciated over that five-year period. For accounting purposes on its income statement, a company must use a method called *straight-line depreciation,* a method of calculating depreciation in which the company determines the actual useful life span of an asset and then divides the purchase price of that asset by that life span. Each year depreciation expenses are recorded for each asset using this straight-line method. Although no cash is actually paid out, the total amount of depreciation is added back to the cash-flow statement.

For tax purposes, companies can be more creative by writing off assets much more quickly and thus reducing their tax burdens at the same pace. One type of write-off enables a company to deduct the full cost of an asset during its first year of use. Other methods enable a company to depreciate assets sooner than the straight-line method. How a company depreciates its assets can have a major impact on how much that company pays in taxes.

Although you won't know how a company depreciated its assets by looking at its cash-flow statement, you will know the adjustment made for depreciation for cash purposes. Remember that depreciation is an expense that must be reported on an income statement, and not a cash outlay.

Financing activities

The financing activities section of a cash-flow statement shows any common stock that was issued or repurchased during the period the report reflects, and any new loan activity. The financial activities section gives you a good idea whether the company is having trouble meeting its daily operating needs and as a result is seeking outside cash. You won't, however, find that new financing always is bad. A company may be in the process of a major growth initiative and may be financing that growth by issuing new debt or common stock.

The bottom line: This section of the cash-flow statement shows a company's total cash flow from financing activities. Table 6-11 compares three successive years of cash-flow totals from financing activities at Home Depot and Lowe's.

Table 6-11	Total Cash Flow from Financing Activities (all numbers in thousands)		
Fiscal Year	*2008*	*2007*	*2006*
Home Depot	(10,639,000)	(203,000)	(1,612,000)
Lowe's	(307,000)	(846,000)	(107,000)

A negative cash flow from financing activities usually means that a company has either paid off debt or repurchased stock. In this case both Home Depot and Lowe's repurchased stock in 2008. A positive cash flow here usually means new stock or debt was issued. Both companies issued new debt during this period as well. Obviously, many combinations of various financing activities can affect the bottom line, but the key for traders is to gain an understanding of why the change occurred and whether the company's reason for making the change was solid enough to improve its profit and growth picture.

Investment activity

This section of the cash-flow statement shows you how a company spends its money for growing long-term assets, such as new buildings or other new acquisitions, including major purchases of property, equipment, and other companies. It also shows you a company's sales of major assets or equity investments in other companies. Tracking investment activities gives investors a good idea of what major long-term capital planning activities have taken place during the period.

The bottom line: This section shows a company's total cash flow from investing activities. Comparing three successive years of investment activities by Home Depot and Lowe's, Table 6-12 indicates that both companies had significant capital outlays that more than likely were for opening new stores in 2006 and 2007. If you've followed the news about these two major home-improvement players, you know they're expanding the numbers of their stores around the country in a battle for market share. Home Depot did slow its expansion efforts in 2008 and decided to sell off some of its non-retail assets, which is reflected in the cash inflow of $4.8 billion in 2008 rather than a cash outlay that year.

Table 6-12	Total Cash Flow from Investing Activities (all numbers in thousands)		
Fiscal Year	*2008*	*2007*	*2006*
Home Depot	4,758,000	(7,647,000)	(4,586,000)
Lowe's	(4,123,000)	(3,715,000)	(3,674,000)

Scouring the Balance Sheet

The balance sheet gives you a snapshot of the company's assets and liabilities at a particular point in time. This differs from the income statement, which gives you operating results of a company during a particular period of time. A *balance sheet* has three sections, including

- An *assets* section that details everything the company owns.

- A *liabilities* section that details the company's debt or any other claims on the company's assets made by creditors.

- A *shareholder's equity* (also called owner's equity) section that lists all the claims made by owners or investors.

The balance sheet gets its name because the total assets of the company are supposed to equal the total claims against it — total liabilities plus total equity.

Assets and liabilities are listed on the balance sheet according to their liquidity, or how quickly and easily they can be converted into cash. Assets or liabilities that are more liquid appear first on the list, while the ones that are increasingly more difficult to convert to cash — long-term assets or liabilities — appear later. The asset section is divided into current assets (the ones that are used up in one year) and long-term assets (the ones whose life spans are longer than a year), as is the liabilities section — current liabilities and long-term liabilities.

Current assets include cash and other assets that can quickly and easily be converted into cash — marketable securities, money market investments, accounts receivables, and inventories. Long-term assets include holdings such as buildings, land, equipment, and sometimes goodwill. Similarly, on the liabilities side, current liabilities include any claims against assets that are due during the next 12 months, such as accounts payable and notes payable. Long-term liabilities are claims due in more than 12 months, such as mortgage or lease payables as well as bonds issued by the company.

Equity accounts include outstanding (remains on the market) preferred shares and/or common stocks and retained earnings. Retained earnings reflect the profits that are reinvested in the company rather than paid out as dividends to owners or shareholders.

Analyzing assets

In analyzing assets, two key ratios to look at are how quickly a company is collecting on its accounts receivable — the *accounts receivable turnover* — and how quickly inventory is sold — the *inventory turnover*.

A two-step process is used to find the accounts receivable turnover. First you must find out how quickly a company turns its accounts receivables into cash using this formula:

Accounts receivable turnover = Sales on account ÷ Average accounts receivable balance

Then you need to find out how quickly a company collects on its accounts by dividing the accounts receivable turnover into 365 to find the average number of days it takes to collect on accounts.

Testing for inventory turnover uses a similar two-step process. First you must find out how quickly inventory turns over during the year using this formula:

Inventory turnover ratio = Cost of goods sold ÷ Average inventory balance

Then you need to divide the inventory turnover ratio into 365 to find the average number of days it takes a company to turn over its inventory. Comparing these results for the companies you're considering can help you determine how well each company is handling the collection of its accounts receivable and the sale of its inventory. Obviously, the faster a company collects on accounts or sells its inventory, the better that company is doing in managing its assets. Compare companies in the same industry to determine how well a company is doing.

Whenever you see accounts receivable rising rapidly, and the number of days to collect on those accounts also is rising, consider it a red flag that signals cash problems likely lie ahead. Whenever you see inventory numbers rising a company can be having a hard time selling its product — which also raises a red flag signalling problems ahead.

We're summarizing these two common ratios so that you know what they mean whenever you see them mentioned by analysts. As a trader, you aren't likely to take the time to do these calculations yourself.

Looking at debt

When considering debt, or what a company owes, the two primary ratios you want to look at are the current ratio and acid, or quick, ratio. You can quickly calculate the *current ratio,* which tests whether a company can make its payments, by looking at the balance sheet and using this formula:

Current ratio = Current assets ÷ Current liabilities

Again, like the other ratios in this chapter, you must compare the ratio of one company to that of other companies in the same industry. A current ratio that's lower than most other companies in the industry can indicate the company is having a problem paying its short-term debts, which, in turn, is a strong sign that bankruptcy may be just around the corner. A current ratio that's significantly higher can be a bad sign too, because it can mean the company isn't using its assets efficiently. For these reasons, traders like to see companies with current ratios that are close to the industry average.

Luckily, you won't have to calculate current ratios, because they're easily found on any Web site that includes fundamental statistics. Using Yahoo! Finance, we found that Home Depot's current ratio is 1.253 and Lowe's is 1.091.

The acid test, or quick ratio, is almost the same as the current ratio; however, the key difference is that inventory value amounts are subtracted from current assets before dividing that result by current liabilities. Many financial institutions take this extra step because inventories aren't as easy to convert to cash. The acid test ratio is calculated by:

Acid test ratio = (Current assets − Inventory) ÷ Current liabilities

The acid test ratio is primarily of interest to financial institutions thinking about making a short-term loan to a company. They look for an acid test ratio of at least 1 to 1 before considering a company a good credit risk. Even though as a trader you're not likely to be in the business of making loans, a company that has problems getting short-term debt is likely to have problems meeting its short-term obligations. As the market recognizes the problem, the company's share price is likely to drop.

Reviewing goodwill

Goodwill is not a tangible asset but rather is usually collected through the years as companies are bought and sold. Goodwill reflects a competitive advantage, such as a strong brand or reputation. When one company buys another and pays more than the tangible assets are worth, the difference is added to the acquirer's balance sheet as goodwill. In other words, it's the premium in price that one company pays for another.

Determining Stock Valuations

By now the key question you're probably asking is, "How do I use all these data to decide how much I should pay for a stock?" Basically, the value of a stock is the amount buyers are willing to pay for the stock and the amount for which sellers are willing to sell the stock under current business conditions. The actual value of a stock shifts throughout the day and usually in a matter of seconds when the trading volume is high.

Fundamental analysis is one of the tools that investors and some traders use to analyze earnings, revenue growth, market share, and future business plans so they can determine the value of the stock and the price they're willing to pay for or sell it. Earnings and earnings growth are key factors and are considered a part of fundamental analysis. Common ratios used to determine a stock's value include the price to earnings multiple, or P/E ratio; price to book multiple, or price/book ratio; return on assets (ROA); and return on equity (ROE). We talk more about how these ratios are calculated in the sections that follow.

After considering all these data, investors decide whether a company's stock is undervalued or overvalued. Although past performance is no guarantee about a company's or stock's future success, fundamental analysts believe collecting and analyzing the appropriate data enables investors to make more of an educated guess about a stock's value.

Earnings

Using the income statement, we've talked extensively about a company's earnings. Remember the three types of earnings figures to consider are

- **Gross profit,** which is calculated after considering the direct costs related to sales

- **Operating income,** which shows a company's profit after subtracting operating expenses

- **Net income,** which is the bottom-line earnings after all expenses, taxes, and interest are subtracted

When you encounter discussions about earnings figures, be certain you know which types of earnings are being discussed for the stock you're eyeing. To be able to compare apples with apples, you must know that you're using the same type of earnings figures.

Projected earnings growth rate

The projected earnings growth rate, which shows how quickly the company is expected to grow, isn't something you'll calculate. What you will find in the fundamental analysis for stocks are earnings growth rate projections made by industry analysts based on their analysis of a company's potential earnings. The earnings growth rate is included on all the Web sites that we mention in Chapter 4 that provide fundamental statistics. When looking for these data, be sure to check out the earnings growth rate potential at a number of those sites.

Continuing the comparison of Home Depot and Lowe's, Yahoo! Finance projected

- Home Depot's earnings growth rate was at –24.3 percent

- Lowe's earnings growth rate was at –7.9 percent

Clearly, at this point in time analysts believe Lowe's will lose less than Home Depot in the future, but they expect losses at both companies.

Eyeing the most fundamental data of all

If we were allowed to choose only one piece of fundamental data to guide our trading, we'd choose the earnings growth rate (you'll sometimes see this called the EPS growth rate — EPS stands for earnings per share). You can use it as a quick summary of a company's performance. Evaluating the entire financial condition of a company isn't necessary when its earnings aren't up to par.

We put only a certain amount of faith in analysts' estimates and don't depend on them when evaluating trading candidates. We're much more interested in actual earnings reported than we are in the analysts' estimates for future earnings. And we're interested only in companies whose earnings are growing, and growing at a faster rate than most other companies. Those companies typically outperform the broad market.

In Canada most of the fundamental research is generated by the full-service investment firms owned by the large banks. Their EPS growth rate projections are a lot more realistic now that the analysts have to certify that their compensation is not related to their views expressed in their EPS reports.

Investor's Business Daily is an excellent source for EPS growth rate data; it publishes a proprietary ranking that shows which companies are growing earnings fastest.

As much as we like this tool, we don't follow the rankings blindly. (And we don't believe the good folks at *IBD* recommend that you do so, either.) *IBD* doesn't distinguish between companies that are earning more and companies that are losing less. That companies can and do turn from losing money to making money is a fact, and that situation can be lucrative for the knowledgeable trader. Call us old-fashioned, but we prefer companies that actually have a history of reporting real, positive earnings.

Figuring Your Ratios: Comparing One Company's Stock to Another

In this section, we show you how to calculate four key ratios — P/E, Price/Book, ROE, and ROA — but luckily you can find all these where fundamental statistics are reported (newspapers, Web sites, and so on — see Chapter 4 for more). Each of these ratios gives you just one more piece in the puzzle of determining how much you want to pay for a stock. By comparing each of the ratios for each of the companies you're considering, you can make a more educated case about the price you want to pay for any stock.

Price/earnings ratio

The *P/E ratio* is probably the one that's quoted more often in news stories. This ratio reflects a comparison of a stock's earnings with its share price. You calculate this ratio using this formula:

P/E ratio = Stock price ÷ Earnings per share

You'll probably find two types of P/E ratios for a stock. The *trailing P/E* is based on earnings reported in previous quarters, and the *forward P/E* is based on projected earnings. At Yahoo! Finance, the trailing P/E for Home Depot was 12.29, and its forward P/E, expectations as of February 3, 2010, was 13.68. Lowe's trailing P/E was 12.28, and its forward P/E, expectations as of February 1, 2010, was 14.16. Little difference exists in the trailing P/E ratios for Home Depot and Lowe's, but analysts seem to favour Lowe's with a higher forward P/E. Historically, market analysts believed a P/E ratio of 10 to 15 was reasonable. For a while, much higher P/Es were tolerated, but during the 2008 market conditions people drifted back to historical P/Es. When comparing companies, you can get a good idea of how the market values each stock by looking at its P/E ratio. While the P/E ratio is actually a percentage, it is rarely stated that way. However, you will sometimes hear it called a price multiple because the P/E ratio represents how much you are paying for each dollar of a company's earnings.

Price/book ratio

The *price/book ratio* compares the market's valuation of a company to the value that the company shows on its financial statements. The higher the ratio, the more the market is willing to pay for a company above its hard assets, which include its buildings, inventory, accounts receivable, and other clearly measurable assets. Companies are more than their measurable assets. Customer loyalty, the value of their locations, and other intangible assets add value to a company. Investors looking to buy based on value rather than growth are more likely to check out the price/book ratio. Price/book ratios are calculated using this formula:

Price/book ratio = Stock price ÷ (Book value − Total liabilities)

Lowe's price/book ratio at Yahoo! Finance was 1.88 and Home Depot's was 2.26. Based on price/book ratio, the market is willing to pay a higher premium for Home Depot's stock.

Return on assets

Return on assets (ROA) shows you how efficiently management uses the company's resources. ROA doesn't, however, show you how well the company is performing for its shareholders. To calculate return on assets, use this formula:

Return on assets = Earnings after taxes ÷ Total assets

Home Depot's ROA at Yahoo! Finance was 7.78 percent; Lowe's was 8.89 percent. Lowe's is doing a more efficient job using its resources based on those two ROA numbers.

Return on equity

Investors are more interested in *return on equity* (ROE), which measures how well a company is doing for its shareholders. This ratio measures how much profit management generates from resources provided by its shareholders. Investors look for companies with high ROEs that show signs of growth. You calculate ROE by using this formula:

Return on equity = Earnings after taxes ÷ Shareholder equity

Home Depot's ROE was 14.40 percent, and Lowe's was 15.51 percent.

The ROEs show that Lowe's is doing a better job for its shareholders, which, again, is reflected in the price investors are willing to pay for its shares.

As a trader, you may not make your buy and sell decisions based on fundamental analysis, but collecting and having access to this information as part of your arsenal certainly helps you to make better and more informed stock choices. Knowing a company has strong fundamentals helps to back up what you're seeing in the technical analysis (see Part III). If you're trying to decide between two stocks whose technical charts are positive, you can use the fundamental analysis to tip the scale toward your best trading opportunity.

Chapter 7

Listening to Analyst Calls

Stock analysts are supposed to be independent oracles who help mere mortal traders understand a company's financial future. Don't count on them to walk on water, however, because they're not always looking to protect the small investor's pocketbook.

A wide spectrum of analysis is undertaken in Canada. Professional authors of investment research range from quality analysts to penny stock promoters. Whenever you read recommendations from an analyst, you must determine whether that analyst is a buy-side analyst, sell-side analyst, or independent analyst before you ever consider using the information he or she is providing.

Analysts get much of their information from conference calls sponsored by companies when they report their earnings or make other key financial announcements. Today, individual investors are invited to listen in on more and more of these calls. You can find out a great deal about a company's prospects by listening in on analyst calls, but the language of these calls can be confusing. This chapter explains the types of analysts, their importance, and the language unique to what they do. We also introduce you to some Internet resources that can make listening in on analyst calls easier.

Getting to Know Your Analysts

If you watch any of the financial news cable television stations, you've probably seen numerous industry analysts frequently touting certain stocks and panning others. Do you know who those analysts represent? Do you know whether they're independent analysts, buy-side analysts, or sell-side analysts? Before deciding whether to follow an analyst's recommendations, be sure you understand who pays his or her salary and what's in it for him or her.

Buy-side analysts: You won't see them

You rarely come in contact with a buy-side analyst, because they work primarily for large institutional investment firms that manage mutual funds or private accounts. Their primary role is analyzing stocks that are bought by the firm for which they work and not necessarily the ones bought by individual investors. Their research rarely is available outside the firm that hired them. Buy-side analysts focus on whether an investment that's under consideration is a good match for the firm's investment strategy and portfolio. In fact, buy-side analysts frequently include information from sell-side analysts as part of their overall research on an investment. You're most likely to hear from a buy-side analyst if you listen to analyst conference calls. They tend to be much harsher on the company officials.

Sell-side analysts: Watch for conflicts

When you read stock analyses from investment dealers, you're more than likely reading information from sell-side analysts. These analysts work primarily for brokerage houses and other financial distribution sources where salespeople sell securities based on the analysts' recommendations.

The primary purpose of sell-side analysts is providing investment advisers with information to help make sales. As long as the interests of the investor, the adviser, and the investment dealer are the same, sell-side analysts' reports can be useful sources of information. A conflict arises, however, when sell-side analysts also are responsible for helping their investment dealers win investment banking business.

New York State Attorney General Eliot Spitzer (yes, *that* Eliot Spitzer) exposed why this conflict is a primary reason for all the scandals you've read about regarding star analysts, such as Henry Blodget of Merrill Lynch (and formerly CIBC Oppenheimer), whose e-mails privately called stocks "dogs," "toast," or "junk" at the same time he and his team were publicly recommending that their customers buy the same stocks. Why do this? Well, according to Spitzer's charges, Blodget's recommendations brought in $115 million in investment banking fees for Merrill Lynch, and Blodget took home $12 million in compensation.

Merrill Lynch was only the first to be exposed. Similar charges were raised against many other firms, including Morgan Stanley, Dean Witter, and Credit Suisse First Boston. Few firms that sell stocks and have an investment banking division avoided the scandal. These companies didn't learn much from the scandals. Merrill Lynch was taken over by Bank of America because of errors made during the mortgage crisis.

At one time in the distant past, analysts were separated from investment banks by what companies called a "Chinese wall." Analysts' work supposedly was kept completely separate from deals that were being generated in a company's investment banking business. At some point, the lines between the two broke down and analysts actually were included in the process of generating deals for mergers, acquisitions, and new stock offerings. By writing glowing reports, analysts helped their companies sign more lucrative investment banking deals, all the while putting their small investors at great risk of losing all their money by buying the recommended stocks. When the market bubble burst in 2000, many of the stocks that were recommended because of these deals, particularly in the Internet, telecommunications, and other high-tech industries, dropped to being worthless, and investors lost billions.

Merrill Lynch, in trying to settle its problems with Spitzer, agreed to publicly disclose its investment banking connections and list its clients. As of June 2002, Merrill Lynch began stating in all its research reports whether it received or will receive fees for investment banking services from any company that was followed by the Merrill Lynch analysts in the prior 12 months. Other companies followed Merrill Lynch's lead in settling their disputes with Spitzer.

The United States Securities and Exchange Commission (SEC) finally stepped into the fray in April 2002 and announced it was broadening the investigation into analysts' roles and was developing new regulations regarding analyst disclosure. The SEC ultimately endorsed rulemaking changes recommended by the New York Stock Exchange and the National Association of Securities Dealers, including the following:

✔ Structural reforms that increase analysts' independence. These reforms include a prohibition on investment banking departments supervising analysts or approving research reports.

✓ A prohibition on tying analysts' compensation to specific investment banking transactions.

✓ A prohibition on offering favourable research to induce business for the firm.

✓ Increased disclosures of conflicts of interest in research reports and public appearances. These disclosures include information about business relationships with or ownership interests in companies that are the subjects of analysts' reports.

✓ Disclosure in research reports of data concerning a firm's ratings, such as the percentage of ratings issued in each of the buy, hold, and sell categories, and a price chart comparing the rated securities' closing prices and the firm's rating or price targets over time.

✓ Restrictions on personal trading by analysts in securities of companies that they analyze and/or report on.

Today, rules are made by FINRA (Financial Industry Regulatory Authority). These rule changes helped investors identify conflicts of interest that can compromise the objectivity of the sell-side analyst's report. Pay close attention to the disclosures and the relationships between the investment dealers and the companies that their analysts' reports cover, and take these connections into consideration when including their buy or sell recommendations in your plans for future stock transactions.

Although Canada can boast of its shares of rogues, we haven't seen something on the scale of what went down between Spitzer and Blodget. For many years, Canadian research analysts have been subject to a thorough regimen of disclosure.

Research disclosures include the following:

✓ **The proportion of buy, sell, and hold reports.** No use relying on research that's meant to be objective if it's always buy, buy, buy!

✓ **Recent underwritings or investment banking services provided for the companies being researched.** You don't need research that's written just to pump up stocks so the researcher's employer can sell you more stocks.

✓ **Conflicts of interest.** Conflicts of interest can arise in many and varied forms. Analysts or their families owning or shorting shares of the companies being covered is a HUGE conflict of interest you need to know about. Similarly, it can be very bad if the analyst's employer is a bank that's lending money too optimistically to the company being analyzed. And watch out for analysts who are compensated or who have their expenses taken care of by the subject of the research — also known as the gravy train. Finally, compensation should not be tied to research recommendations (in other words, analysts are not paid less for writing the truth).

Independent analysts: Where are they?

You're probably wondering where these *independent analysts* — people you can trust who don't have investment banking connections — really are. Although they do exist, most work for wealthy individuals or institutional investors and provide research for people who manage portfolios of much more than a million dollars and pay fees of at least $25,000 per year.

No one really knows exactly how many independent analysts are out there. Estimates range from 100 to several hundred, but their ranks surely will grow now that independent research will be a required part of selling to individual investors.

In addition to independent research that you probably see distributed by your investment dealer, as a small investor you can turn to some of the major investment research firms such as Morningstar (www.morningstar.ca) and Standard & Poor's (www.standardandpoors.com). They offer services to individual investors through their publications and Internet sites at more reasonable fees than many of the small independent analyst firms. Nevertheless, you need to bear in mind that even these analysts are answering to the companies or wealthy individuals that pay the greatest share of their costs.

The Importance of Analysts

No matter whose report you're reading, remember that the analyst's primary income is coming either from the investment dealer or the large institutional clients that he or she serves. Analysts rate stocks on whether you need to consider purchasing them, but no standardized rating system exists. In Table 7-1 we offer the three most common breakdowns you can expect to see.

Table 7-1   Common Stock Recommendations from Analysts

Analysis by Company A	Analysis by Company B	Analysis by Company C
Buy	Strong Buy	Recommended List
Outperform	Buy	Trading Buy
Neutral	Hold	Market Outperformer
Underperform	Sell	Market Perform
Avoid		Market Underperformer

You can see from this table that you must understand how a company's analysts rate stocks for that company's recommendations to have any value. Company A's "Buy" recommendation is its highest, but Company B uses

"Strong Buy" for its highest rating, and Company C uses "Recommended List" for its top choice. Merely seeing that a stock is recommended as a "Buy" by a particular analyst means little if you don't know which rating system is being used.

Unfortunately, when it comes to stock analysis, if the information is free it's probably no better than that free lunch you're always looking to find. Someone has to pay the analyst, and if it isn't you, you must find out who is footing the bill before you use that advice to make decisions.

The best way to use analysts' reports is to think of them as just one tool in your bucket of trading tools. Analysts' opinions are one good way to find out about an industry or a stock, but they're not the final word about what you need to do. Only your own research using fundamental and technical analysis can help you make your investment decisions. We discuss fundamental analysis tools in Chapters 5 and 6 and technical analysis tools in Part III.

Tracking how a company's doing

Analysts are good resources for finding historical data about how a company or industry is doing. Their reports usually summarize at least five years of data and frequently provide a historical perspective for the industry and the company that goes back many more years. In addition, analysts make projections about the earnings potential of the company they're analyzing and indicate why they believe those projections by including information about new products being developed or currently being tested at various stages of market development.

These reports help you track how a company is doing so you can find the gems that may indicate when to expect a company to break out of a current trading trend. For example, if an analyst covering a pharmaceutical company mentions that a new drug is under consideration by the Food and Drug Administration, you may look for news stories about the status of that drug and monitor the stock for indications that drug approval may soon be announced. Watching the technical charts may help you jump in at just the right time and catch the upward trend as positive news is announced. Stocks usually start to move in advance of news.

Providing access to analyst calls

In addition to reading reports, you can track companies by listening in on *analyst calls.* Some calls are sponsored by the companies themselves to review annual or quarterly results, and others are sponsored by independent analysts.

Company-sponsored calls

Analyst calls sponsored by companies more often are earnings conference calls primarily for institutional investors as well as Bay Street and Wall Street analysts. They occur on either a quarterly, semiannual, or annual basis, and can be the richest sources of information concerning a company's fundamentals and future prospects.

Senior management — usually the chief executive officer (CEO), president, and chief financial officer (CFO) — talks about the company's financial reports and then answers questions during these calls. The calls sometimes are scheduled to coincide with announcements of major changes in a company's leadership or other breaking news about the company. After a formal statement, senior management answers questions from analysts. That's when you usually can get the most up-to-date information about the company and how management views its financial performance and projections. We discuss how to read between the lines and get the most out of these calls in the next section of this chapter.

Access to these calls used to be limited to professional analysts and institutional investors, but today more than 80 percent of companies that sponsor analyst calls open them to the media and individual investors, according to a survey conducted by the American National Investor Relations Institute. This change primarily is credited to the SEC's Fair Disclosure (FD) Regulation, which requires companies to make public all major announcements that can impact the value of the stock within 24 hours of informing any company outsiders. This rule helps level the information playing field for individual investors.

Analysts no longer can count on getting two or three days of lead time on major announcements, which heretofore helped them inform major investors about company news. Often that amount of lead time enabled analysts to recommend buy or sell decisions to their key clients, but that same practice hurt small investors and traders who weren't privy to the news. Some complain this new rule actually hurt the flow of information, because companies clammed up in private conversations with analysts, making it harder for the analysts to write their investigative reports. Since the regulation first took effect in 2000, the fair disclosure rule helped to level the information playing field.

Independent analyst–sponsored calls

Firms that provide independent analysis also sponsor calls primarily for their wealthy and institutional clients. During these calls, analysts often discuss breaking news about a company or an industry that they follow. Doing so gives their clients an opportunity to discuss key concerns directly with the analysts. Unless you're a client, opportunities for listening in on these calls are rare.

Seeking insider information

Investors began seeking insider information about companies long before the scandals that you now read about almost daily. In fact, one of the first stories ever told about trading on insider information involved the startup of one of today's leading financial information services — Reuters. Julius Reuter started his news service in response to the desire investors had for insider information and how it could impact stock prices. In 1849, Reuter used trained homing pigeons to fly information about closing stock prices from Europe's mainland across the English Channel to England, thus giving his subscribers a jump on news about a stock so they'd be able to react before other, less informed investors received the information. This story highlights a simple but powerful secret of investing: *Information is power.* Investors with privileged access to information hold a distinct advantage over other investors who don't have the same access.

Just to give you an idea of how insider information was used by analysts more recently, here are a couple of examples. In February 1999, during a tour of the headquarters of Compaq Computer Corporation, the company's treasurer told a group of big-time investors that he was concerned about softness in the software industry. Compaq shares dropped 14 percent before most individual investors ever discovered such a concern existed. In September 1999, executives at Apple Computer Inc. called analysts to alert them that an earthquake in Taiwan disrupted the production of iBook and Powerbook notebook computers. The Apple execs wanted to warn analysts that the company would not meet its numbers for the quarter. The stock fell 7 percent in four days, and again, by the time most investors found out, it was too late. The new SEC fair disclosure rule attempts to prevent this kind of favoured treatment for insiders.

Listening to Analyst Calls

Most company conference calls start with a welcome to all call participants, followed by a discussion of the financial results being released or the purpose the company has designated for the call. After the CEO, president, and CFO make their statements, other key managers may comment on the results before the call is opened to questions from the listening audience.

The question-and-answer portion of the call usually is the most revealing and enables you to judge just how confident senior managers are with their reporting. It's when you're most likely to hear information that hasn't been revealed in press releases or formal annual or quarterly reports. Analysts and institutional investors usually are given the first shot at asking questions, meaning before other listeners, the press, or individual investors get their turn. Not all companies permit individual investors to ask questions. Even when you can't ask any questions, listening to responses to the questions posed by analysts, institutional investors, and the media still is worthwhile.

Be sure to listen closely; chances are good that any question you may have will be answered during the question-and-answer period. If not, you can always write or call the company's investor relations division to get an answer to your specific question.

Understanding the analysts' language

We recommend that before your first call you get familiar with some of the language you'll hear. We discuss most of the common terminology in Chapter 6, including earnings per share (EPS), EPS growth, net income, cash, and cash equivalents. However, some terms are unique to the analyst call world. These include:

- ✔ **Hockey stick:** When companies say their revenues come in like a hockey stick, company officials are not exactly talking about getting hit with a puck. Instead, they're talking about the *shape* of a hockey stick. Because most of their revenues are booked in the final days of the quarter, revenue charts take on the appearance of a hockey stick. Most companies, in fact, book revenues this way, because sales incentives are designed to encourage the sales force to close their contracts before the end of a quarter. Salespeople have to meet their quotas, and companies that are planning purchases frequently delay those decisions until near the end of a quarter so they can negotiate the best deals when the salespeople are most desperate. You've probably done the same thing yourself when buying a car or other major item.

- ✔ **Lumpy:** Nope, the CEO isn't talking about poorly cooked oatmeal when he or she says revenues or orders were lumpy. This term means that sales were uneven during the quarter, with some weeks having low order rates and others having high order rates. The key is finding out why sales were lumpy and whether lumpy sales are normal for the company.

- ✔ **Run rate:** Don't worry, you won't be asked how fast you can run a race. The run rate is the way senior management talks about how its current performance can be projected over a period of time. For example, if the current quarter's revenues show a $1 million monthly run rate, then you can expect annual revenues to total close to $12 million. This concept may work for companies with steady earnings but not for companies whose products primarily are seasonal. For example, if a retail company reports a run rate of $1 million per month during the fourth quarter, which of course includes holiday sales, you won't expect that performance to be indicative of a full 12-month performance. You must be certain you understand a company's revenue picture before counting on run-rate numbers.

> ✔ ***Burn rate:*** Nope, nothing to do with matchsticks or fireworks. *Burn rate* refers to negative cash flow. If a company has monthly expenses of $1 million, no revenue, and only $6 million in the bank, then its burn rate tells you it will be bankrupt or raising more capital within six months.

If you hear other terminology that you don't understand, write it down so you can research it and thus be ready for the next time you hear it.

Developing your listening skills

In addition to *what* senior management is saying, you also need to listen to *how* they're saying it. If management is happy with the results, they'll probably be upbeat and talking about a rosy future for the company. On the other hand, if management isn't so happy with the results, the mood probably will be downbeat and apologetic as they try to explain why the company didn't perform as expected and, of course, make excuses for their failure to meet expectations.

Learn to listen and read between the company lines. Try to listen in on every earnings call. The first one you hear may not mean much unless you know how the results differ from previous reports and projections. Before that first call, you need to read analysts' reports and become as familiar as possible with the company's earnings history. After you've followed a certain company's calls for a while, the information presented will mean much more to you. Among the many indicators that may help you determine your trading activity are signs relating to earnings expectations, revenue growth, analysts' moods, company facts, and future projections.

Earnings expectations

Whether a company is meeting its own projections and analysts' expectations is the most important clue about how a company is doing and how the stock market will react to its periodic reports. If the company fails to meet expectations, the market will likely punish the stock by driving the price down, and that can point to a good trading opportunity. If you believe the setback is temporary and the company's long-term prospects look good, you may want to wait for the stock to bottom out before buying it. If you think failing periodic expectations is a sign of long-term bad news, and you hold a position in the stock, you may want to sell it as soon as possible. If you don't own it, you may want to consider shorting the stock. We discuss shorting a stock at length in Chapter 18.

Revenue growth

Listen for information that indicates whether revenue growth kept pace with earnings growth. This factor becomes even more critical whenever the economy slows down, because a company may play with or manipulate the numbers in a practice that's known as *window dressing*, or making sure that earnings meet expectations. However, manipulating revenues is much more difficult. Growth in revenues is the key to continued earnings growth in the future.

Although manipulating earnings may be difficult, we've seen companies do it successfully for at least a few quarters and, in some cases, a few years. A number of companies caught in recent scandals successfully manipulated these numbers with creative methods of booking revenue. One place where you may want to watch for signs of revenue manipulation is accounts receivable. If receivables rise dramatically above historical balances, one of two things are likely — the company is having a hard time collecting on its accounts, or the company is booking fictitious revenue. Manipulation may also be detected when a company reports revenue for items sold that actually is greater than the company has the capacity to produce.

Canadian telecom Nortel brings such creativity to mind. In a nutshell, Nortel's customers couldn't afford to buy Nortel's products, so Nortel lent them the money and then reported the sale! The phrase at the time that described that fad was a deadly form of vendor take-back financing. RIP, Nortel.

You may notice analysts questioning revenue-growth figures in great detail. This examination by analysts can be a sign that they suspect problems with the numbers. Detecting any of these signs while listening to a call can be a sign of possible trouble ahead, and you need to take a closer look before buying the stock or holding what you already have.

Analysts' moods

You can find out a great deal about how analysts are responding to a company's report by merely listening to the tone of their questions. By listening to how analysts are asking questions and what questions they are asking, you can judge whether the analysts are downbeat on company prospects, especially if they're asking increasingly probing questions. On the other hand, you may notice that analysts are upbeat and encouraging senior management to talk even more positively about their results and future plans. When you've followed the analysts' calls for a company during several quarters, recognizing whether the mood has changed won't be difficult. When analysts receive news positively, they often start their questions with some kind of congratulatory remark.

Be sure to jot down the names of analysts, especially the ones making positive remarks. The positive remarks from analysts with sell-side orientation may not be as good a sign as the positive remarks from buy-side analysts. If you don't know what type of analyst is commenting, research his or her affiliations and leanings after the call.

Buy-side analysts carry the most weight whenever they're indicating a positive reaction to the company's financial news. Many buy-side analysts who attend analyst calls already have a stake in the company, so they have a vested interest in putting a positive spin on the news. If they're positive, they'll likely revise their earnings estimates upward, which can be the first indication that they'll recommend additional buys and the stock may be getting ready to enter an upward trend. This positive spin can give you the first sign of a good trading opportunity, so watch your technical analysis for any signals of a potential breakout. We discuss more about breakouts in Chapter 10.

Just the facts, ma'am

The best way to judge whether senior management is confident in their reporting is determining how quickly they respond to questions. If senior managers are confident with their numbers, they respond to questions quickly, taking little time to think their responses through. If senior managers are unsure of their reports, they're more likely to take a good deal of time checking through their papers to answer even the simplest questions. You definitely need to think twice about buying or holding stock in a company whose management shows a lack of confidence in reporting their numbers.

The future

You're likely to get a good reading about how senior managers view the company's future prospects by listening to their vision for the company and whether the results actually demonstrate that they are fulfilling that vision. When managers are successfully fulfilling their vision, they clearly articulate their view of the company's future and how they plan to get there. Ask yourself whether management inspires you with its vision. If not, managers most likely are not inspiring their employees, which can be an early sign that the company is heading on a downward trend.

Employee satisfaction

Happy employees are a good sign that a company will be able to meet its future expectations. If, during the call, you hear that the company is having trouble attracting new employees or retaining its existing staff, you may be looking at a sign of trouble on the horizon. High employee turnover is bad for future growth, and so is having trouble finding and recruiting qualified employees.

Analyst conference calls are best used as a research tool and not for taking an immediate action based solely on the information you gather from them. Consider them just one more way of gaining more knowledge about a stock you're thinking about buying, or of tracking stocks after you've already bought them. Day traders and swing traders sometimes use the information from analyst calls to trade after hours, but such trades can be highly risky. We talk more about these two trading strategies in Chapters 16 and 17.

Locating Company Calls

Many companies list information about their upcoming earnings reports and analyst calls on their company Web sites, while others simply post an audio version after the event. Some companies offer their investors a service that alerts them to upcoming events. If these services are not available for the companies you plan to follow, your best way of tracking upcoming calls is through one of two online sites: VCall (`www.investorcalendar.com`) and BestCalls (`www.bestcalls.com`).

VCall is the leading Webcaster for official investor relations events. Many but not all companies use its services to run their events online. This Web site offers you free access to live and archived corporate communications. In addition to the calls, you can find copies of financial information released by the company. VCall also enables you to set up e-mail alerts for the companies you track that are served by VCall.

BestCalls is the leading resource site for locating earnings conferences on the Internet. Although VCall is the leading provider for companies that play host to calls, the only company calls that are listed on VCall's site are for companies that use its services. BestCalls, on the other hand, is the largest single source for tracking analyst call schedules with links to the location for these calls and access to archived calls. Thousands of companies list their conferences and analyst calls on this site, and you can set up an e-mail alert for any company you want to follow. BestCalls charges membership fees to access the entire site and fees for transcripts of older calls. You may be able to find a link for free from the investor relations section of a company's Web site.

Identifying Trends in the Stock Analyst Community

A new regulatory climate came to Canada after the Bre-X Minerals scandal in 1997, when this massive fraud involved a so-called gold mine with an apparent market capitalization of almost $6 billion. As a result, the Toronto Stock Exchange had to hire Standard & Poor's to police the choice of companies for its Composite Index. In the United States, it arrived in the wake of abuses exposed when the tech stock bubble of the early 2000s burst. Regulations now control the flow of information between companies and analysts — and, ultimately, what information makes its way to you as an outside investor or trader.

Some traders believe that the new restrictions that ban selective disclosure to friendly analysts or key investors actually hurt the flow of information to the general public. Regulations require that any information disclosed to analysts or key investors that can affect the value of the company must be disclosed to the general public within 24 hours, even if the information wasn't part of a planned report.

The preference is for making announcements about material information at the same time for everyone, but sometimes during meetings with analysts or institutional investors information is shared inadvertently. For example, if analysts find out information during a company tour, the company then is required to put out a press release disclosing the same information to the general public. Some analysts believe this is making the preparation of their reports much more difficult than it needs to be.

Newer regulations, however, have halted some commonplace industry practices, including closed meetings with analysts and institutional investors. Lawyers for many companies warn senior managers to be careful about responding to calls from individual analysts. Some companies require that any contact with analysts first be evaluated and approved through their legal advisers.

Regulations also impact *roadshows,* which are marketing tours that introduce a company's new securities offerings. The regulators permit these events but give clear guidance that they now need to be more like oral offers that are designed to avoid the prohibition against written or broadcast offers made outside the official prospectus of the offering. American regulators believe these roadshows are best conducted in the open to all investors and have voiced objections to having two separate roadshows, one for institutional investors and another more watered down version for retail investors. Some legal experts also advise companies to be careful about whether they include outside analysts, those not employed by the underwriter of the offering, as part of the roadshow. Including outside analysts, some believe, can be viewed as selective disclosure, which violates Regulation FD in the United States.

The biggest regulatory changes you'll see as an individual investor or trader relate to disclosures that must be made in research reports, including a requirement that securities firms must disclose any compensation they receive for investment banking services they provide during the three months following the public offering for a covered company. In addition, firms that are members of some exchanges must disclose when they stop coverage of a public company. Many times this type of news generates unfavourable publicity for the company and can result in a drop in stock prices. In addition to these big disclosures, analysts' research reports now must include information about the relationships among the analysts, underwriters, and stock issuer.

One international investment firm has to provide such a large array of disclosures due to its global presence that it needs four pages of type in a font smaller than the one you are reading now. Often the research disclosure is longer than the research report itself!

Operating in this type of fish bowl may make companies and analysts nervous, but it nevertheless should balance the cards for individual investors. Look carefully for these disclosures as you read analysts' reports and take advantage of your newfound access to information by attending analysts' earnings conferences and being part of the insider pool rather than a passive outsider waiting to be fed information by the financial media or professional analysts.

Part III
Reading the Charts: Technical Analysis

The 5th Wave — By Rich Tennant

"Trendlines? Channels? Breakouts? I say we stick the money in the ground like always, and then feed this guy to the sharks."

In this part . . .

You discover how to read and interpret stock price charts as we describe their virtues and usefulness, together with the weaknesses of chart analysis. We cover the basics of constructing a stock price chart, and then delve into identifying distinct patterns that lead to profitable trades. In addition, we talk about trends, how to spot them, and why they're so important, and we explore how computer-generated indicators and oscillators can enhance your analytical skills.

Chapter 8

Reading the Tea Leaves: Does Technical Analysis Work?

*E*veryone knows that foretelling the future is a tough thing to do, especially when money is involved. Whether your prognosticating tool of choice is a Ouija board or a Magic 8 Ball, knowing exactly what the future holds is difficult.

Investors and traders are always looking for an edge in forecasting stock prices to improve their trading results. The method of choice for many investors is *fundamental analysis,* which we describe in Chapters 5, 6, and 7. For some traders, on the other hand, *technical analysis,* as described here and in Chapters 9–11, is the way to go.

Although some overlap exists between fundamental and technical analyses, you find dyed-in-the-wool, true believers in both camps, and they argue that their way is best, even going so far as to say the opposite way is worse than useless. For our money, the truth lies somewhere in between these two extremes.

Understanding the Mythology

A *technician* — that's someone who reads charts — believes you can use price charts and market statistics to develop a profitable trading plan. Some technicians even say that price charts foretell where a stock's price is heading simply by showing where it has been. Detractors argue that technical analysis is merely another name for fortune telling, a charlatan's moniker that avoids entanglements with local authorities and the securities regulators.

Had Madame Cleo, that deposed temptress of tarot cards, made her living foretelling stock prices, she might still be in business. Likewise, had she lived in earlier times, she might have been revered by the masses and the high priests for her fortune-telling skills instead of being scorned as a fraud.

In ancient Rome, tracking the stars, the planets, and the behaviour of birds was popular, and so was inspecting the entrails of sacrificial animals. Although a bit gruesome, the *haruspex* — that's the expert gut checker — was highly regarded. As an *augur,* an official diviner in ancient Rome, Madame Cleo would have been consulted to foretell events and reveal the gods' reactions to any future courses of action. She would have been in the limelight and riding as high as she was right before the U.S. Federal Trade Commission brought her into check. Although it may have been bogus, Madame Cleo couldn't have hoped for more.

In spite of Madame Cleo's fate, fortune-tellers still ply their trade. Are the most successful the ones who divine future price movements by reading the entrails of stock price charts? That's what a cadre of academic financial experts thinks. To the uninitiated, price charts are merely squiggles and lines on a page. The academics apparently believe, just like augurs of old, that technicians track those squiggles and lines as a means of predicting price behaviour and attempting to divine a particular stock's future course of action.

Thankfully, the market entrails viewed by technicians aren't as gruesome as the ones analyzed by the haruspex. Nevertheless, academics and fundamental analysts often regard technicians in the same light as *haruspices* — little more than an expert gut checker — but the analogy isn't really valid. Technical analysis is not a forecasting tool. It is a trading tool and nothing more.

There is a tale, no doubt apocryphal, about a technician who approached Warren Buffett with some wonderful technical analysis as a sure way to beat the market. The "Oracle of Omaha" applied the analysis and came to a neutral conclusion. Then he instructed that all the original charts be turned upside down and the same analysis applied. The conclusion was the same. Buffett's alleged quotations are: "I realized technical analysis didn't work when I turned the charts upside down and didn't get a different answer," and "If past history was all there was to the game, the richest people would be librarians."

Technical analysis does not turn water into wine. It's simply a useful tool you may choose to use in building your investment skill set.

Understanding the Methodology

Although technicians try to anticipate the future and make trading plans based on price-chart squiggles, technical analysis is a far cry from reading tea leaves or tarot cards. Instead of predicting the future, technical analysis is used to identify events that are likely to occur, and to make trading plans in case they do and alternative plans in case they do not. Technicians use a logical framework to identify price trends, turning points, trading ranges, and breakouts. These important trading concepts are covered in Chapters 9 through 11.

To understand the technical analyst's methods, you need to be familiar with these technical analysis concepts:

- Everything is in the price.
- Price movements are not (always) random.
- Price changes are caused by an imbalance between supply and demand.

Finding everything in the price

The stock market is so efficient that everything that's currently known about a company is priced into its stock. In other words, the current price reflects the combined wisdom of everyone in the market, including corporate insiders, pension funds, mutual funds, individual investors, stock analysts, fundamental analysts, technicians, publishers, media, regulators, and you.

Technical analysis provides a synopsis of all the fundamental and psychological factors that affect the price of a stock. Although we personally think putting all your eggs in the price basket is taking the point to an extreme, that's why some technicians don't even try to evaluate the fundamentals. Why bother trying to outsmart the smartest when everything's in the price?

The technician's understanding of why a stock's price moves is not important. Technicians don't care whether the price movement was caused by the most recent analyst's report or by the flapping of a butterfly's wings in China. They are concerned only with

- What is the price now?
- What is the price history?

Technical analysts examine current prices relative to the histories of price movements to understand and plan for what may happen next. Fundamental analysts ask why, trying to understand what piece of news causes a particular rise in price or what bit of insider knowledge causes a sell off. Technicians try to see everything the price represents and base their trades only on what they see.

You can't know what causes every ripple in the price continuum. So why try?

Realizing price movements are not always random

Sometimes prices move higher. Sometimes they move lower. And sometimes prices move back and forth within a tight trading range. When prices move higher or lower, we say prices are *trending.* The trading-range periods between trending periods often appear to be random price movements, and at times they may actually be random. But when you zoom in to view the price movements within those seemingly random trading-range periods, you will find the trading range is made up of many mini trends. The closer you look, the less random these price movements appear, and that is the crux of technical analysis. These are important concepts for trading and are covered more fully in Chapter 10.

At its simplest, technical analysis identifies the periods of time during which trends occur. In general, technicians want to base their trades on trending markets. The idea is determining when trends are beginning and when they're ending. But which trend? Are you the type of trader who is interested in the little mini trends that make up a trading range? Or are you most interested in trading longer-lasting trends?

The trick to technical trading, therefore, is identifying a stock's price trend within the time frame during which you want to buy or sell it. Depending on the length of time you plan to hold the stock, you want to base your trades on analyses done in the corresponding time frame. We are primarily concerned with long-lasting trends that span many weeks or months. In that case, you'll want to analyze charts showing daily and weekly prices. If, instead, you plan to hold your stock for no more than a few hours or a few days, you'll want to analyze charts showing intraday prices. When looking at intraday price charts, you will see many examples of mini trends and trading ranges. However, if you're buying a stock and holding your position for weeks or months, those mini intraday trends and trading ranges are meaningless. We discuss these concepts more fully in Chapter 9.

Balancing supply and demand

If you've ever watched the nightly business news, you've probably heard reporters claim that stocks rose because more buyers were looking for stocks than sellers were willing to part with them. At some level, that's hogwash. Even novice investors realize that every trade must have a buyer and a seller.

What the reporter really means is that the supply and demand were out of balance and that price is a function of supply and demand. In macroeconomics, this concept is illustrated using a freely traded commodity like wheat. When farmers grow more wheat than bakers need, the price of wheat falls. When bakers need more wheat than farmers grew, bakers bid higher prices to get the wheat they need.

In many ways, the price of a stock works just like the price of wheat. When buyers want to buy more shares of a stock than sellers are willing or able to sell, buyers bid the stock price higher until they find sellers willing to part with their shares. Conversely, when sellers can't find enough buyers, they offer their shares at lower and lower prices until enough buyers can be found.

Changes in a company's business plan, a new competitor, anything really, can throw the balance between supply and demand out of whack. Realizing that imbalances cause prices to move — and not the news itself — is the point where technical analysis is concerned.

Understanding where you've been

Technicians examine price history, trading volume, and additional market statistics to evaluate the balance between supply and demand. The conceptual framework is easy to understand. As long as prices are rising, demand exceeds supply, and buyers are more interested in buying than sellers are in selling. The reverse is equally true. When prices are falling, supply exceeds demand, and sellers are more interested in selling than buyers are in buying. When a stock trades within a tight range of prices, a balance between supply and demand has been achieved. This situation is evident on the price chart when a stock trades within a trading range. Examples are shown in Chapter 9.

Technical analysis helps identify these kinds of scenarios. Technicians examine charts in search of the price levels where buying pressure stops a stock's price from falling further or where selling pressure squashes a rally.

Here's a hypothetical scenario to illustrate that point. A high-profile investment adviser issues a recommendation to buy shares of XYZ, which closed at $18.50 the day before and has traded in a tight price range of $17 to $18.75 during the past four months. The recommendation to buy is in effect only if the stock trades for less than $19 a share. The idea is not necessarily to buy the instant that a recommendation is made, but rather to buy at a good price.

Taking the hypothetical example a step further, say that the investment adviser has a wide following. Invariably, the recommendation is quickly followed by a surge in the volume of buyers purchasing shares of XYZ that ultimately pushes the price of the stock to $21.

Buying surges based on these kinds of recommendations have a tendency to stall out and return to the buy-under price (in this case $19) after all the early buyers make their trades. Patient subscribers of this adviser have seen this movie many times before, so they wait for a pullback, and place a limit order near the $19 price. (We discuss limit orders in Chapter 2.) Enough patient subscribers usually are in the market for the stock to keep its price from falling further.

Now imagine you're watching this stock without knowledge of the investment adviser's recommendation. The steps that you'd likely see the price of XYZ shares take during the course of a week or two include:

1. **XYZ breaking out of its trading range and rallying on high volume**

2. **XYZ pulling back on low volume**

3. **High-volume buying of XYZ resuming as the price falls near $19**

This type of market activity is what technicians wait for. You will see this scenario play out over and over again, both in individual stocks, in exchange-traded funds, and in the general market indexes. Chapter 9 covers this technique in more detail, but for now, know that it is a textbook example of a *trading-range breakout* defined by the following:

- A high-volume breakout after a long period of range-bound trading
- A low-volume pullback
- High-volume rally to new highs

If you were interested in this stock, you may have taken a position. In fact, given this setup, the three logical places where a technician takes a position are

- **At the breakout:** Buy as soon as the stock trades through the resistance at the upper end of the trading range.

- **At the pullback:** Buy immediately as the stock begins trading higher after the low-volume pullback.

✔ **At the double top:** When the stock retraces the move from the pullback to its high price, it's called a *double top*. Buy when the stock makes a new high for the move.

Of these three alternatives, our favourite is the middle one, because buying at the pullback is a relatively low-risk, high-reward trade. Our least favourite alternative is the last one, trading the double top as the stock makes a new high, because it is the riskiest of the three. Both the breakout and the pullback trades are covered in much more detail, including example charts, in Chapter 9.

As long as technical analysis helps you get a good entry price on your trade and keep your losses small, you'll have a powerful trading tool at your disposal.

Understanding where you're headed

Technical analysis helps you find out where in the ups and downs of the market buyers took action in the past. If you have a hint where buyers have stepped in before, you can reasonably expect that they will do so again in the future. When they do as you expect, you need to be able to trade on that information profitably.

If they don't do as you expect, you may have to bust your trade, and yet you've still discovered a great deal of valuable information. You hope that the price you pay for that knowledge isn't too great, but you nevertheless know more than you did before. You know that the last wave of buying exhausts demand, and thus you need to begin looking for further evidence of a reversal.

You don't have to adhere to arguments that technical analysis is a good forecasting tool merely to recognize that it's a useful trading tool. If you combine technical analysis with some fundamental analysis, you can soon get to the point where you see the merits of both disciplines.

Answering the Detractors

A few arguments against technical analysis actually make some sense, but an entire category of lame complaints also exists. For example, some people argue that no technicians have been successful over the long run and that no technician has mustered the stature or success of illustrious market moguls like Sir John Templeton, Warren Buffett, Benjamin Graham, Peter Lynch, or Peter Cundill.

As if to further this argument, they point to some infamous technician who blew up his portfolio in spectacular fashion. Then a few years later, they harp on another well-known technician who made a boneheaded call, and then it happened again, and therefore technical analysis is useless.

The impulse to counter these arguments with a list of high-profile fundamental analysts who also blew client portfolios, however, is misguided. Even a litany of disasters wouldn't disprove the usefulness of fundamental analysis any more than a list of high-profile successes proves that fundamental analysis is the only way to make money in stocks. Why, then, should anyone accept that either proves technical analysis is useless?

In fact, many successful technicians have long, profitable trading careers. Canadian technicians worthy of mention include Don Vialoux, Skot Kortje, and Donald Dony, MFTA (Canada's first master of financial technical analysis). Although most technicians toil in self-imposed obscurity, some are prominent and outspoken. For example, John W. Henry, who owns the Boston Red Sox, made his fortune as a trend-following technician, but missed the mark in the volatility of the market in 2006 and 2007 so he lost most of his clients. Additional examples include Ed Seykota, a trader with 35 years' experience and one of the original *Market Wizards,* and Bill Dunn of Dunn Capital Management Inc. This is just a tiny sample of the many successful independent traders and fund managers who employ technical analysis tools to make trading decisions. But they do not always read the tea leaves correctly, as we saw with John W. Henry. It's an art — not an exact science.

A related argument about a chart-reading challenge that no technician has ever attempted (or would even consider) works like this: The technical analyst is given one half of a price chart with all identifying information removed. From that information, the technician is supposed to tell whether the stock's price was higher or lower at any point in the second half of the chart.

Of course, nobody ever claims the prize for having accomplished this feat, and that, therefore, is supposed to be proof that no technician ever has enough confidence in technical analysis to even try. Accomplished technicians aren't any better at telling the future than a haruspex or tarot-card reader — and neither, for that matter, are fundamental analysts. Technical analysis is not fortune telling, it's simply a trading tool.

Walking randomly

The *random walk theory* has nothing to do with hiking without a map, but instead is an academic theory that says stock prices are completely random. What happened to a stock yesterday has nothing to do with what happens to its price tomorrow.

Furthermore, this theory claims that the market is so efficient that consistently outperforming broad-based market indexes is impossible. In other words, any edge that you may gain from fundamental analysis, technical analysis, or tea leaves is useless and expensive. After all, transaction costs far outweigh any performance improvement that your analysis provides.

Armed with computer models and reams of study results, academic experts cling to these efficient-market hypotheses as gospel. Several challenges oppose their argument. No less an authority than the Federal Reserve Bank of New York published a study showing that using support and resistance levels (see Chapter 9) improved trading results for several firms. Additionally, articles published in the *Journal of Finance* suggest that trading based on moving averages and head and shoulder reversal patterns outperformed the market averages. (We discuss reversal patterns in Chapter 9, and moving averages in Chapter 11.)

So do you think this is proof that technical analysis is effective all the time? Of course not. But it casts doubt about the validity of the random walk theory, especially the part that technical analysis cannot be used to consistently improve results compared to the market averages.

A more recent theory comes from Leonard Mlodinow in his best-selling book *The Drunkard's Walk*. The author discusses the random nature of most financial data, which resemble the unpredictable steps of a drunk.

Debating these arguments to a logical conclusion is nearly impossible. Even when you use technical analysis successfully, random walkers claim your performance is the result of random chance — nothing more than good luck. Don't believe them. Instead, believe that luck favours the prepared mind.

Watching trading signals known to all

Anyone who cares to look can see exactly the same patterns and has access to the same indicators as every other trader. There is nothing new under the sun — or in the markets.

Although some traders create proprietary indicators to gain a trading edge, many more use well-known off-the-shelf trading tools. The patterns and indicators described in Chapters 9, 10, and 11 are all well known. Some are freely available on the Internet for anyone to use. Thus, if everyone sees the same thing, how can you use those trading signals profitably? The question is perfectly legitimate.

Although everyone sees the same patterns and the same indicators, this equality is a strength rather than a weakness. Technical analysis gives you insight into what future actions you can expect from your fellow market participants. With practice, you can use that information to construct a consistently profitable trading plan.

After you become familiar with traditional patterns and indicators, you can incorporate your experience and market knowledge into your trading plans and thus come to an understanding about when to use specific tools and when results are meaningless. From these plans, you can find out when a trading signal works and when it fails. You can make trades based on indicators and patterns that help and ignore the rest.

Many widely known indicators and trading patterns exist, but we personally use only a handful of the simplest ones. Your results will differ from ours. You may trade in a different time frame than we do, or you may choose a different set of tools altogether. As long as your tools improve your trading, continue using them.

Telling Fortunes or Planning Trades?

Cutting to the chase, you probably guessed by now that you're never going to foretell the future with technical analysis. Technical analysis, instead, is simply a useful trading tool.

Successful trading does not mean that you have to be right all the time or even half the time. You don't have to tell the future. Technical analysis is an excellent tool for managing your money, controlling your losses, and enabling your profits to run (see Chapter 12 for more money management information).

Even people who base their trades on fundamental factors can use chart analysis to help them time market entry and exit points and gauge price volatility and risk. Using technical analysis successfully means

- ✔ Being patient
- ✔ Finding out how to identify and use a small number of patterns and indicators
- ✔ Becoming proficient at finding these patterns and profitably trading on them
- ✔ Adding methodically to your tool kit to improve your trading results

Remember that no method is foolproof. Nothing ensures successful trades 100 percent of the time. But technical analysis is an excellent tool for improving your trading results.

Chapter 9

Reading Bar Charts Is Easy (Really)

Stock charts come in many flavours. Some prominent ones include point-and-figure charts, candlestick charts, and the ever-popular bar charts, which we use throughout this book.

Bar charts are easy to create, interpret, and maintain. Furthermore, charting tools and analysis techniques for bar charts apply to stocks, bonds, options, indexes, and futures, and are applicable across any time frame in which you may want to trade. In addition, most chart patterns work for *long* (buy first, sell later) and *short* (sell first, buy later) *trades.*

This chapter shows you how to draw price charts for a single stock, for an index such as the S&P/TSX Composite Index or the S&P 500, or for an exchange-traded fund, and recognize simple single-day trading patterns. In addition, you find out how to identify trends and trading ranges and how to look for key transition points that often lead to good trading opportunities. Charting is a visual methodology, so you'll find many example charts used throughout this chapter. Examine them carefully. You'll want to quickly identify the patterns we describe here when evaluating charts for your own trading.

Creating a Price Chart

Traders used to create their charts by hand. Today, however, many charting alternatives and options are available, including easy-to-use computer software and easily accessible Internet sites, both of which are discussed in Chapter 4. You may, of course, still want to create charts by hand; that's something we encourage you to do — at least for a little while. Making your own charts is easy, a great way to discover charting concepts, and an excellent way of getting a feel for the markets.

A chart of stock prices shares characteristics with other charts with which you're probably familiar. These kinds of charts typically are made up of two axes; the *horizontal axis* represents time, and the *vertical axis* represents price. One unusual feature of a stock chart is that its vertical axis, the price axis, usually is shown on the right, as in Figure 9-1. The most current prices are shown on the right-hand side of the chart, and so are the newest trading signals. You always trade while those signals are on the right edge of a chart, so having the price axis closest to the most crucial part of the chart makes sense.

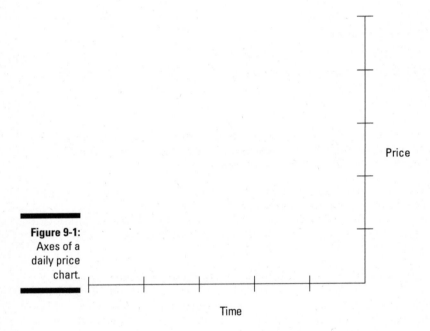

Figure 9-1:
Axes of a daily price chart.

Price

Time

Creating a single price bar

Regardless of whether your chart is an *intraday chart* (showing fluctuations throughout a trading day) or a chart of daily or weekly prices, the format of the price bar is the same. Each bar represents the results for a single trading period. On a chart that provides daily information, for example, each bar represents the results for a single trading day.

Most stock-price bar charts show four important prices on each bar:

- ✔ **Open:** The price recorded for the first trade
- ✔ **High:** The highest price trade during the trading period

✔ **Low:** The lowest price trade during the trading period

✔ **Close:** The price recorded for the last trade

By convention, a daily bar chart shows trades for the Toronto Stock Exchange (TSX) and the New York Stock Exchange (NYSE) trading day — from 9:30 a.m. to 4:00 p.m. ET — but some charting packages include optional after-hours results (prices from trades that occur after the market closes) as part of each daily bar. Likewise, some charting packages omit the opening prices on intraday charts. The opening price on an intraday chart (almost) always is the same as the closing price for the previous bar, so omitting it is of little consequence. However, omitting the opening price on daily, weekly, and monthly charts diminishes the usefulness of the chart, so avoid charts that don't provide all four prices.

Figure 9-2 shows a single price bar. The full range of prices traded throughout the period is shown by the vertical bar. The opening price is shown as a small line on the left-hand side of the bar, and the closing price is shown by a similar line on the right-hand side of the bar.

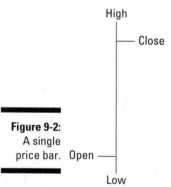

Figure 9-2:
A single
price bar.

This identical format is used for all time periods. For example, an intraday chart may use 1-minute bars, where each bar spans all the prices for your stock that occur during trades over a full minute. Common time frames for stock price charts are

✔ **1-minute bars:** Each bar represents one minute of trading.

✔ **5-minute bars:** Each bar represents five minutes of trading.

✔ **10-minute bars:** Each bar represents ten minutes of trading.

✔ **15-minute bars:** Each bar represents 15 minutes of trading.

✔ **60-minute bars:** Each bar represents 60 minutes of trading.

> ✔ **Daily bars**: Each bar represents one full day of trading.
>
> ✔ **Weekly bars:** Each bar represents one week of trading.
>
> ✔ **Monthly bars:** Each bar represents one full month of trading.

In our own trading, we typically monitor weekly charts, daily charts, one or two intraday charts, and either 60-minute bars for stocks and exchange-traded funds or 5-minute bars for indexes. We cover our chart selection and methodology more fully in Chapter 13.

Measuring volume

In addition to prices, bar charts often show the volume, or the number of shares traded during the given time period represented by each bar. On a daily chart, trading volume shows the total number of shares traded throughout the day. By convention, the volume is shown as a separate bar graph and usually is shown directly underneath the price chart. Figure 9-3 shows an example.

Volume (the number of shares sold) is used as a confirming indicator. In other words, if a price bar shows bullish activity (which is discussed later in the section on "Identifying Simple Single-Day Patterns"), that bullishness is confirmed by a higher-than-average trading volume. However, that bullish indication may diminish if trading volume is lower than average.

Volume also is used to gauge institutional participation in a stock. Significant trading volume often signals that large institutional investors — mutual funds, billionaires, pension funds, insurance companies, hedge funds, and others — are placing orders to buy or sell a stock. When prices rise and volume is strong, you usually can infer that institutions are accumulating positions in the stock. The reverse also is true. When prices fall and trading volume is high, large institutions may be liquidating positions, which is considered a bearish development.

Low-volume price changes are less meaningful, at least from a technical perspective, than high-volume changes. That's why technicians say, "Volume confirms price."

Price Bars

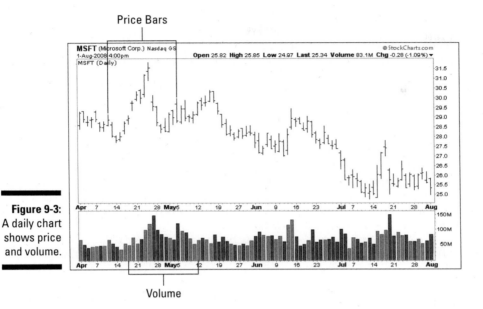

Figure 9-3:
A daily chart
shows price
and volume.

Volume

Colouring charts

Displaying price and volume bars in colour is common on charts. When using colour, be sure to use contrasting colours so you can distinguish up days from down days. One prominent charting package, for example, defaults to green for up days and red for down days. A prominent Internet site defaults to black for up days and red for down. Most charting services enable you to configure colours to suit yourself.

Identifying Simple Single-Day Patterns

The goal of chart reading is determining whether buyers or sellers are in control of the price. In a bull market, shareholders may be willing to sell, but only if they can coax higher prices from buyers. In a bear market, buyers are able to negotiate a better price when sellers are more eager to sell than buyers are to buy.

You're trying to infer the market's underlying psychology by looking at the history of price movements. Inferring that as prices rise, buyers are more interested in buying than sellers are in selling is a fair observation. In a rising market, buyers must continue bidding prices higher to convince sellers to part with their shares. Rising prices attract additional buyers, who must continue to bid prices higher to convince even more reluctant sellers to part with their shares.

Single-bar patterns

The most bullish thing that a market can do is go higher. Although technicians typically view each bar within the context of its neighbouring bars, each individual bar has something to tell the careful observer. Figure 9-4, for example, shows a *bullish single-bar pattern*.

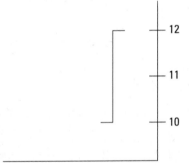

Figure 9-4:
A single bullish bar.

In the example in the figure, buyers bid prices higher throughout the day. The opening price of $10 also is the lowest trade for the day. The daily range shown on the bar is $2, and the stock closed at $12, the high for the day.

If you're keeping score (and as a trader, believe us, you are), the bulls gained ground and clearly are ahead for the day. Bears holding short positions were hurt where it hurts the most — in their pocketbooks. A trader takes a short position by borrowing shares of stock and selling them in the hope of making money if the stock price falls. This trade loses money if the stock's price rises. The mechanics of selling short are described in Chapter 14. The example in Figure 9-4 shows the stock opening at the extreme low and closing at its extreme high, but the pattern nevertheless is just as bullish when the stock opens near its low and then closes near its high.

Figure 9-5 shows a *bearish single-bar pattern*. The stock opened at $11.75; traded to $12, the high for the day; fell to $10, the daily low; and then closed at $10.25. The stock doesn't have to close at the low for the day for it to be bearish. Closing near the low is good enough.

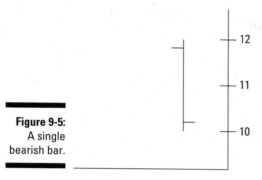

Figure 9-5:
A single
bearish bar.

These single-day patterns are helpful to the trader who's trying to understand the underpinnings of the markets. Whether these patterns present a trading opportunity depends on the stock's recent history and whether its trading volume confirms the pattern (see the earlier section on "Measuring volume"). We give you several examples later in this chapter in the section "Searching for Transitions," where a bullish single-bar pattern triggers a buy signal.

Reversal patterns

A *reversal bar* is another single-bar pattern that shows a stock opening and closing at the same end of its trading range. Figure 9-6 shows a *bullish single-bar reversal* where the stock opens at the high, trades lower through part of the day, and by the close, the stock regains all its losses and closes at its highest intraday price.

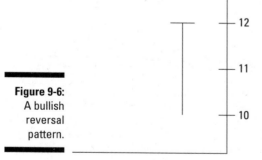

Figure 9-6:
A bullish
reversal
pattern.

During the early part of the trading sessions depicted in the bullish reversal pattern, buyers were willing to buy only if sellers lowered their offering (asking) prices. By the end of the day, the tide had turned and roles were reversed, with sellers willing to sell but only at higher prices. This situation is another win for the bulls, because they were able to stop the price slide and recover all the intraday losses.

Figure 9-7 shows a *bearish reversal pattern*. In this case, the stock opens at $10.25, rallies during the day to $12, but closes at the $10 low.

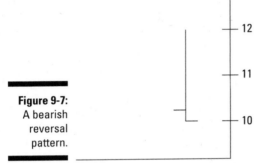

Figure 9-7:
A bearish reversal pattern.

Reversal patterns often represent a powerful single-bar trading pattern. Whenever a bullish reversal bar is preceded by several periods of falling prices, for example, its pattern often represents a buying opportunity. On the other hand, when a bearish reversal bar is preceded by a rising trend, it may be a signal to close a long position or initiate a short position. We describe selling short in Chapter 14.

Not all price bars, however, present specific trading opportunities. Some bars are neutral by themselves, but add to a stock's history when viewed in context. Through charts, you can use a stock's visual historical record to develop your trading plan, as you'll see in the following sections.

Identifying Trends and Trading Ranges

Technical analysis helps you identify trends, discovering when one begins and ends. Our style of trading, *position trading,* looks for the persistent trend, a trend that lasts for at least several weeks to several months, perhaps even longer. Day traders and swing traders who buy and sell in the shortest of terms also look for trends to trade. In fact, the distinction between a day trader, a swing trader, and a position trader is the length of the trend that each is hoping to find. Swing trading and day trading are discussed in Chapters 16 and 17, respectively. If you're really interested, check out *Swing Trading For Dummies* by Omar Bassal and *Day Trading For Dummies* by Ann C. Logue (both published by Wiley).

Following trends is an effective trading strategy, especially for new traders. To follow trends successfully, you first need to identify and distinguish between stocks and markets exhibiting trends and their counterparts, trading within specific price ranges.

Identifying a trading range

Stocks are either trending up or down or trading within a confined price range. The latter are said to be *range bound* or stuck in a trading range, never trading higher than the high nor lower than the low during a specific time frame. You also hear range-bound stocks described as consolidating or building a base. Although some subtle distinctions may exist among these terms, we nevertheless use them interchangeably.

In general, we're not interested in trading range-bound stocks. Trading ranges can persist for long periods of time. Some may even last for years. For a position trader, having money in a range-bound stock represents wasted opportunity. You won't lose money, but you won't make any either. Instead, we are interested in identifying range-bound stocks because they have the potential to begin trending. We patiently watch these stocks for a signal indicating the trading range may end and a trend may begin. Stocks that break out of a long-lasting trading range often begin trends that can be traded profitably.

Trading ranges are easy to spot after the fact, but anticipating when a stock is about to enter or exit a trading range is nearly impossible. For this and other reasons, range-bound stocks are difficult to trade, especially for new traders. Some short-term traders are able to trade range-bound stocks successfully, so it isn't impossible, but we encourage you first to become a proficient trend trader before attempting to trade stocks stuck in trading ranges. We describe tools you can use in trading-range situations in Chapter 11. In Chapter 10, we discuss what to do if a stock you own stops trending and becomes range bound.

Identifying a trading range is best done visually. Figure 9-8 shows a chart of Time Warner Inc. (TWX) stock in a range-bound pattern.

Time Warner spent more than nine months trading between $13.50 and $16.50. Notice how the price moves up and down but always between those levels, never making much progress one way or the other. Also notice the lines drawn on the chart near $13.50 and $16.50. These lines show support and resistance levels, respectively, and are discussed in the "Support and resistance: Not just for undergarments" section later in this chapter.

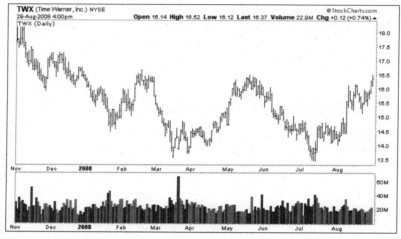

Spotting a trend

Now contrast the Time Warner chart in Figure 9-8 with the chart of Ryanair Holdings (RYAAY) in Figure 9-9. RYAAY appears quite different from the range-bound stock. Notice the steady stair-step march upward as the stock rises higher and higher.

Even in a strong upward trend, stocks rarely go straight up. You often see some reversals and mini-consolidations in a trend that cause the stair-stepped look.

That stair-stepped upward march is an identifying characteristic of an *uptrend*. Although defining it quantitatively is possible, seeing an uptrend on a chart is easy and that's the way it often is done. As long as a stock price continues to reach higher intermittent highs, and its new lows don't fall below previous lows, the uptrend remains intact. Chapter 10 discusses trends and these stair-step patterns in more detail.

Stocks can also *downtrend;* a series of lower highs and lower lows is as much of a trend as its upward-bound counterpart. See Figure 9-10, a chart showing Comerica Inc. in a downtrend.

Figure 9-10: Comerica's stock in a downtrend.

Time frame matters

The time frame of your chart determines your trading perspective.

You may notice that the price lines of a range-bound stock are made up of many small trends. If you look at an intraday chart of Time Warner stock (TWX) that spanned the 25 or so days of trading from April 14, 2008, through May 15, 2008, TWX appears to be in an uptrend.

In fact, TWX was in a trend during that period. However, when you step back and observe a broader historical record of TWX's trading pattern by looking at the daily and weekly charts, you can easily see that the multi-day trend actually was confined within the prevailing trading range.

Although short-term swing traders and day traders make a living basing their trading on these mini- and microtrends, doing so isn't our cup of tea. We caution you that consistently trading range-bound stocks profitably is very difficult to do.

Searching for Transitions

A stock can transition from a downtrend to an uptrend in several different ways. It can, for example, fall precipitously, turn on a dime, and begin heading higher. Furthermore, a stock can fall, bounce around in a trading range for a while, and begin a new trend — up or down — as it breaks from the trading range.

Although turning on a dime from downtrending to uptrending sometimes presents profitable trading opportunities, these transitions are difficult to identify, and are even more difficult to base a trade on. Additional tools of technical analysis to unearth these transitions are explained in Chapters 10 and 11. Rather than trying to score big on sharp transitions, we recommend searching for stocks making the transition to trending after a period of range-bound trading lasting at least six to eight weeks, preferably longer.

Support and resistance: Not just for undergarments

The transition from range-bound to trending is relatively easy to identify visually and is the easiest to trade profitably. To find the transition, you must be familiar with the concept of support and resistance. You will see support and resistance used in many contexts. For example, they are used to identify a trading range, as discussed in this section. They are also used to help identify when a trend has reached its end, as we discuss in Chapter 10.

For an example of how support and resistance levels are shown on a chart, refer to Figure 9-8, the chart showing TWX stuck in a trading range. The support line shown on this chart is at approximately $13.50; the resistance line is shown near $16.50.

Support is always the lower trading-range boundary; *resistance* is always the upper trading-range boundary.

When technicians talk about support, they mean the price where buyers are willing to buy enough stock to stop the price from falling. Said another way, when sellers see enough buying interest at the support price, they may still be willing to sell, but, as for now, they'll sell only if they can coax buyers to raise their bids. Buyers are now eager to buy, so they're willing to bid a little more to complete the transaction. The result: Prices end their descent and begin heading higher.

The reverse is true as the stock price approaches the resistance level. Buyers begin losing interest as the stock reaches elevated prices. Eager sellers must lower their offer (asking) price to complete the transaction, which causes prices to stop rising and begin falling.

Support levels and resistance levels often are determined visually by means of a chart. Knowing the exact price where lines of support and resistance need to be drawn is difficult, and traders may differ on where to draw these lines. Some choose the extreme, plotting intraday highs and lows of a trading range during a specific time frame to establish those levels. We prefer using closing prices on a daily or weekly bar chart to define the upper and lower boundaries within the trading range. If you're analyzing an intraday chart, use the last trade price on each bar when drawing the support and resistance levels. In our opinion, closing prices (or last prices) have more significance and better represent the consensus of traders and investors. Ultimately, the choice is yours.

Technical analysis is not an exact science. And as such, thinking of support and resistance levels as areas of support or zones of resistance is probably better than viewing them in terms of specific prices or single lines on a chart, even though that's how they appear.

Finding a breakout

A stock remains stuck in its trading range as long as it bounces between zones of support and resistance. Short-term traders may be interested in these movements, but as a position trader you're looking for a more substantial trend, so you must wait for something to change the status quo and cause the stock to break out of its trading range.

A *breakout* sometimes signals the transition of a stock trading within a range to a new uptrend or downtrend. When breaking out to the upside, we want to see the resistance zone violated by a significant amount, certainly by more than 5 or 10 cents. More important, we want to see the stock trade through its resistance zone on much higher volume than the average. Ideally, volume needs to be at least 50 percent higher than average. More volume is even better. Remember that volume confirms price.

Figure 9-11 shows a chart of Baxter International Inc. (BAX), a textbook example of a stock breaking out of a trading range. BAX had been trading within a narrow range from mid 2005 through June 2006. We drew the support line just above $34.50 and the resistance line near $38.00. The support and resistance levels were tested several times in 2006.

On July 20, 2006, BAX opened well above its previous close, traded through the zone of resistance, and closed at $38.88. This pattern — where a stock's opening price is well above its previous close and moves up, breaking out of its trading range — is called a *breakout gap,* which we discuss more fully in Chapter 10. Although not a requirement for a stock to break out of its trading range, a breakout gap does bolster the case for this rise in prices to be a transition from trading within a range to a new uptrend. Trading volume was almost 8 million shares, or almost triple the average daily volume of 2.7 million shares.

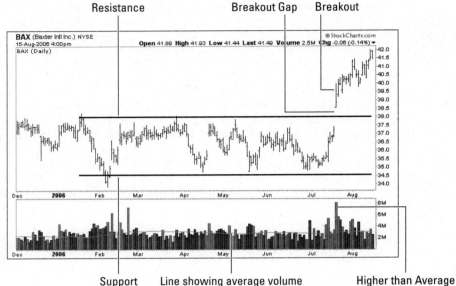

Figure 9-11:
Baxter
International
Inc. stock
breaks out
of its trading
range.

As the chart shows, BAX continued to trade higher. Although you cannot see it in Figure 9-11, BAX continued its rally through May 2007.

The BAX breakout was an almost picture-perfect setup for a trading opportunity. Baxter is a leading stock in a leading industry. The stock built a solid trading-range base and broke out on higher-than-average volume. Then BAX went on to rally for almost a year. Nice. We discuss ways to identify when a trend has come to an end, and when to close your trade to realize your profits, in Chapter 10.

Waiting patiently for winning patterns

We can hear the gears grinding from here. Yes, it's a nice trade . . . but you're probably saying to yourself, "Couldn't I have bought BAX for about $35.00 several times between February 2006 and June 2006? Why wait until the breakout drives my entry price up?"

The answer: Finding a good trading signal is important; avoiding bad trading signals is more important.

Foretelling the future is hard. Of course hindsight is going to tell you that buying BAX at $35.00 would've earned you more money than buying it above $38. But when the price was $35.00, how could you know that BAX wouldn't stay in its trading range for many more months or years? Or how could you tell that BAX wasn't going to break out of its trading range to the downside, and start trending lower?

It happens. In fact, if the stock had traded below its zone of support, technical analysis would've suggested a potential opportunity to sell BAX short.

Another important reason for waiting for a breakout is that when you enter a trade, you need an exit strategy. Exit strategies are discussed more fully in Chapters 12 through 14, but for now, know that you need technical signals to show you when to exit your position, the same way you needed them to enter the position in the first place. If you're trying to buy stocks at the bottom and then sell them at the top, few signals are available to tell you whether your entry signal has failed.

Fine-tuning your trading-range breakout strategy

Three ways you can fine-tune your trading-range breakout strategy are by

- ✔ Observing that breakouts from long trading ranges tend to result in more profitable buying and selling than breakouts from shorter trading ranges.

- ✔ Understanding that breakouts from tight trading ranges, where price fluctuations are confined to a relatively narrow price range, usually result in better trades than when trading-range price fluctuations are wide.

- ✔ Waiting for a short while — at least one day, possibly two or three — to confirm the trading range breakout can be helpful. Waiting to see whether the stock falls back into the trading range before you take a position can save you from a negative market reaction. Running into a wave of selling immediately after a breakout is not uncommon, and the way the stock reacts to that selling is just as important as the breakout itself.

Consistently snagging the lowest price is nearly impossible, regardless of whether you use technical analysis, fundamental analysis, a Ouija board, Madame Cleo, or follow the best prognosticators in the business. Technical analysis can help you find transitions, but it can't tell the future. As a technician, you never (almost never) buy your stocks at their lowest prices, and you rarely exit your positions at the highest prices.

However, if you wait for a solid trading signal, you can ride the middle part of the trend for a large portion of the move. Try not to be greedy. The middle part of the trend is a very profitable place to trade.

Sipping from a cup and saucer

Another widely followed transitional formation is called a cup and handle. In a *cup and handle formation,* a stock's price levels form a rounded curving bottom that looks a bit like a cup or a saucer, which often is followed by a modest shakeout formation that, if you use your imagination, looks a bit like the handle on a coffee cup.

Figure 9-12 shows a chart of the Apple Inc. (AAPL) stock that illustrates the cup and handle formation.

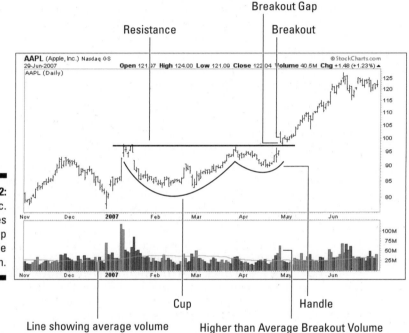

Figure 9-12: Apple Inc. stock prices show a cup and handle pattern.

The entry strategy for this pattern is similar to that used for the trading range breakout. The trigger occurs when the stock price breaks above the handle on high volume. In the Apple example, it occurs in late April, and is accompanied by a small breakout gap.

Notice that the stock traded in a very narrow range during the next couple of days, retesting the former area of resistance. As often is the case, that former resistance level actually provided support after it was crossed. You'll see this phenomenon occur frequently.

The cup and handle is a reliable trading pattern, but that doesn't mean the pattern never fails. It does, and you need an exit strategy for when it does, just like every other trade. We discuss exit strategies in Chapter 12.

Deciding what to do with a double bottom

Another transition pattern that often leads to profitable trading opportunities is the double bottom. Visually, a *double bottom* looks like a "W" on the chart, so it is very easy to see. However, a double bottom doesn't need to form a perfect "W" to be valid. In fact, we actually prefer the right-hand trough to be a little lower than the left-hand trough. When a minor new low forms, it tends to shake out the weakest owners of the stock and makes it much easier for bulls to drive the price higher.

Figure 9-13 shows a well-formed double bottom on the Newmont Mining Corp. (NEM) stock chart. The left-hand trough occurred in June 2007; the right-hand trough in August 2007.

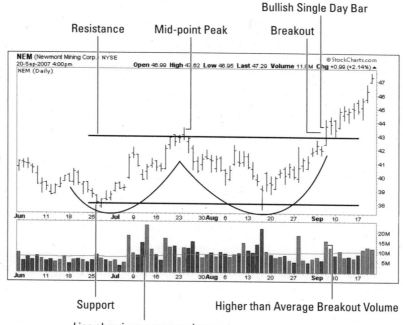

Figure 9-13: Newmont Mining Corp. stock reaches a double bottom.

The entry criteria for this pattern are similar to that of the trading-range breakout. In this case, the trigger point occurs when the stock breaks above the mid-point peak between the two troughs. This peak is sometimes called the *pivot point.* Ideally, higher-than-average volume confirms the trigger.

The trigger price on the chart is just below $43.00, which corresponds to the $42.91 close on July 24. The stock gapped above the trigger point on September 6 with a volume of more than 15 million shares. That's 50 percent more than the average daily trading volume.

Also notice the bullish single-day bar pattern on the breakout. The stock pulled back to test resistance at the mid-point close price and then rallied.

An alternative double-bottom strategy

One scenario where aggressive traders may want to anticipate the formation of a double-bottom pattern is when the "W" is particularly deep and the pivot is many points away from the trough. When that happens, taking a position as the stock is forming the right-hand trough sometimes makes sense.

If the price holds near or just below the left-hand trough, and volume confirms the reversal, then aggressive traders can enter a position. You may also want to enter a position if signals from other single-day patterns confirm the reversal. The risk is relatively small, and the potential reward is relatively large. If the stock falls below the lowest low, you'll know your trade has failed and you must exit. Otherwise, hold the position until the stock tests the pivot point (see previous section).

Using the NEM chart in Figure 9-13 to illustrate this strategy, the buy trigger occurred on August 16 when NEM showed the single-day reversal pattern at the bottom of the trough. Your entry point would be the next trading day, and your stop would be below $37.60, the low for that reversal bar.

Looking at other patterns

Many other reversal patterns are published in technical analysis books and magazines, but the ones in the preceding few sections, we believe, are the most reliable.

Inexperienced traders always want to find the Holy Grail, that pattern or indicator that enables them to profitably trade the turn-on-a-dime "V" pattern. In truth, however, "V" bottoms don't happen all that often. And when they do, many reasons express why it's probably not the best trading opportunity available to you. If you talk shop with other traders, you're certain to hear them discuss many esoteric patterns. We know them, but we rarely trade them. The simple techniques we've shown you in this chapter will enable you to trade profitably. No need to look for the esoteric when the simple does the job just as well.

Chapter 10

Following Trends for Fun and Profit

. . . .

In This Chapter

▶ Spotting uptrends and downtrends

▶ Finding areas of support and resistance within a trend

▶ Identifying gaps

▶ Understanding continuation and retracement patterns

▶ Planning for failed trading signals

. . . .

*T*echnical analysis helps you identify new price trends and look for endings to existing trends. Being able to identify those two extreme end points means you can develop a powerful, profitable trend-following trading system. Technical analysis can also help you evaluate the persistence of a trend, which is useful for finding secondary entry points and generating short-term trading signals.

In this chapter, we discuss trading strategies for several trend-following techniques. We also look at methods for identifying continuation patterns, retracement patterns, and reversal patterns, together with strategies for dealing with the inevitable failed trading signal.

Identifying Trends

Identifying a trend is relatively straightforward. Instinctively, you know it when you see it. Visual techniques and calculated indicators both can be used to identify trend signals. We discuss visual identification techniques in this chapter. We cover calculated indicators in Chapter 11.

A steadily rising or falling stock is a *trending stock.* But if you watch stocks for any period of time, you know that they rarely go straight up or down. Instead, you see a stair-step effect in which a stock rises several steps and then falls back. Talking about a trend as a series of intermittent highs interrupted by intermittent lows makes good sense. So an *uptrend,* then, is a series of higher intermittent highs and higher intermittent lows. Conversely, a *downtrend* is a series of lower intermittent highs followed by lower intermittent lows.

Figure 10-1 shows a price chart of Polycom Inc. (PLCM) stock exhibiting a series of higher intermittent highs and higher intermittent lows. (From here on out, for simplicity's sake, we call these higher highs and higher lows.)

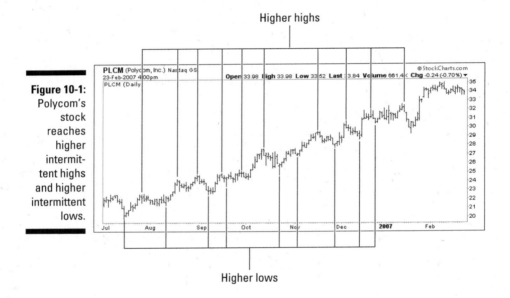

Figure 10-1: Polycom's stock reaches higher intermittent highs and higher intermittent lows.

The PLCM example shows the type of trends that you hope follow the breakout patterns we discuss in Chapter 9. As long as the pattern of higher highs and higher lows continues, you can participate in a profitable trade.

Figure 10-2 shows a downtrending price chart of American International Group's (AIG) stock that identifies its series of lower highs and lower lows. You may recall hearing about the government bailout of AIG during the credit crisis. You may also notice that the company's stock performance signalled trouble long before the credit crisis began.

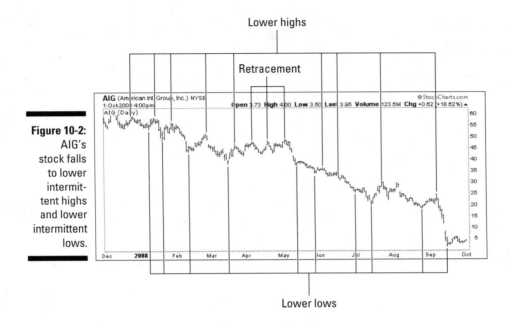

Figure 10-2:
AIG's
stock falls
to lower
intermit-
tent highs
and lower
intermittent
lows.

Supporting and Resisting Trends

You may have noticed in Figure 10-2 that a higher intermittent high formed in the midst of the downtrend exhibited by the chart. That anomaly is identified as a retracement on the chart (see the "Withstanding Retracements" section later in the chapter). It happened again a few months later. Although the series of lower highs and lower lows appeared to have been broken, AIG's downtrend remained intact and continued its fall.

In an uptrend, as long as the pattern of higher highs and higher lows continues, you can say that the trend persists. The converse (lower highs and lower lows) is true in a downtrend. Unfortunately, you cannot say that breaks in these patterns signal the end of any trends.

Sometimes you see an uptrend pattern broken when the stock fails to reach a new high or when it makes a lower intermittent low. You may actually see several of these disconcerting lower lows, only to witness the resumption of a strong uptrend. As such, you need to anticipate these eventual hiccups as you plan your trading strategy, and you need tools to help you determine whether a stock is still trending or the trend has reached its end.

Drawing trend lines to show support

Trend lines are drawn underneath a trend, much as support lines are drawn underneath a trading range as described in Chapter 9. And just like the support line, trend lines show areas of trading-range support that can be used to trigger short-term trading signals as you monitor the progress of a trend.

If you remember your days in geometry class, you'll recall that only two points are needed to define any line. Knowing which points to choose is the trick when drawing a trend line. You may, for example, choose to have the trend line touching two or more of the intermittent lows, as is the case in Figure 10-3. Or you may choose to draw the trend line based on the lowest closing prices between those intermittent lows.

Figure 10-3:
Finding a
trend line.

Unfortunately, drawing trend lines is not a precise discipline, and no universal consensus exists for where and how to draw them. In fact, you're not likely to find any two traders drawing trend lines in exactly the same place for the same stock. Furthermore, you'll drive yourself crazy trying to touch all the important lows with your trend line.

Trend lines are drawn to fit historical data. That the trend rides atop the trend line is not surprising, given that you drew it that way. However, whether that trend line represents the actual trend or is able to generate reliable trading signals is constantly in doubt.

So many variables apply. You might, for example, draw the trend line on a traditional price scale as we've done here, but that trend line will look very different from one drawn on a log or semi-log scale that shows percentage price changes. It's hard to know which is the better choice. Also, trend lines are often drawn using the oldest historical data, but newer data are more relevant for generating trading signals. As such, constantly questioning your information and continually updating your trend line is a good habit to follow.

Watching the price bar cross below the trend line can be disturbing; it can signal the end of the trend, or it may mean that you need to redraw the trend lines. Unfortunately, when the stock price closes below the trend line you can't know whether the penetration represents the end of the trend or just another opportunity to redraw the trend line to conform to the newest price data.

An alternative technique for drawing the trend line reduces the ambiguity just a bit. Instead of drawing the trend line from left to right, the way most people instinctively do, draw the trend line backward, or from right to left. Using the two most recent intermittent lows in the trend, draw the trend line backward as long as it is meaningful, then project the trend line toward the right. This approach has a couple of benefits:

- ✔ The slope of the trend line is more closely aligned with the most recent trading data, which usually are more relevant to your trading decisions.

- ✔ You'll resign yourself to the necessity of continually redrawing your trend lines based on the newest data.

Surfing channels

Traders use a _channel_ to identify potential entry and exit points during a trend. Channel lines are formed when a line is drawn parallel with the trend line across a trend's intermittent highs. This _top channel line_ is analogous to the resistance line in a trading range, which we discuss in Chapter 9. The original trend line then becomes the _bottom channel line_. Figure 10-4 shows an example of a channel.

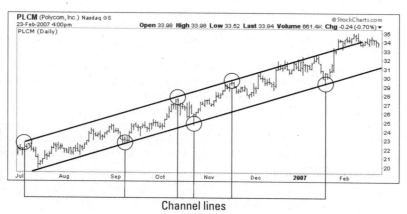

Figure 10-4:
A channel.

Channel lines

Trending and channelling strategies

The strategies for using trend lines and channels are similar. When an uptrending stock approaches the trend line or the bottom channel line, short-term traders often see an opportunity to take a position in the direction of the dominant trend. As long as the stock's price does not fall through this support level, they will hold the position. Position traders, on the other hand, may use these same conditions to validate their existing positions as still viable. If, however, the stock closes below the trend line and remains below it for longer than a day or two, position traders *and* short-term traders must consider the possibility that the trend has reached its end. It's even possible that the trend has reversed.

It may seem perverse, but when an upwardly trending stock breaches the top channel line, it's not always good news. The stock may be overextended. At the very least, it's an indication to traders to pay close attention. In Figure 10-4, PLCM rose outside of its top channel line several times. The trend failed soon afterward (but that isn't shown in Figure 10-4).

Trend lines and channels work better across longer periods of time. A stock price that violates a long-running, persistent trend or channel line on a weekly chart provides more meaningful guidance than when it breeches a support line on a daily chart or an intraday chart. In our experience, short-term trend lines add little information that isn't already present in the steady march of higher highs and higher lows.

When a stock breaks a short-term trend line, we believe it's best to step back one time increment to evaluate the situation. For example, if you're trading based primarily on daily chart data, display a weekly chart and examine the trend line and the series of intermittent highs and lows. If the march of higher highs and higher lows remains intact on the weekly chart, you may want to give your position a little room to work itself out. However, if a longer time frame shows a break in the pattern of higher highs and higher lows, consider exiting your position right away.

We use trend lines for guidance while trading, but rarely do we make decisions solely on the basis of a trend-line penetration. Although initiating short-term positions in the direction of the dominant trend is possible by using channels to enter and exit the position, doing so is very difficult, and few traders are able to engage in that practice profitably. Some traders even take this concept one step further by trying to take positions in opposition to the dominant trend as the stock price approaches the upper channel line. We believe trading in the direction opposite that of a dominant trend and a stock's fundamental picture is foolhardy and an excellent way to lose a substantial portion of your trading capital.

Bottom line: Trend lines and channels are additional tools you can use to monitor the progress of a stock price trend. They can be used to help identify trading opportunities, but we recommend they not be your primary method of determining entry and exit points.

Seeing Gaps

A *price gap* forms on a bar chart when the opening price of the current bar is above or below the closing price of the previous bar. Gaps occur mostly on daily charts, sometimes on weekly charts, and rarely on intraday charts. Depending on the circumstances, gaps can show continuation and reversal patterns, and they can signal an opportunity to enter or exit a position.

Some gaps are obvious and some are subtle. For example, if the opening price is above the previous close, but the low of the current bar is below the previous high, then those bars overlap and the gap is hard to spot. Many traders simply ignore that type of gap. If, however, the low of the current bar is obviously higher than the high of the previous bar, that will draw the attention of most traders. Examples of obvious gaps are shown in the following sections.

Gaps are divided into several broad categories based on where the gap occurs. These categories determine your trading strategy and are discussed in the sections that follow.

Common gap

Gaps that occur within a trading range, as described in Chapter 9, can be either a *common gap* or a *breakout gap*. If the gap occurs in the middle of the trading range, far from either the support or resistance level, it is a common gap. Common gaps occur frequently and are, well, rather common. They rarely provide meaningful trading opportunities. Ignoring them usually is the best policy. Figure 10-5 shows several common gaps and a breakout gap.

Breakout or breakaway gap

When a stock price exceeds a high of a price range during a specific time frame or falls below the low during that same period and simultaneously forms a gap, traders describe that situation as a *breakout* or *breakaway gap*. A breakout gap often provides excellent trading signals to enter a new position, in the direction of the gap. Figure 10-5 shows an example of a breakout gap from a long-standing trading range. We discuss trading strategies for trading range breakouts in Chapter 9.

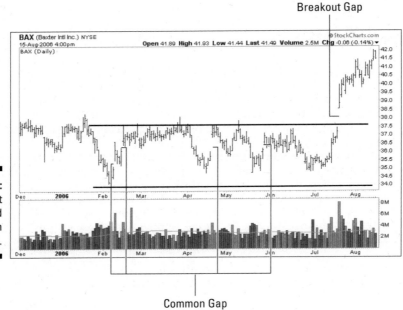

Figure 10-5: Breakout gap and common gaps.

Continuation gap

A *continuation gap* is also known as a runaway gap or an acceleration gap. This type of gap occurs within an uptrend when the open price of the current bar is higher than the close price of the previous bar. If the low of the current bar is also obviously above the high of the previous bar, this gap usually indicates that the trend is very strong. Continuation gaps may also occur in downtrends. The defining characteristics are opposite those of the uptrend.

Figure 10-6 shows several examples of continuation gaps in a downtrend. Some short-term traders may use a continuation gap as a signal to enter a position in the direction of the gap. Position traders may use this same signal to confirm that a current trade remains viable. You sometimes see a series of runaway gaps occur in close proximity to each other, and these gaps usually are a strong confirmation of the prevailing trend. However, continuation gaps also warrant caution, because they can turn into an exhaustion gap.

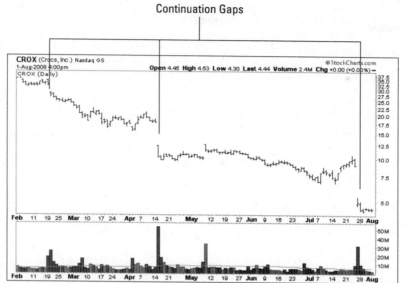

Figure 10-6:
Continuation
gap.

Exhaustion gap

Exhaustion gaps occur at or near the ends of strong trends. Unfortunately, the defining characteristics for an exhaustion gap are virtually identical to those for a continuation gap. Exhaustion gaps are often accompanied by very large volume, which is one clue that the gap may not be a continuation gap. Otherwise, distinguishing an exhaustion gap from a continuation gap is sometimes impossible, until the stock price changes direction. By that time, it is usually obvious that something is wrong with the trade and you should exit your position.

In Figure 10-6, we actually assume the final gap is a continuation gap, because if the stock price continues its trend, it will become one. If, however, the stock price reverses, the gap may be classified as an exhaustion gap. Reversal patterns are discussed in Chapter 9. Sometimes, an exhaustion gap turns into an island gap.

Island gap

An *island gap,* or an island reversal (Figure 10-7), forms when a trend changes direction. The pattern is actually two gaps that isolate either a single bar or a short series of bars from the dominant trend and the new trend. An island gap usually is a good indicator that the prior trend has been extinguished and can be used to signal an exit from an existing position. You may also use an island gap to initiate a new position, but only if the direction of the new trend aligns with the stock's underlying fundamental condition. Be sure to review the "Dealing with Failed Signals" section in this chapter before initiating any positions based on an island gap.

Figure 10-7:
Island gap.

Island Gap

Waving Flags and Pennants

Flag and pennant patterns represent areas of consolidation on a trend chart. You've already encountered these patterns, just not by name. In a series of higher highs and higher lows, these patterns form the basis for the higher lows. In other words, the higher lows are made of flag and pennant patterns.

A *pennant pattern* looks like, well, a pennant. Support and resistance lines converge into a point forming what looks like a small pennant shape. A *flag pattern,* on the other hand, is bounded by parallel lines. All these patterns almost always fly counter to the prevailing trend, but the direction in which they're flying is not actually a requirement.

Figure 10-8 shows examples of flags and pennants on the chart of a trending stock.

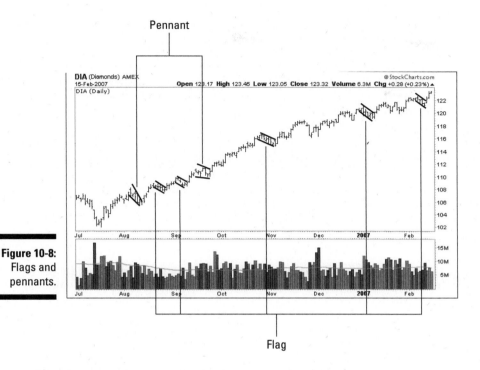

Figure 10-8:
Flags and
pennants.

The key for each of these patterns is the breakout. If the breakout from the formation is in the direction of the established trend, then the trend continues. If not, it's possible that the trend is over.

Flags and pennants typically are associated with a trend, but you may also see these patterns within the confines of a trading range. A flag or pennant forming near the top of a trading range hints of an eventual breakout. The flag or pennant pattern shows the stock consolidating near the top of the trading range, and that suggests that selling pressure is diminishing and the stock is preparing to test the zone of resistance.

Withstanding Retracements

A *retracement* occurs when a trending stock revisits recent prices. You've already seen many examples. When a stock makes a higher intermediate high and then a higher intermediate low, that is a retracement. A trading range as discussed in Chapter 9 can also be considered a retracement. You may hear a retracement called a price consolidation or a pullback, but the concept is the same.

Flags and pennants are relatively simple forms of retracement patterns. More complex retracements can occur within the confines of a trend, and like their simpler counterparts they don't actually signal the end of the trend. Unfortunately, complex retracements cause confusion and consternation for traders when they occur. Besides being difficult to anticipate, they send out conflicting signals to traders trying to make sense of which trading-plan adjustments are needed.

Three-step and five-step retracements

In an uptrend, you sometimes see breaks in the pattern of higher highs and higher lows when the stock price fails to reach a new high or makes a lower intermittent low. You may see several occurrences of these worrisome lower lows and lower highs happen one right after the other followed by a resumption of a strong uptrend.

You will see a couple of these benign multistep patterns frequently occur in the midst of a strong trend, so it's useful to watch for them. A *three-step retracement* makes at least one lower intermittent high and one lower intermittent low. A *five-step retracement* makes two lower highs and two lower lows. Multistep retracements also occur when a downtrending stock makes higher highs and higher lows.

Figure 10-9 shows an example of a five-step retracement that ultimately resolves in the direction of the prevailing trend. The five steps are identified, along with the corresponding intermittent highs and lows.

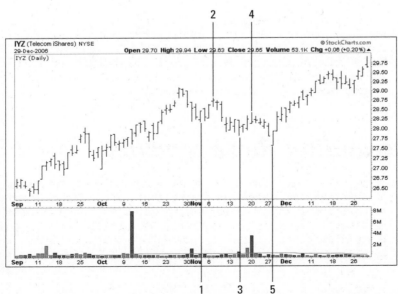

Figure 10-9:
Five-step retracement pattern.

Trust us when we tell you that situations like these are disconcerting whenever you're holding a position. They're not, however, absolute signals that a trend has reached its end. Knowing when a trend has ended, however, is nearly impossible, so you need a plan for dealing with it when it happens.

Where the multistep retracement occurs within a trend has some bearing on what plan you choose. If the stock price has just broken out of a long trading range and then falters, you may want to wait for a subsequent attempt to break out of the trading range, but closing the position is probably best. Look for trading opportunities elsewhere.

If a stock price starts what may be a three-step or a five-step retracement after a long period of trending, and your position is profitable, you may want to see how the retracement plays out. Absent any obvious sell signals, such as an island reversal or a downside breakout from a flag, pennant, or trading range formation, you can wait to see how the retracement resolves itself.

Checking out a chart that reflects a longer time frame can be helpful. For example, you can examine a weekly chart when the retracement occurs on the daily chart. If the trend shows no signs of faltering on the weekly chart, hold your position. If the stock recovers and heads higher, so much the better, but if it establishes another lower high and trades below its next lower low, it's time to exit.

Finally, considering fundamental factors before making your decision makes good sense. If a company's deteriorating financial situation is an underlying cause of the retracement, then exiting your position makes sense. You also need to be aware of the cycle the economy is in when making your decision. If the economy is approaching a turning point as your stock's technical situation deteriorates, getting out of the position usually is a good idea.

Dealing with subsequent trading ranges

A trading range or a cup and handle formation, like the ones we describe in Chapter 9, also are complex consolidation patterns. A trend that's interrupted by a period of range-bound trading may indicate either a pause before the trend resumes or the end of the trend. The only way of knowing which way the trend will go is to watch for the breakout. Unfortunately, you may be in for a long wait.

In the retracement pattern shown in Figure 10-9, you can make a valid argument interpreting the five-step retracement as a cup and handle formation. Technical analysis is an imprecise discipline, so you may encounter ambiguous situations like this. The results in this case were the same regardless of your interpretation. The stock broke out of its nine-week complex consolidation pattern and resumed its trend.

Breakouts that occur in the direction of the prevailing trend may indicate that the trend has farther to run, but they may also be a prelude to a failed breakout signal. Trading-range breakouts provide the strongest signals when they result in a change of direction from the previous trend.

Dealing with Failed Signals

All trading signals are subject to failure. Sometimes, things just don't work out as planned. However, even a failed signal provides additional information that you can use to revise your trading plans. In fact, sometimes the best trading signals are the direct result of a failed signal.

Trapping bulls and bears

Breakouts from trading ranges and cup and handle patterns sometimes fail. These failures happen to bullish and bearish signals, and when they fail it is called a *trap*. The two kinds of traps are

- ✔ **Bull traps,** which occur after an upside breakout. The stock breaks out of its trading range to the upside but then reverses back into the trading range and ultimately breaks out to the down side.

- ✔ **Bear traps,** which occur after a downside breakout. This opposite scenario to the bull trap often is very bullish. The stock reverses course and reenters the trading range. If a bear trap occurs within a trading range that's preceded by a long period of declining prices, it often represents an excellent buying opportunity, because it's a sign that selling pressure has evaporated in the stock, which thus is likely to attempt an upside breakout.

Whenever you see a potential bear trap taking place and the stock meets all of your fundamental criteria, you may want to enter a long position as soon as the stock price reenters the trading range.

Filling the gaps

A gap that's forming usually is interpreted as a signal that the prevailing trend will continue. If a stock reverses and retraces prices within the gap, we say that the gap has been filled. A gap that's filled negates the trading signal that it generated.

When dealing with a breakout gap, a stock price that falls back through the trading range resistance zone and fills the gap is likely to be a bearish development. Similarly, when a continuation gap is filled, you need to consider it a failed signal and exit your position. The same is true for an island gap. If prices trade back into the area of the isolated island, the trading signal has failed and you need to exit your position.

Deciding whether to reverse directions

A bear trap shows an example of where taking a position based on a failed signal makes sense. If, however, you already have a position and the signal fails, exiting your position is a wise choice — you're letting the market sort out its psychosis without risking your money.

You also need to consider economic and fundamental factors when deciding how to handle a failed signal. Acting on a contrary signal makes sense only when economic and fundamental conditions support the decision.

For example, if a bullish signal fails and becomes a bearish signal, selling a stock short makes sense only if it's fundamentally weak and the stock's sector is in decline. Conversely, if a bear trap occurs and generates a buy signal, taking a position in the stock makes sense only if its earnings are strong and growing, its sector is performing well, and the economy is on an upswing.

Chapter 11

Calculating Indicators and Oscillators

*T*he personal computer ushered in a new era for technical analysts. Today's Internet-connected computers offer data access and analytic capabilities at speeds that were impossible only a decade or two ago. That's not to say that calculated indicators and oscillators weren't used before the PC, but rather that these indicators were so difficult to calculate and maintain that few technicians performed these calculations for themselves. Even fewer had access to real-time analysis tools that traders now take for granted.

However, the ease of calculating, modifying, testing, and using computer-generated trading tools is as much a curse as it is a blessing. New traders often shun visual pattern analysis, instead preferring computer-generated indicators and oscillators. To do so is a mistake. Although the perceived precision of these calculations seems to add to their allure, you nevertheless need to be aware that computer-generated analysis tools are not necessarily more accurate, and neither are computers able to generate higher-quality trading signals than visual pattern analysis.

The indicators and oscillators that we describe in this chapter provide you with additional insight into the technical condition of a stock or the market; however, they can't provide faultless trading signals. No indicator works in every situation, finds every opportunity, and generates only accurate trading signals.

As a new trader, you risk paralysis by analysis by trying to follow too many indicators. You have too many choices. This chapter describes how to create and use a tiny subset of the tools that are available in today's charting packages. We recommend that you become familiar with a small set of tools that can help you trade profitably, rather than learning how every available tool works. Find out how to trade profitably using this subset of tools before deciding what you need to add to your toolbox.

The computer-generated tools that we use every day are described in this chapter. Two types of moving averages are discussed, along with the moving average convergence divergence indicator (MACD) and the stochastic oscillator. In addition, the powerful concept of relative strength is described.

These tools are but a tiny subset of the technical analysis tools that are available online or in software charting packages. And yet this subset is more than enough to get you started as a profitable trader. Become familiar with these tools. Play around with them using historical data to see when they work and when they fail, and try to understand why. That way, you can know when the tools can help you and when they can't.

The Ins and Outs of Moving Averages

A *moving average* is a trading indicator that shows the direction and magnitude of a trend over a fixed period of time. Some traders call it a *price overlay,* because it's superimposed over the price data in a bar chart. Moving averages visually smooth out the data on a price chart to help make trend identification less subjective. All moving averages follow a stock's price trend but can't predict changes. They report only what has happened.

As its name implies, a *moving average* shows the average of a stock's up-and-down price movements during a specific period of time. A stock's daily closing price usually is the value being averaged, but any value on a price chart can be displayed as a moving average. Some traders, for example, prefer using the mid-point between daily high and low prices for the moving average calculation, but you can also use the opening, high, or low prices or any coincident value on a price chart, including volume.

You'll find that moving averages are used as indicators by themselves or in conjunction with other indicators. They are also the building blocks for other indicators and oscillators such as the moving average convergence/divergence (MACD) invented by Gerald Appel in the 1960s. Before discussing how the MACD is used (see the section "Discovering MACD" later in the chapter), we must explain moving averages and how they are calculated. In this section we describe two of the many types of moving averages.

Simple moving average

A simple moving average (SMA) is simple to calculate and simple to use. To calculate it, you add a number of prices together and then divide by the number of prices you added.

An example makes the SMA clearer. In this example, a nine-day moving average of Intel's (INTC) closing price is calculated throughout May 2008 and then is plotted on a price chart. To start the SMA calculation, use the closing prices shown in Table 11-1. Add the first nine closing prices together, from May 1 through May 13, and divide by 9. The resulting value is placed alongside the ninth trading day, May 13, and each subsequent day in the month.

Table 11-1   Simple Moving Average of Intel (INTC) Closing Price

Date	Close	SMA
5/1/2008	22.81	
5/2/2008	23.09	
5/5/2008	22.91	
5/6/2008	23.23	
5/7/2008	22.83	
5/8/2008	23.05	
5/9/2008	23.02	
5/12/2008	23.29	
5/13/2008	23.41	23.07
5/14/2008	23.49	23.15
5/15/2008	24.60	23.31
5/16/2008	24.63	23.51
5/19/2008	24.51	23.65
5/20/2008	23.73	23.75
5/21/2008	23.31	23.78
5/22/2008	23.53	23.83
5/23/2008	23.06	23.81
5/27/2008	23.25	23.79
5/28/2008	23.12	23.75
5/29/2008	22.80	23.55
5/30/2008	22.84	23.35

Figure 11-1 shows a bar chart associated with the price data in Table 11-1. The SMA data are superimposed on the bar chart's price data. Notice that you need nine prices before you can plot the first SMA point. In other words, the first SMA point appears on the ninth price bar, and the first eight price bars do not display an SMA value.

To calculate the second SMA point, add the prices from May 2 through May 14 together, divide by 9, and place the result as the SMA data point next to May 14. Another way to think of calculating SMAs is that you drop the oldest price in the calculation and add the closing price from the next price bar. Continue this series by dropping the oldest price, adding the newest price, and dividing by 9 for the remainder of the month.

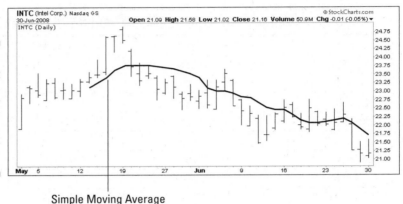

Figure 11-1:
This chart reveals a nine-day simple moving average for Intel stock.

Simple Moving Average

If you're mathematically inclined, here's what the series looks like as an equation:

$$SMA = (P_{[1]} + P_{[2]} + P_{[3]} + \dots P_{[N]}) \div N$$

Where: N is the number of periods in the SMA

$P_{[N]}$ is the price being averaged (usually the closing price)

Traders used to calculate SMAs by hand, but fortunately, computers now relieve traders from this rather mundane chore. The way you use a moving average in your trading is discussed in the next section.

Exponential moving average

Another commonly used moving average is the exponential moving average (EMA), which can be superimposed on a bar chart in the same manner as an SMA. The EMA is also used as the basis for other indicators, such as the MACD (moving average convergence divergence) indicator, which we discuss later in this chapter.

Although the calculation for an EMA looks a bit daunting, in practice it's simple. In fact, it's easier to calculate than an SMA, and besides, your charting package will do it for you. Here are the calculations:

$EMA_{[today]} = (Price_{[today]} \times K) + (EMA_{[yesterday]} \times (1 - K))$

Where: N = The length of the EMA

$K = 2 \div (N + 1)$

$Price_{[today]}$ = The current closing price

$EMA_{[yesterday]}$ = The previous EMA value

$EMA_{[today]}$ = The now current EMA value

The start of the calculation is handled in one of two ways. You can either begin by creating a simple average of the first fixed number (N) of periods and use that value to seed the EMA calculation, or you can use the first data point (typically the closing price) as the seed and then calculate the EMA from that point forward. You'll see other traders handling it both ways, but the latter method makes more sense to us. It's the method used in calculating the EMA amounts in Table 11-2, which shows a nine-day EMA calculation for Intel throughout May 2008. The EMA value for May 1 is seeded with that day's closing price of $23.29. The actual EMA calculation begins with the May 2 closing price. For comparison, we include the results of the earlier SMA calculation to illustrate the difference between an EMA and an SMA.

Table 11-2	Exponential Moving Average of Intel (INTC)		
Date	*Close*	*EMA*	*SMA*
5/1/2008	22.81	22.81	
5/2/2008	23.09	22.87	
5/5/2008	22.91	22.87	
5/6/2008	23.23	22.95	
5/7/2008	22.83	22.92	
5/8/2008	23.05	22.95	
5/9/2008	23.02	22.96	
5/12/2008	23.29	23.03	
5/13/2008	23.41	23.10	23.07
5/14/2008	23.49	23.18	23.15
5/15/2008	24.60	23.47	23.31
5/16/2008	24.63	23.70	23.51
5/19/2008	24.51	23.86	23.65
5/20/2008	23.73	23.83	23.75
5/21/2008	23.31	23.73	23.78
5/22/2008	23.53	23.69	23.83

(continued)

Table 11-2 *(continued)*

Date	Close	EMA	SMA
5/23/2008	23.06	23.56	23.81
5/27/2008	23.25	23.50	23.79
5/28/2008	23.12	23.42	23.75
5/29/2008	22.80	23.30	23.55
5/30/2008	22.84	23.21	23.35

In this example, the EMA doesn't show the same nine-day lag at the beginning of the chart as the SMA. Notice that the results of the moving average calculations also differ. Figure 11-2 shows the data from Table 11-2 plotted on a chart. The EMA data are shown as a solid dark line. For comparison, the SMA data are also plotted using a lighter line. (StockCharts.com, our chart vendor, handles both the EMA and SMA differently than we've shown here. They use historical data to calculate the first EMA data point, and they automatically fill in the missing data on the charts for the first N periods in the SMA calculation.)

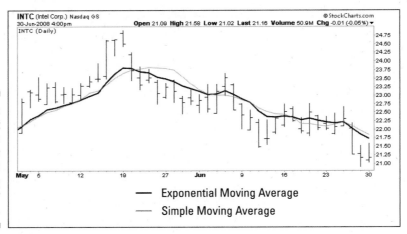

Figure 11-2:
This chart reveals a nine-day exponential moving average for Intel stock.

Comparing SMA and EMA

The SMA and EMA are used regularly by position and short-term traders alike. Each moving average has its strengths and weaknesses. Which one you choose is somewhat a matter of personal preference, but one probably is better suited than the other in several situations. As position traders, we use both. We use a relatively long-term SMA to help signal exit points, and we use EMAs whenever we rely on the MACD indicator (see the "Discovering MACD" section, later in the chapter).

Consistency

An SMA has the benefit of being consistently calculated from one charting package to the next. If you ask for a nine-period SMA, you can be certain that the result will be identical to every other nine-period SMA for the same stock during the same time period (as long as no errors have occurred in the price data — it's rare, but it happens).

Unfortunately, EMAs are not always consistent, because of the way the EMA is calculated — the starting point matters. You actually need more data when calculating an EMA than was used in the example in Table 11-2. In theory, you need to use all the price data available for any individual stock. In practice, however, that rarely is done. Some charting software packages enable you to specify how much data are used when calculating an EMA, but most Internet charting sites do not. The result: One charting vendor may calculate EMA values that are significantly different than the ones provided by another.

Discovering that you're basing your trading decisions on an inaccurate moving average is more than a bit disconcerting. This problem occurs with short-period calculations such as the nine-day EMA example in Table 11-2, but it is especially problematic for longer-term EMA calculations. Unfortunately, the only thing you can do is ask your chart supplier how much data it uses when calculating an EMA and then verify the resulting EMA by hand. Otherwise, you risk making trading decisions on faulty data. Also, if you use more than one charting package, make sure they both use the same method to calculate the EMA.

Reaction time

In general, short-term traders are more likely to employ EMA, but position traders are more inclined to use SMA. The EMA usually is closer to the current closing price, which tends to make it change direction faster than the SMA. As a result, an EMA is likely to be quicker in signalling short-term trend changes.

The SMA probably is the better indicator for identifying long-term changes in a trend. Unfortunately, those signals are likely to take more time to appear than the ones generated by a comparable EMA. The method used to calculate the SMA causes it to react to price changes a bit slower, and that's the trade-off for getting a signal that is potentially more reliable.

Sensitivity

An unfortunate result of the method of calculating an SMA is that every time you add a price, another price falls off the back end of the equation. In other words, each new SMA data point is affected by two prices, the most recent closing price and the oldest closing price in the calculation. Ideally, you want the most recent data having a greater influence on your indicators than the impact of older data. But in an SMA, the oldest price affects the newest SMA point with the same weight as the newest price.

EMA calculations eliminate that problem. Each data point affects the EMA only once. You never have to drop the oldest price as a new price is added. For that reason, the EMA has a much longer memory than the SMA. Every price ever used in calculating EMA has some small effect. As an added benefit, EMA calculations place additional weight on the most recent price.

To understand how this works, examine the role played by the *coefficient K* in an EMA calculation. In the earlier example showing a nine-period EMA, the value of K (the newest price) is 0.20, or 20 percent.

$$\text{For } N = 9; K = 2 / (N + 1) \rightarrow K = 2 / (9 + 1) = 2 / 10 = .20 = 20 \text{ percent}$$

This means every new price added to the calculation represents 20 percent of the value of the EMA, while all the previous data represent 80 percent of it. The implication: The oldest data always have an impact, but slowly fade away, and newer data have a greater influence on the EMA value and the placement of the EMA data point.

Notice also that as the EMA period, represented by N, grows larger, the value of K becomes smaller, which means that each new data point has less influence on the EMA as the period grows larger.

Interpreting and using moving averages

Traders use moving averages to trigger buy and sell signals. In general, when a moving average slopes upward, you can infer that the trend is up, and when the moving average slopes downward, the trend is down.

One simple mechanical strategy that some traders employ works like this:

- ✔ Buy when the moving average slopes upward *and* the closing price crosses above the moving average.
- ✔ Close the position when the price closes below the moving average.

> ✔ Sell short when the moving average slopes downward *and* the closing price crosses below the moving average.
>
> ✔ Close the short position when the price closes above the moving average.

Although simple crossover strategies like this are remarkably effective in some trending situations, they're equally ineffective in others. Many variables must be in alignment for this approach to work. For example, the stock must be trending (see Chapter 10), and the period for the moving average must be chosen carefully for the indicator to be effective. These trend-following systems fail miserably when a stock is range bound (see Chapter 9).

Figure 11-3 shows an example of this simple mechanical strategy on a chart of the Dow Diamonds (DIA), an exchange-traded fund that mirrors the Dow Jones Industrial Average. The chart is shown with a 30-day SMA.

The DIA showed a double bottom (see Chapter 10) in June and July 2006. Using the trading rules of this simple mechanical strategy, the first buy signal occurred on July 24, 2006, when the stock closed above the SMA as the SMA turned higher. Although the DIA traded below the SMA several times, it did not close below the SMA and generate a sell signal until February 27, 2007.

Figure 11-3:
Chart of
the Dow
Diamonds
ETF stock
with a
30-day
SMA.

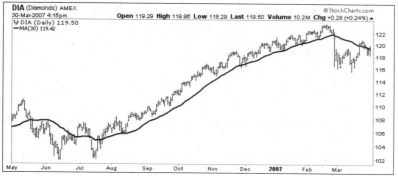

As it turns out, this sell signal was triggered during a retracement (see Chapter 10). Although it is not shown on this chart, the DIA ultimately traded quite a bit higher. Unfortunately, the simple mechanical system did not generate another buy signal until the trend was almost completely exhausted.

This points out the difficulty you face when your trading strategy is based on a moving-average or any trend-following system. When a stock is range bound or in a retracement, it's difficult to know whether the buy and sell signals that the moving average crossover strategy generates are good entry or exit signals. Keeping an eye on these complex retracement patterns (which we discuss at length in Chapter 10) helps you recognize that DIA may have entered a period of retracement — another way of saying the stock is trading within a range — in March and April 2007. You can't know for sure whether DIA will break out of its consolidation to the upside or the downside until after the breakout actually occurs.

From our perspective, waiting for the breakout causes you little, if any, harm. When DIA entered a retracement pattern in March 2007, the economic cycle appeared to be ascending and not ready to peak. Other traders, however, argue that you risk missed opportunities elsewhere when you're waiting on position in a range-bound stock to break out. Although that argument is valid, and favours action on the SMA sell signal, we're still inclined to wait for the breakout before deciding.

We normally want some sort of confirmation signal before entering or exiting any position in a stock or exchange-traded fund. For example, we might temper the buy signal in the simple mechanical strategy described earlier with a requirement that the stock price remains above its SMA for several days after the initial signal before entering a position. The same is true for the sell, or close, signal. You want the stock to close below the SMA for several days, or you'd like to see another coincident sell signal — perhaps one of the visual patterns we discuss in Chapter 10 — before exiting your position. We use a long-period SMA to provide one of several signals to exit from existing positions. For example, if the price closes below a relatively long-term moving average and remains below it for a couple of days, we use that signal to exit our position.

Support and resistance factors

In addition to their trend-following abilities, moving averages also tend to provide support and resistance in stock prices that are trending up or down. When a price is trending higher, you often see the stock trade down toward the moving average only to reverse course and head higher. The same is true in reverse for stock prices that are trending lower. You often see a downtrending stock move up toward its moving average before heading lower. The moving average acts as an area of resistance.

Back in Figure 11-3, uptrending DIA approached its 30-day moving average in mid-August, November, December, January, and February. After each lull, DIA headed higher. Short-term traders use these opportunities to enter positions in the direction of the dominant trend. When moving averages show a stock is trending higher by sloping upward, for example, short-term traders buy into a position when the stock price closes near or just below the moving average so they can ride the trend to sell at a higher price later on. Position traders also can use these signals as second-chance entry points whenever they miss the first breakout. This strategy is called *buying on a pullback*.

Deciding the moving average time frame

Perhaps the most difficult decision you have to make when creating a moving average is determining the length or period that best fits the situation. Regardless of whether you select an EMA or an SMA, shorter periods yield more signals, but a greater percentage of those signals are false, and longer moving-average periods yield fewer signals, but a greater percentage of those signals are true. One hitch: Signals occur later in longer-term moving averages than they do in shorter-term ones.

In general, the shorter your trading horizon, the shorter the moving average you want to select. For us, a nine-period moving average is nearly useless. It generates too many signals that we have no intention of following. More isn't always better. We want our technical analysis tools to provide better signals, not more, because although getting good signals is important, avoiding bad signals is even more so.

To reiterate, we rarely use short-term moving averages to generate buy signals. Instead, we use a long-period SMA to monitor the health of a trend. Typically, we select either a 30-day or 50-day SMA, depending on the duration of the existing trend and prevailing economic conditions. If a trend has existed for a relatively long period of time, we choose the 50-day SMA as an exit indicator. However, if the economy appears to be nearing a peak, as described in Chapter 5, then we tend to tighten our exit procedures and shorten the SMA. See Chapter 13 for more on trading strategies and exit procedures.

Traders can fall into a trap when trying to fine-tune the moving average — or any indicator, for that matter — for a specific stock or situation. Logically, testing many different moving average periods using historical data to find the one that generates the most profitable trades and the fewest losing trades seems right, and charting software packages enable you to do just that to your heart's content.

However, you'll soon discover that what worked when using historical data often fails miserably when trading real money in real time. This problem is well known to statisticians and economists who build mathematic models to forecast future events. It is called *curve fitting*, because you are moulding your model to fit the historical data. We talk about this problem more in Chapter 15. For now, know that fine-tuning an indicator for a specific stock or index rarely has any predictive value and you must avoid it. You simply can't trade using historical data. You're better off settling on a moving average period that satisfies the requirements for a great many situations, rather than trying to fine-tune the time frame of a moving average to fit each stock.

Understanding Stochastic Oscillators

The *stochastic oscillator* indicates momentum and attempts to show buying and selling pressure. This indicator compares current closing prices with the recent range of high to low prices and displays the results on a chart. Stochastic oscillator values cycle, or oscillate, between zero and 100 percent.

Calculating stochastic oscillators

The typical stochastic oscillator is measured across a 14-day period, but a different time frame can be specified. Here's the calculation:

%K = 100 × (closing price – lowest low (N)) ÷ (highest high (N) – lowest low (N))

%D = 3-period moving average of %K

Where: N is the number of periods used in the calculation (usually 14)

This calculation describes a fast stochastic. The names %K and %D, respectively, identify the stochastic oscillator and the signal line. We typically use a variation of this indicator that's called a slow stochastic. The slow stochastic oscillator calculation is

%K = 3-period moving average of (100 × (closing price – lowest low (N)) ÷ (highest high (N) – lowest low (N)))

%D = 3-period moving average of %K

Where: N is the number of periods used in the calculation (usually 14)

In effect, the slow stochastic uses the %D value from the fast stochastic calculation as its starting point. Although the fast and slow stochastics look similar when plotted on a chart, the slow stochastic is smoother and less jumpy. It generates fewer and more reliable trading signals, but the signals appear more slowly than with the fast stochastic. ***Note:*** You will find that some charting packages permit you to specify different values for the moving average period, and some even permit you to change from an SMA to an EMA.

Interpreting stochastic oscillators

As we mention earlier, the stochastic oscillator cycles between zero and 100 percent. Readings of more than 80 percent imply an overbought condition. Readings of less than 20 percent are interpreted as an oversold condition. As with most indicators, an overbought condition can be resolved if a stock trades lower or enters a period of consolidation. Similarly, an oversold condition can be resolved if a stock trades higher or enters a period of consolidation.

Overbought and oversold conditions can persist for long periods of time; therefore, readings that stay above 80 percent or below 20 percent are not enough to generate trading signals. Instead, stochastic oscillator signals are generated

- ✔ When the stochastic oscillator moves from below to above 20 percent, triggering a buy signal

- ✔ When the stochastic oscillator moves from above to below 80 percent, triggering a sell signal

Figure 11-4 shows a slow stochastic oscillator on a price chart for Apple (AAPL). Note the transitions from below to above 20 percent that occurred in February, April, August, and November. All three represented good entry opportunities for this uptrend. Also note that the stochastic buy signals coincided with a retracement pattern. Finally, note that few of the indicator's sell signals, where the stochastic oscillator crosses below 80 percent, represented good selling or shorting opportunities while Apple was trending higher.

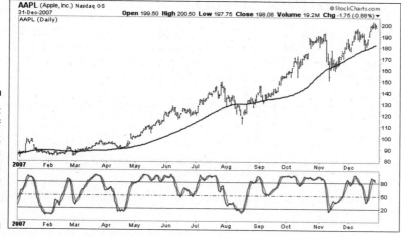

Figure 11-4:
Chart of
Apple stock
prices
includes
a slow
stochastic
oscillator.

Some traders use a *stochastic oscillator crossover strategy,* where buy signals are triggered when %K crosses above %D and sell signals are triggered when %K crosses below %D. For our style of trading, that generates too many signals, a very high percentage of which are false, as you can see in Figure 11-4.

The stochastic oscillator is most useful when it's used in conjunction with other indicators. When a stock is trending, the stochastic oscillator is useful in finding entry points within a dominant trend. In an uptrend, for example, a buy signal that's generated when the stochastic oscillator moves from below to above 20 percent is likely to be a good one. The stochastic oscillator signals many overbought conditions within an uptrend and rarely generates useful sell signals. It also works well in trading-range situations, and you'll find short-term traders who use it to trigger buy and sell signals when a stock is in a trading range.

Discovering MACD

The *moving average convergence divergence indicator* (MACD) is a trend-following momentum indicator. MACD is designed to generate trend-following trading signals based on moving average crossovers while overcoming problems associated with many other trend-following indicators. MACD also acts as a momentum oscillator, showing when a trend is gaining strength or losing momentum as it cycles above and below a centre zero line. MACD is an excellent indicator and an integral part of our trading toolset.

Calculating MACD

Charting packages routinely calculate MACD for you, but knowing how this indicator is created is important for gaining a better understanding of how it works. The MACD calculation isn't complex; it's just three exponential moving averages. Here are the steps:

1. Calculate a 12-period EMA (see the earlier section on "Exponential moving average").

2. Calculate a 26-period EMA.

3. Subtract the 26-period EMA from the 12-period EMA to create the MACD line.

4. Use the resulting MACD line to calculate a 9-period EMA to create the signal line.

5. Plot the MACD as a solid line; plot the signal line as either a dashed or lighter-coloured line.

An additional indicator, the MACD histogram, is usually shown as part of the MACD. It uses a histogram to show the difference between the MACD line and the signal line. The histogram is plotted above the zero line when the MACD line is above the signal line, below the zero line when the signal line is above MACD, and at zero when they cross.

Figure 11-5 shows a weekly chart of AGCO Corp. (AG) along with an MACD indicator and an MACD histogram. When using MACD, we prefer weekly charts. That's how the indicator was originally designed to be used, and for our style of trading a weekly MACD indicator provides more useful information about the strength and direction of a trend and potential trend reversals. You will find that other traders use this indicator for both longer and shorter periods as well.

Figure 11-5:
A weekly
chart of
AGCO Corp.
stock with
MACD and
MACD his-
togram.

AG experienced a long period of consolidation before starting to rally in early 2006. The stock continued its ascent through 2006 and 2007. Notice the corresponding periods on the MACD. The MACD line (the solid line) crosses over the zero centre line during the third week in February. This was a buy signal for this stock. You might also notice that the MACD line crossed the signal line in early January 2006. This MACD crossover signal is another early indication suggesting a possible new uptrend. See Chapter 13 for more about how we use this signal.

Using MACD

MACD provides a remarkable amount of information in a concise format. As you can see in Figure 11-5, MACD oscillates above and below a centre zero line and is a good indicator for showing the direction of the dominant trend, signalling

✔ An uptrend when the MACD line crosses above the centre line

✔ A downtrend when the MACD line crosses below the centre line

Some short-term traders use the signal line to trigger

✔ Buy signals when the MACD line crosses above the signal line

✔ Sell signals when the MACD line crosses below the signal line

We don't, however, find that short-term technique to be very reliable because it generates too many false signals. Instead, we prefer using the position of the MACD line relative to the zero line as an indication that the stock has begun trending.

Figure 11-6 shows a chart of weekly prices for the S&P 500 Depository Receipts, sometimes called SPDRs or spyders (the stock symbol is SPY). SPY is an exchange-traded fund that tracks the S&P 500 index.

Notice how the SPY establishes a series of higher highs and higher lows during the period from June through October 2007, but the MACD line establishes a series of lower highs during this period. This creates what's known as a divergent pattern. This particular example of a divergent pattern is a bearish divergence. In a bearish divergence, the stock establishes a series of higher lows and higher highs, while the MACD establishes a series of lower highs. A bullish divergence is the reverse: the stock establishes a series of lower lows and lower highs, while the MACD establishes a series of higher highs.

Divergences that occur in the same direction as the dominant trend are often useful for entering positions. However, a divergence that is counter to the dominant trend is less likely to be a reliable trading signal. For example, a bearish divergence in a dominant uptrend is rarely a good signal to enter a short position. This type of bearish divergence may, however, signal that the stock has entered, or is about to enter, a period of retracement.

This bearish divergence on SPY is best interpreted as a signal showing that the momentum of the multiyear S&P 500 bull market was slowing. In fact, the market peaked in October 2007 and remained in a downtrend for many months.

Each time the MACD line crosses above or below the signal line suggests a potential change in the direction of the dominant trend. Although this is not an outright buy signal or sell signal, it does suggest a change may be in the wind. In the case of a bearish divergence, the best way to exploit that information is to monitor individual stocks and ETFs for weakness, and either close long positions when they deteriorate, or initiate new short positions as they present themselves. In Chapter 13, we provide additional ideas to help integrate the information generated by the MACD indicator into a useful trading strategy.

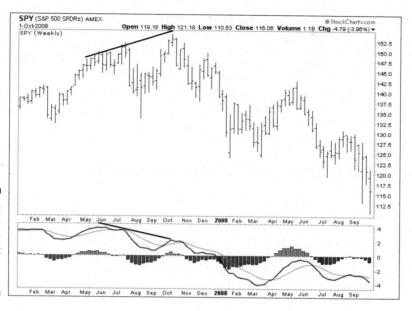

Figure 11-6:
Chart of the
SPY shows
a divergent
MACD
pattern.

Most charting packages enable you to fine-tune the MACD calculation. Many traders vary the 12-, 26-, and 9-week values. Although nothing is inherently wrong with this approach, you nevertheless risk the curve-fitting problem whenever you try to find parameters that give you better results for a specific stock. That said, Gerald Appel, the man who developed MACD, uses values different than the original 12, 26, and 9. He also uses different values to generate buy signals than he does to generate sell signals. So feel free to experiment and have fun after you gain some experience with the default parameters. Because MACD is prone to whipsaw (causing you to lose potential profit), many technicians now use MACD as a monitoring tool. Whipsaw is like whiplash caused by a violent jerk in the opposite direction when you get hit from behind. Traders can buy shares just before they fall in value or sell shares just before they go up in value by reading the MACD tealeaves too closely.

Revealing Relative Strength

Relative strength measures the performance of one stock against another, or, more commonly, against the performance of an index such as the S&P 500. The idea is to determine how the stock is performing compared with the broad market.

Unfortunately, you may run across another indicator with a similar name when working with your charting software. The other indicator is called the *relative strength index* (RSI) and it is something completely different from the relative strength discussed here. RSI is an oscillator that is used in a similar way as the stochastic oscillator described earlier. To keep the two separate, we suggest you call the RSI by its initials and use the phrase "relative strength" when you mean to compare the performance of a stock against a broad-based index or another stock.

Calculating relative strength

Among the many ways you can calculate relative strength is simply dividing the stock price by the index value and plotting the result, like this:

> Relative strength No. 1 = Stock price ÷ Index value

Another technique compares the price of the stock during a given period of time against the index during the same period. Our preference is comparing percentage changes during the same period. The calculation looks like this:

> Relative strength No. 2 = Percentage change in stock price ÷ Percentage change in index value

Either of these approaches, or any other that you may invent, can be plotted on a stock chart. Some Internet sites provide a relative strength capability; see www.stockcharts.com/charts/performance for an example. Unfortunately, if you're using a charting software package, you'll probably have to program it into your system by using its formula-editing capabilities.

Or, you can look it up. *Investor's Business Daily* has a proprietary calculation for relative strength that ranks stocks based on their six-month performance. It is a handy tool.

Putting relative strength to work

The goal when examining a stock's relative strength is not necessarily to find the best-performing stocks in the universe of all stocks, but rather to find stocks that are performing better than the average stock as each stock signals a buy.

Relative strength is one of the final pieces to the technical analysis puzzle. You've found a trading candidate when you find a stock that:

- ✔ Exhibits fundamentals as a strong company
- ✔ Has earnings that are growing faster than average
- ✔ Functions well in a strong sector
- ✔ Operates in a growing economy
- ✔ Is approaching a technical buy signal on its bar chart
- ✔ Performs better than the average stock

These characteristics favour a long position, of course. For short-position candidates, reverse each criterion.

Part IV

Developing Strategies for When to Buy and Sell Stocks

The 5th Wave   By Rich Tennant

"Sell."

In this part . . .

All the pieces come together in this part, where we show you how to get started as a trader and use fundamental analysis and technical analysis to develop a profitable strategy. In addition, we show you how to create a trading system of your own that matches your trading goals and your personality, and we explain how you can effectively implement that strategy and work with your adviser or discount broker to enter trading positions and exit them under the right circumstances. But most important of all, in this part we show you how to manage your money to achieve profitable results.

Chapter 12

Money Management Techniques: When to Hold 'em, When to Fold 'em

---

In This Chapter

▶ Building your trading characteristics

▶ Trading successfully and cutting your losses

▶ Managing your holdings

▶ Protecting your money

▶ Knowing your risks

You may find this hard to believe, but some successful traders have more losing trades than winning trades. How? Their profits from winning trades overwhelm the losses from losing trades. The key to this success is knowing when to hold 'em and when to fold 'em — disciplined money management. You must develop a discipline that keeps your losses under control by quickly closing losing positions. The trick is to follow the rules you set. Good money management minimizes your trading losses when they occur and helps you realize a profit when it hits you right in the old kisser. Recognizing winners and losers — and setting your target prices before ever entering a position — is crucial to your money management strategy. In this chapter, we give you a set of rules to follow to get started.

Identifying Important Characteristics of a Successful Trader

Successful traders share a common trait. You'll find that they all successfully manage their money. The critical points of successful money management may be difficult to implement, but they're easy to identify. They include

✔ Planning your trades carefully by identifying entry and exit points

✔ Minimizing losses by ruthlessly adhering to your stop-loss points

✔ Protecting your profits with trailing stops

✔ Exiting your position when the trend ends

When using technical analysis to make your trades, you won't get the lowest entry price or the highest exit price. That means you will always leave something on the table. The idea is identifying when a trend has begun, entering the position, and riding the trend until it ends.

Opening the Door to Successful Trading

Because your way to successful trading is disciplined money management, the key to opening that door to success is developing a plan for your trades and sticking to that plan, even if it goes against what your gut tells you. Sometimes you think you've picked what seems like the perfect stock, but then it just doesn't perform the way you expected.

Before entering that trade, you need to set an entry point, the price at which you'll enter a trade, and an exit point where you will exit the trade if it goes poorly. Don't deviate from your plan, even if it means accepting the fact that you made a mistake. We discuss setting entry and exit points in the section "Protecting Your Principal." For more info about entering and exiting positions, check out Chapters 10 and 11.

Although it may be cliché, it's nevertheless true: Cut your losses short and let your profits run. In other words, fold (sell) when your losses first appear and hold as your profits continue to build.

Your most important money management goal is to get out of losing positions as quickly as possible. After taking normal up and down price fluctuations (as discussed in Chapters 9 and 10) into consideration, you must develop a method of recognizing when a stock is not behaving the way you expected, and as a result be prepared to close a losing position before it consumes too much of your trading capital. Try to keep losses below 5 or 6 percent for any position. Or you could think in terms of your total trading capital and try to keep the loss from any single position below 1 or 2 percent. Unfortunately, achieving a balance between recognizing your losers and dumping them in time (knowing when to fold 'em) is more difficult than it sounds.

Managing Your Inventory

To be successful, you need to treat trading as a business and stocks as your business inventory. Just like any other business, you must carefully manage your inventory to succeed. Factors paramount to successful trading are:

- ✔ **Viewing trading as a business.** You trade to make money. Sometimes you pick the wrong stock and have to accept a loss. Losses are a part of any business. The key to good business planning is minimizing losses.

- ✔ **Overcoming the most common trader's dilemma.** Many traders get caught up in the moment, trying to defend their position even as it moves in the wrong direction. When your choices no longer make good business sense, you must quickly make cold, hard decisions and decisively act to cut losses short.

- ✔ **Approaching the solution to your trading dilemma as if it's a business problem to solve.** Sell when you stand the chance of making a healthy profit or when you must accept that you've made a mistake and it's time to move on. Select your entry and exit target points before you buy the first share.

Thinking of trading as a business

So, how do you start thinking of trading as a business? Conceptually, it's simple. Like any other business, traders have fixed costs; variable costs; finite amounts of working capital, assets, and liabilities; fickle customers (or fickle market conditions); fickle vendors (market conditions again); and inventory. Managing these business factors results in either profits or losses, and you, of course, want to maximize the profits and minimize the losses. The most important step you can take in treating trading as a business is thinking of the contents of your portfolio as your inventory.

Traders need to manage their businesses with the same clear-eyed, cold-hearted detachment as any successful business owner. But many traders, even the experienced, find thinking about trading as a business a difficult task. They make a decision, take a position, and stick with it regardless of how far prices go down — even when their stock flushes farther down the toilet.

Recognizing the trader's dilemma

Selling is hard. For some reason it's emotionally more difficult to close a position, especially a losing position, than it is to open it. Traders rationalize holding a losing position by saying to themselves, "I'll give it some room to work out, it's only a paper loss." But that rationalization can be foolhardy. You never hear traders describe a winning trade as a paper gain, and you shouldn't rationalize losing positions that way, either.

Falling in love

Traders fall in love with their stocks. It's not hard to understand how falling in love with a stock can happen. You spend many a late night finding the right stock. You evaluate the economy, find a strong sector, research the financial condition of the top companies in the sector, and check the charts. You may even use the company's products or services yourself. You're a customer.

You didn't mean for it to happen, but you try to justify your actions as nothing more than a fling . . . really. You find a stock that looks promising, and then something clicks. You hardly notice at first, but now you're in love. So you enter your trade, and . . . your stock's price goes the wrong way. Which way is the wrong way depends on your position. If you own the stock and its price falls, obviously that's the wrong way. But if you sell the stock short, the wrong way is if its price rises. We discuss the mechanics of selling short in Chapter 14. Either way, you're losing money.

Breaking up is hard to do

After all the late nights, the hard work, and the brilliant analysis, you may end up asking yourself, "How could I have been so wrong?" You're not alone. We just kept thinking: "How can everyone else be so wrong? This is a great stock. It has to go up. We'll wait for everyone else to come to their senses, to realize the error of their ways, and then this trade will turn out just fine."

The idea that the market may not love your stock, too, sometimes is hard to swallow. After you've taken a position, a psychological quirk (everyone has it) makes you want to be right. Somehow, you need to overcome this quirk. Otherwise, it can lead to many losses and possibly to financial ruin.

Finding a better plan

Approaching the trader's dilemma as though it were a business problem for you to solve can be helpful. The business of women's fashions provides an analogy that will do so nicely. The fashion industry works in obvious cycles. For example, you see long-term cycles at work as hemlines rise and fall and even longer cycles as you witness periodic mysteries that cause Capri pants and bell-bottom trousers to appear and just as easily disappear. You also see shorter cycles as clothing for the current season is discounted to make way for the next season's fashions. These shorter seasonal cycles illustrate the day-to-day issues that traders face.

Picking stock for the seasons

As spring approaches, retailers stock up on colourful, lightweight merchandise. You may even see swimsuits before then for those lucky souls who head to the tropics to escape the frosty chill. Fall clothes start showing up in stores as summer heats up. Before summer is over, heavier-weight clothes, including a selection of winter coats, begin appearing on clothing racks.

Ideally, retailers try to sell all their winter coats — and all their bathing suits and spring outfits — before the next season arrives, but that rarely happens. Retailers often have unsold inventory as the end of the season approaches.

Cleaning out the stock

You can use a couple of alternatives for handling unsold seasonal inventory, but neither is pleasant. The retailer can store the merchandise until next year, but storage costs carry charges that eat into capital. The greatest cost of storing merchandise is the lost opportunity. The retailer's capital gets locked up in unsold merchandise and thus can't be used to buy current-season inventory that's more in demand. Making matters worse is the fact that fashions offer no guarantee they'll remain fashionable, so selling this year's inventory next year may be impossible.

Another alternative is marking down the price of merchandise beginning relatively early in the season and continuing to do so until all the merchandise is sold. This approach quickly

- Frees up capital the retailer then can use to buy newer inventory
- Stops the accrual of carrying charges
- Clears out storage and display space
- Avoids the risk that the merchandise will become worthless in the future

This solution is better, even though it sometimes means selling the merchandise below cost.

Clothiers buy inventory to sell it at a profit. They know their costs, and they determine the profits they want to earn from the sale of each item. Retailers try to earn as much profit as possible, but start cutting prices whenever sales don't happen quickly enough. Retailers cannot afford to fall in love with their winter coats. They need the space and capital for spring merchandise. They don't get choked up when it's time to sell.

Keeping your inventory current

Managing your trading business as if you were a retail merchant is a good idea. The cycle of economic expansion, peak, recession, and trough, as described in Chapter 5, is somewhat akin to the four seasons. Your stocks are your inventory. Their prices rise and are discounted in anticipation of the changing economic cycles, as described in Chapter 13. And your trading account is your working capital. Just like the retail merchant, your goal is to protect your principal — your working capital — so you can stay in business.

However, you may find that some factors differ. The stock market is, of course, a much more efficient pricing mechanism than the retail clothing industry. You can't set the price of merchandise; the market does it for you. You can take several approaches to keep your trading inventory current. Many traders use trend analysis and relative strength analysis, as described in Chapters 10 and 11, to try to take positions in the best performing stocks and sectors. Some traders also track general market conditions, quarterly and annual OSC and SEC filings, company announcements, and key analysts' reports, as described in Chapters 5, 6, and 7.

We tend to combine both approaches in the ways we trade. We want to own strong stocks in strong sectors, and we want to know how well the companies manage their businesses. Although any changes in these elements are worth a look-see, we don't have immediate hair-trigger reactions. We do sometimes replace positions that begin to underperform, relative to the market, with emerging leaders, and yet we show a little extra patience with positions that are profitable but are beginning to slightly underperform. If, however, a stock position starts losing money, then we close the position without a second thought. The goal is to protect your trading capital, and we show you some techniques and examples to accomplish this in the next section.

Protecting Your Principal

In the same way that retail merchants face the possibility of holding on to their stock of winter coats that may fall out of style, you can avoid the risk of owning a stock that falls out of favour with other investors and loses its value. By acting quickly when you see changes in the market, you can avoid losing a large chunk of your trading capital (or *principal*). As long as you get out of your position quickly, your trading capital won't be tied up in a losing stock position any longer, and you'll escape the losing trade with most of your cash intact. More importantly, you'll be able to trade another day.

It makes sense, of course, to hold on to a stock as long as its price is appreciating. However, being mindful of when your stock price begins to fall is important. You must have a plan for dealing with losing trades or deteriorating profits. Time to fold up the stock and get out!

If your goal is to keep trading for a long time, the only way to do that is to not lose too much money. This might seem patently obvious, but you would be surprised by how few investors, and even some traders, make capital preservation their highest priority. To avoid that mistake, it helps if you keep these important goals in mind as you trade:

- ✔ Protect your principal first.
- ✔ Don't let a large profit turn into a small profit.
- ✔ Don't let a small profit turn into a loss.
- ✔ Don't let a small loss turn into a large loss.

Recovering from a large loss: It ain't easy

When thinking about protecting your principal, accept that taking a small loss is better than risking a larger one. You need to understand how badly (and quickly) things can go wrong, and how that can result in a loss of a huge chunk of your capital with little chance of recovering it. To illustrate, check out an example of the impact that large losses can have on your money.

Perhaps you bought XYZ stock for $10 per share. The stock falls to $9, representing a $1 loss. You've lost 10 percent of the original price of the stock. To recover from that loss the stock price must rise from $9 to $10, but notice that 10 percent of $9 is only 90 cents. In other words, your stock must gain more than 10 percent to recover from a 10 percent loss. Here's how to review the math using percentages.

To find the percentage loss, push or click on the respective percent button on your calculator or in a computer spreadsheet, or simply divide $1 by $10.

$$\$10 - \$9 = \$1 \rightarrow \$1 \div \$10 = 0.10 \rightarrow 0.10 \times 100 = 10\%$$

To find the percentage gain required to recover that $1 loss — again notice that your stock is now a $9 stock and that 10 percent of $9 is only 90 cents, not $1 — divide $1 by $9.

$$\$1 \div \$9 = 0.1111 \rightarrow 0.1111 \times 100 = 11.11\%$$

In other words, your $9 stock needs to gain a little more than 11 percent to get back to even.

For losses of less than 10 percent, the required gain isn't significantly greater than the loss you've just experienced. But for larger losses, the problem grows unmanageably. Look at Table 12-1 to see what we mean.

Table 12-1	Percentage Gain Required to Recover Loss
Loss of	*Percentage Gain Required to Recover Loss*
5%	5.2%
10%	11.1%
25%	33.3%
50%	100%
75%	300%
100%	Game Over

Getting a stock to go up 5 or even 10 percent is hard enough. It seems irrational to hope for a stock that's fallen by 50 percent to quickly recover 100 percent, or for one that's fallen by 75 percent to ever recover 300 percent.

Selling quickly and avoiding large losses is a much better course. Otherwise, you'll be out of trading capital, and out of business, in a mighty quick hurry.

Setting a target price for handling losses

The most important concept of protecting your principal is accepting the fact that you made a mistake and moving on. Sell that loser. Don't let a small loss turn into a large one. Before entering a trade, make sure you set a target price that you're willing to initially pay for a stock, and set a target price for selling it if the trade results in a loss.

Setting a stop-loss price (or, as traders say, "setting your stop") is more akin to an art than a science. You can employ several techniques for determining your stop-loss price. One that others often advocate, but we don't recommend, is choosing a predetermined percentage loss as your stop-loss price. We think using technical analysis (see Chapters 9 and 10) to identify when a trade has failed is a better approach. Here's an example.

Figure 12-1 is a daily price chart of the Gold Trust Shares (GLD) exchange-traded fund that shows support and resistance lines, respectively, drawn on the chart at approximately $63.62 and $67.47 and indicates the ETF has just broken out of a long trading range on high-volume. Support, resistance, and breakouts are discussed in Chapter 9. The breakout is identified on the chart.

Figure 12-1 represents a picture-perfect setup for entering a trade. As discussed in Chapter 9, your entry point for this trade occurs above $67.50 when the ETF breaks through the resistance line. But how do you handle the trade if it doesn't work out? Or, perhaps a better question to ask is, how do you know when the trade has failed?

Why traders use percentages to describe results

Why do traders use percentages to describe their results? Because it's a simple way of accurately comparing the results of one trade with the results of another — as a percentage, a $1 gain on a $10 stock is identical to a $10 gain on a $100 stock. The price per share is not as important as the percentage gain (or loss) or the total gain (or loss). Look at it like this: If you have $1,000 in your trading account, you can buy 100 shares of a $10 stock, or you can buy 10 shares of a $100 stock. If the price of either stock rises by 10 percent, your account total is the same in either case — $1,100. A 10 percent rise in a $10 stock is $1. A 10 percent rise in a $100 stock is $10. But the total amount of money earned is the same in either scenario.

If you think in terms of percentage gains or losses, you can correctly compare the results of one trade with that of another. The actual price of a stock, and the actual number of points gained or lost, isn't as important as the size of the move in percentage terms. Although you can buy many more shares of the lower-priced stock, it's equally difficult for either stock to move 10 percent. If you think about it like this, you'll see that no reason exists to favour the lower-priced stock, even if you can buy more shares, over the higher-priced stock.

One of several approaches suggests that if the breakout fails (the price declines below the resistance level), you need to exit your position immediately. For the GLD example in Figure 12-1, if the ETF were to fall below the resistance line ($67.47) after it breaks out above it, you should exit.

Another approach suggests that if the ETF falls below the mid-point of the trading range, in this case somewhere around $65.50, then the breakout buy signal has failed. In that case, you can use any price below $65.50 as the stop-loss price to exit from this position.

In the first scenario, the financial risk is small. As long as you get good fill prices (fills) on both your entry and exit orders, your risk should be no more than $1.00 to $2.00 per share, which reflects a loss of only 1.5 percent to 3 percent on the trade. We discuss fills further in Chapter 15.

In the second approach, the risk is greater. The difference between the $67.47 breakout price and the $65.50 stop-loss price is $1.97, but the breakout gap means your actual fill price will be $67.90 or more, resulting in a greater percentage risk on the trade. Poor fills on either entry or exit orders increase the amount at risk.

The trade-off between the two approaches is clear. The first one risks a smaller amount before triggering the exit trade, but is prone to whipsaws (see Chapter 11), which means you may be bumped out of a potentially winning trade. The second risks a greater amount but is less prone to whipsaws. In general, shorter-term swing traders and day traders (see Chapters 16 and 17) are more likely to choose the first, and position traders who expect to hold a trade for several weeks or months are more likely to choose the second.

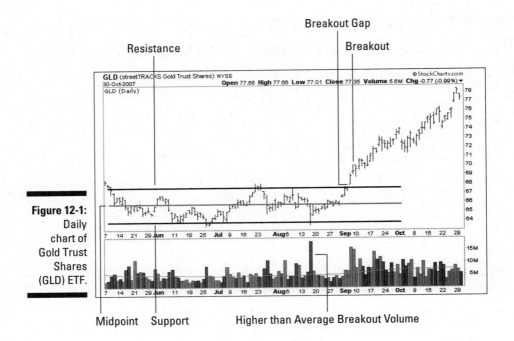

Figure 12-1:
Daily
chart of
Gold Trust
Shares
(GLD) ETF.

Either approach is rational, so choose the one you can live with. If you start second-guessing your stop-loss points they're no longer useful, so be sure to use an approach that you'll honour. Using the first approach may make more sense for new position traders, so tight stops can serve as educational tools. You'll risk less on each trade but you'll be subject to a few whipsaws, and you'll get into the habit of selling when you have small losses. And that's a good habit to learn.

Determining good trading candidates

Whether the ETF in this example (Figure 12-1) is a good trading candidate is open to discussion. From a technical perspective (see Chapter 9), it has many of the characteristics of a good setup. The same is true for the fundamental point of view. The price of the Gold Trust ETF correlates closely with the rate of inflation and with many commodity prices, both of which had been rising. It also has an inverse correlation to the value of the U.S. dollar, which has been losing value for years.

However, GLD had been in an uptrend from 2001 through early 2006. The ETF then traded in an increasingly tighter range that lasted through the period shown in Figure 12-1. After a long run up in price like this, you must be circumspect about any stock or ETF, even following the long consolidation period in this example. Although stocks can continue to rise in price for very long periods of time, neither stocks nor ETFs grow to infinity or beyond.

Even though the technical and fundamental conditions favoured this trade, these late-to-the-party setups do not always work out. That's why we like to keep our stops very tight in this kind of a situation. As it turned out, this trade was profitable. GLD rallied into the first part of 2008 and peaked over $100 before ultimately breaking down.

This example is applicable to any *new* trading position. To find good trading candidates, you need to decide whether the trade makes sense from financial and technical perspectives. Then you'll be better able to identify a trading pattern that clearly shows a good entry point and identifies the price point when the original trading signal has failed. Only then can you place a stop-loss order nearby to reduce your risk of losing too much of your precious trading capital. Only under those circumstances should you enter the trade.

Strategies for handling profitable trades

Profitable trades are somewhat easier to handle than losses, but they're not without complications. You must decide whether you want to leave your stop-loss point where it is or try to lock in a small profit by moving it up.

You obviously want to try to keep any profit from turning into a loss. For example, say you enter the GLD trade in the Figure 12-1 example, and a few days after entering the order it remains in positive territory with a small profit. For this discussion, assume that your original stop price is $65.50, the mid-point of the trading range. Your choice is to leave the stop where it is or move it above the resistance line, to $67.50. If you choose the former, and the stock trades below $65.50, your formerly profitable trade will be closed for a loss. If you choose the latter, you will be stopped out if GLD trades below $65.50. You must now decide whether to move your stop-loss order to protect the small profit, or leave the stop where it is to keep from jeopardizing the stock's chances of gaining more.

This balancing act is delicate. You're trying to catch a bigger trend higher and ride it, which argues for leaving the stop where it is for a little while longer. But sooner, rather than later, you'll want to move your stop-loss above your entry price. This decision becomes easier as the position progresses. As your profit grows, you'll want to continue adjusting your exit points upward. This is called a *trailing stop,* and is discussed in the section "Using trailing stops."

Breaking the pattern of higher highs and higher lows

Trends are easy to see on charts. Examine Figure 12-2, and you can easily identify the trend that carried the price of this GLD ETF from less than $65 per share to $100 per share in six months' time. In this case, the ETF creates a series of higher highs followed by higher lows, interspersed with several retracements. See Chapter 10 for more on trends, higher highs and higher lows, and retracements.

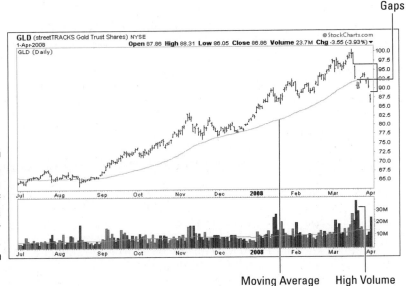

Gaps

Moving Average   High Volume

Figure 12-2:
Broken
pattern of
higher highs
and higher
lows.

Although this pattern sometimes is difficult to define rigorously, you can easily identify it on a chart. Take note that the ETF's price appears to ride the moving average line (see Chapter 11) as it progresses. As a trader, this kind of trend is the type you want, and like, to ride for as long as you can, because it'll make you some money.

Figure 12-2 also provides a couple of clues that this trend came to an end in March 2008. Notice the price gaps (see Chapter 10) that occur in March, and the accompanying high trading volume. These gaps are your first hint that the ETF may be in trouble. Another hint is shown at the point where the line indicating the ETF's price closes significantly below its moving average. A third hint occurs when the stock fails to reach a higher price after the gap occurs.

Any one of these events may carry enough weight for you to close your position. Taken together, they clearly signal that the upward trend probably is over, and you need to exit your position.

Using trailing stops

After you've entered a position and it becomes profitable, you want to move your stop to protect your profits. This is known as a trailing stop, because you keep moving it higher as your profits grow. In an uptrend, a stock makes intermittent higher highs and intermittent higher lows (see Chapter 10). Use the higher lows to define your stop points. After the ETF has made a higher high, reset the stop to either the most recent higher low, or the one just before it. Using Figure 12-2, after the ETF reaches a new high in early October, you should reset the stop using the most recent interim closing low around $72.00.

Tracking market indexes

Individual stocks and entire sectors of similar stocks regularly fall in and out of fashion. Sometimes these changes happen in a grand way, such as when the financial sector fell out of favour in 2007 and 2008.

Look at the weekly chart of the S&P 500 Index in Figure 12-3. Although the S&P 500 index peaked in October 2007, by 2008 it had formed a lower high and lower low below its recent intermittent lows. The price also closed well below its 52-week moving average. By the time 2008 rolled around, the vast majority of financial stocks were in worse shape than the broad market index — a prime example of a dramatic shift in market conditions. If you were trading at the time, you could

- ✔ Sell your positions when you saw that prices, market fundamentals, and technical indicators were simultaneously deteriorating.
- ✔ Wait out the market, hoping things would get better.

If you held financial stocks during that time and chose the second option, you took a much greater loss by selling later. Unfortunately, many buy-and-hold investors unwisely believed that the downturn was a temporary blip and that financial investments would remain viable. In fact, a number of companies never recovered and some no longer are trading.

The right choice then, as usual, was to close your positions. By following these simple strategies, you'd have had more than enough information to know things were not going according to plan. Although you wouldn't have sold your stocks at the highest prices, neither would you have ridden them to their ultimate lows. By selling, you protect your profits and your trading capital, so you can trade another day.

Knowing when a trend is complete is just as difficult as knowing when it began. You can't trade with perfect knowledge, and you can't predict the future — neither can we. But you can use these tools to identify when a trend is likely to begin, and when it's likely to end. And if you use excellent money management, you're likely to trade profitably.

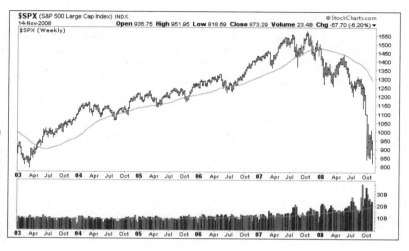

Figure 12-3:
Weekly
chart of
the S&P
500 Index,
2003–2008.

Understanding Your Risks

You need to look at the risks that traders face. The three general categories are market risks, investment risks, and trading risks.

Market risks

Market risks are pretty much out of your control. Of course you understand the risk that the markets are bound to rise and fall, but understanding the risks you face when they do helps you manage your money better. Three key risks that you can manage as a trader are

- **Inflation risk:** Although inflation is a risk that traders rarely consider, it nevertheless impacts people who are afraid to take risks. You definitely can't be a trader if you're afraid of taking risks. Basically, the risk that this factor poses is that your money won't grow fast enough to exceed the increases in costs that inflation causes. As you know, the basics — housing, clothing, energy expenses, and food — increase in price each year. By investing in monetary vehicles that don't keep pace with inflation, you actually end up losing money.

- **Marketability risk:** This factor relates to how liquid your investment is. If you're restricted from selling your investment when you want to do so, your target selling point won't mean much. For most stock traders, this factor isn't an issue, but if, for example, you choose to invest in a small company whose stock isn't traded on one of the major stock markets, you risk not being able to close your stock position when the time is right.

✔ **Currency translation risk:** Currency translation refers to disparities in trading stocks of companies in foreign countries. It's only a factor when you trade foreign stocks, because you then must be concerned with fluctuations between the values of your local currency and the currency in the country where the company is located. Even if the stock increases in price, you can still lose money based on the currency exchange rate. If the value of your currency rises against the other currency, your investment can be worth less when you convert it back.

Investment risks

Investment risks relate directly to how you invest your money and manage your entry and exit trades. Two critical risks you must manage are

✔ **Opportunity risk:** This kind of risk involves balancing your trade-offs. When you trade, you establish a position that ties up money that otherwise can be used elsewhere. After you choose a stock and buy it, you lose the opportunity to buy something else that may strike your fancy, until you trade out of the first position. Essentially, you can miss other opportunities while your money's tied up in another position.

✔ **Concentration risk:** This kind of risk happens when you put too many eggs in one basket. You may think you've found that hot stock that's going to make you a millionaire, so you decide to invest a huge portion of your principal into that stock. By concentrating so much of your money on one investment, you also concentrate the risks associated with that investment and with the possibility of losing it all.

Trading risks

Risks that are unique to trading increase simultaneously with increases in trading volume. Swing traders and day traders often see a greater impact caused by these risks than do position traders, but everyone needs to be aware of these issues. See Chapters 16 and 17 for more information about swing trading and day trading, respectively. Risks associated with trading are

✔ **Slippage risk:** Hidden costs associated with every transaction are the focus of this risk factor. Every time you enter or exit a position, your account balance dwindles by a small amount. Every time you execute a trade, you subject yourself to the problem of buying at the ask price but selling at the bid price. The ask price is the lowest price available for the stock that you want. The bid price is the highest price someone is willing to pay for shares you own. Unfortunately, the bid price is always less than the ask price. Although you can mitigate bid/ask problems by using limit orders, doing so subjects you to the risk that your order won't get filled. The amounts for each trade may at first seem small, but as your trading volume increases, so do the amounts you lose to slippage. Trade only the stocks of the large, liquid companies so your bid/ask spread causes negligible slippage.

✔ **Poor execution risk:** This problem occurs whenever your investment adviser or discount broker has a difficult time filling your order, which can result from any number of factors, including fast market conditions, poor availability of stock, or the absence of other buyers and sellers. The result is always the same: The price you expect is somewhat different than the price you actually receive. Although you can mitigate this problem to a degree by using limit orders, you still risk having the stock trade through your limit price and not getting your order filled at all. Ditto: trade large, liquid companies.

✔ **Gap risk:** This kind of risk comes into play whenever a break in trading occurs. Sometimes a stock opens at a price significantly higher or lower than its previous close, and sometimes a stock trades right through your exit price. For example, a stock may close at $25 a share today and open tomorrow morning at $20. If your planned exit price is $24, and you have a stop order in place, your order is likely to be filled at the opening price or worse. Price gaps created in this way occur most often at the open. And although relatively rare, a gap also can occur during the trading day whenever surprising news is reported or trading halts. We hope you have more nice gap profits than losses — they both occur regularly, so keep your spirit and optimism high.

Chapter 13

Using Fundamental and Technical Analyses for Optimum Strategy

Knowing the current state of the economy can help you improve your trading results. However, knowing the current state of the market is crucial, because you obviously want to buy stocks in a bull market and sell them, or short them, in a bear market. Besides the obvious, you also want a strategy for trading stocks during market transitions and consolidation phases.

As a result, you need a method for identifying and categorizing the differing phases of bull and bear markets. We recommend using the six phases in the list that follows. Doing so enables you to adjust your trading strategies for each phase of the market, regardless of whether you're trading stocks, bonds, indexes, futures, or options. The six phases of the market are

- ✓ **Bullish transition:** The market is transitioning from a bear market to a bull market.

- ✓ **Bull market:** A persistent rising trend in the market.

- ✓ **Bullish pullback:** A bull market in the midst of a pullback.

- ✓ **Bearish transition:** The market is transitioning from a bull market to a bear market.

- ✓ **Bear market:** A persistent downtrend.

- ✓ **Bearish pullback:** A bear market in the midst of a consolidation.

This chapter shows you how to identify these phases of the market using the techniques of fundamental and technical analyses that we describe throughout this book. Although no single detail or event can enable you to out-and-out declare a bull market or bear market, we address many small details that, when taken together, enable you to make informed conclusions. Likewise, distinguishing a transition phase from a pullback phase can be difficult. This chapter helps you methodically analyze the economy, the market, leading and lagging sectors, and individual stocks, so you can identify the particular phase a market is in. Furthermore, this chapter describes unified trading strategies that are built around these market phases.

Seeing the Big Picture

Identifying the current economic climate is the first step toward identifying the current phase of the markets. Only a tiny fraction of available economic data is required to develop a snapshot of the economy from which you can infer the current state of the markets. The conditions that you need to know (and questions you need to ask) to be able to evaluate and determine the cycle that the economy currently is in are

- ✔ Where are interest rates headed? Are they rising, falling, or staying the same?

- ✔ What are officials of the BoC and the Fed doing now? What are they likely to do in the future?

- ✔ How is business performing in general? Is industrial production rising or falling?

- ✔ Which sectors are leading and which are lagging? Are economically sensitive stocks appreciating or declining in value, or are traders currently favouring defensive stocks?

This information is crucial for determining the cycle in which the economy currently is functioning. (For more about economic cycles, see Chapter 5.) Fortunately, the economic picture doesn't change quickly, so taking the temperature of the economy, if you will, can be a weekly or monthly exercise. Ultimately, maintaining a background knowledge of the cycles through which the economy is passing helps you identify current phases of the markets, which, in turn, can help you make better trading decisions.

Knowing when monetary policy is your friend

Current interest rates and interest rate trends help determine the current position of the economy within the business cycle. Low interest rates are associated with economic troughs and high rates with economic peaks. In a nutshell, lower rates stimulate economic activity and higher rates slow it down. But the time lag between the interest rate change and any reaction by the economy often is a long one, making monetary policy an imprecise indicator. Nevertheless, you can use interest rates to get a rough idea about the current economic landscape.

Interest rate reductions generally are good news for the stock market. The opposite also is true. When the monetary policy raises interest rates, stocks normally react poorly. Either way, stock markets may not react immediately, and unfortunately, many months can pass before either the stock market or the economy responds in either direction to the monetary action. Although the old stock market saying "three steps and a stumble" doesn't always hold true, markets do often head lower after rates are raised for the third time.

In short, falling interest rates typically lead to a rising economy and to a market that's changing from a bear market to a bull market — in other words, a bullish transition. Ultimately, a bullish transition leads to a new bull market. Conversely, however, rising interest rates sooner or later lead to a market that's changing from a bull market to a bear market — a bearish transition, and ultimately a bear market. The problem: No consistent timetable exists that enables you to anticipate when these changes will occur, so you should use interest rate changes only as a hint that a transition may be coming and wait for an additional confirmation before you act on a trading strategy.

Keeping an eye on industrial production and capacity utilization

In addition to interest rates, industrial production and capacity utilization are other indicators that provide insight into the health of the economy. Once again Statistics Canada comes to the rescue, with industrial capacity utilization rates; you can glean the ratio of actual output to potential output at www.statcan.gc.ca/daily. You can monitor industrial production in the U.S. by keeping track of the Federal Reserve's monthly report, "Industrial Production and Capacity Utilization," at www.federalreserve.gov/releases/G17/Current/default.htm. You can find release dates at www.federalreserve.gov/releases/g17/default.htm.

New economic growth is suggested when industrial production statistics start inching higher, a sign that usually indicates the market either is entering a bullish transition or will soon do so. Similarly, robust growth numbers often accompany a bull market phase. Conversely, levelling off or falling industrial production data show that a bearish transition can be expected. And finally, a bear market phase often accompanies falling production data.

Watching sector rotation

Monitoring leading and lagging economic sectors (see Chapter 5) provides direct insight into the current state of the stock market, because some industries tend to perform well at the beginning of an economic expansion and others tend to perform relatively well as the economy cools. Traders often try to anticipate changes in the economy by watching specific sectors that they know have tendencies to rise or fall in specific patterns that coincide with one economic or market cycle. These patterned tendencies are called *sector rotation*. Although you won't see picture-perfect sector rotation with every cycle, you will see enough similarities from cycle to cycle to enable you to gain additional insight into the current phase of the economy and the stock market.

Sectors that perform well during specific economic cycles and market phases are described in the following sections.

Anticipating a new bull market

Economic conditions that foster a new bull market include low interest rates and hints that industrial production is beginning to rise. Traders who monitor these economic conditions often respond to them by buying the stocks of cyclical and technology-based companies. Bullish transition phases usually begin in this manner.

The stocks of companies whose business is sensitive to the economic cycle have traditionally been called cyclical stocks. Within the past few decades, technology-based companies have joined these so-called cyclical companies as bellwether economic indicators. The stocks of cyclical and technology-based companies, and the companies themselves, perform best when interest rates are low. Increased sales of their products drive industrial production numbers higher. These companies usually lead the market and often rally before an economic trough, or recession, completely bottoms out. Unfortunately, traders jump the gun as often as they get it right, so whenever you see cyclical and tech stocks begin to rally, it pays to be skeptical. Rather than jump to the conclusion that a sector rally means a bull market is just around the corner, instead consider that it potentially indicates only a bullish transition.

Industries known for making up cyclical sectors include

- Automobile and automotive component manufacturers

- Consumer durable manufacturers that produce products such as appliances and consumer electronics

- Retailers, such as department stores, big-box discounters, and specialty retailers (excluding food, beverage, pharmaceutical, and other nondurable retailers)

- Media companies, such as movie studios, radio and television companies, and book publishers

- Hotels, restaurants, and entertainment and other leisure companies

Watching the economy rebound

Strength in the industrial sectors is a condition that usually indicates the markets may be entering a bull market phase. As the economy begins showing signs of growth, we often see a rally in industrial sectors. Large industrial companies often need to borrow money to increase production, a factor that makes them sensitive to interest rate changes. These companies tend to perform best in a low-interest-rate environment. Rising industrial production that drives industrial-sector earnings and stock prices higher is no coincidence.

Companies in the industrial sectors include

- Building products manufacturers

- Construction and engineering firms

- Aerospace and defence companies

- Electrical equipment manufacturers

- Airlines and air freight, transportation, and infrastructure companies

- Major manufacturing conglomerates (which are widely diversified companies such as Alberta's ATCO, Ontario's Onex Corp., GE, United Technologies, and Tyco before it split into three new companies during 2007)

Approaching a market top

When the economy is firing on all cylinders, industrial production is robust, and interest rates are beginning to rise. However, the stock market is trying to anticipate what happens next and it's probably nearing its peak. The stocks of basic material, energy, and consumer staples companies tend to do well under these conditions. When you begin to see strength in the consumer staples sector, search for confirmation of a bearish transitional phase.

Companies in the basic industry and materials sectors include

- Metals and mining companies
- Chemical companies
- Construction material companies
- Forest-product companies, including paper, packaging, and container companies

The energy sectors include

- Oil and natural gas exploration and drilling services
- Coal and coal processing
- Refineries

Companies in the consumer staple sectors include

- Food and beverage companies
- Household product companies and other consumer staples companies, such as personal-care product companies
- Retailers, specifically food, beverage, drug, and other nondurable goods retailers

Weathering a bear market

Healthcare and other service-sector stocks often perform better than the average stock as the economy peaks and as bullish market tendencies fade to bearish outlooks. The stocks of utility and financial companies also tend to perform better than average during bear markets, because they're considered safe havens from the accompanying tide of rising interest rates and flattening industrial production. As these stocks begin showing higher relative strength, it's time to move your indicator from bearish transition to a bear market phase.

Consumer service sectors include

- Healthcare equipment and supplies companies
- Healthcare providers
- Pharmaceutical and biotechnology companies

The utility sector includes

- ✔ Electric power generation and distribution companies
- ✔ Natural gas distribution companies
- ✔ Water utilities companies

Companies in the financial sectors include

- ✔ Diversified financial service companies, including banks and investment dealers and mutual fund managers
- ✔ Insurance companies

Taking a relatively long point of view as you monitor the markets for sector rotation is a good idea. By that we mean you're not interested in the day-by-day ups and downs, but rather you're trying to evaluate sector performance during periods of many weeks and even months. Remembering that bull markets tend to lift prices for all stocks is also important. So when you monitor sector performance, you try to find the sectors that are performing better than others. In bear markets, stocks that hold their values, for example, will outperform all stocks that have falling prices.

Finding the dominant trend

The idea is to own stocks during bull markets, and sell them, or short them (see Chapter 14), during bear markets. In other words, you want to trade with the *dominant trend*. The stock market tends to lead the economy, so using the market's performance as your primary reference to find the dominant trend makes sense. Combining your analysis of the dominant market trend with the background knowledge you gained from analyzing interest rates, industrial production data, and sector rotation helps you refine the way you categorize the current phase of the market. That kind of refinement means your trading performance will improve when you can make trades with the dominant trend or market phase on your side.

Looking at weekly index charts

Only a handful of tools are needed to determine the dominant trend or phase of the market. We use two, the weekly charts of broad market indexes and the bullish percent index, which is discussed in the next section. Significant changes in the markets happen slowly, and thus show up better in weekly charts than they do in daily charts, because insignificant changes are filtered out.

We typically monitor charts of the major indexes such as the S&P/TSX Composite Index, the S&P 500 (SPX), or the Nasdaq Composite Index (COMPX). Doing so makes visually identifying bull markets and bear markets easy. They appear as trends, exactly like the ones shown on the stock charts in Chapter 10. A bull market appears as a series of higher highs and higher lows on weekly index charts. A bear market appears as a series of lower highs and lower lows. These are the dominant trends.

Pullback patterns, such as the flag, pennant, and other retracement patterns discussed in Chapter 10, correspond to the bullish pullback and bearish pullback conditions. And bullish transition and bearish transition phases may signal a trend reversal, in much the same way that reversal patterns and trading ranges often lead to a change in direction.

Figure 13-1 shows the phases of a bull market using a weekly chart of the Nasdaq Composite Index. Figure 13-2 shows the phases of a bear market using an earlier weekly chart of the Nasdaq Composite Index.

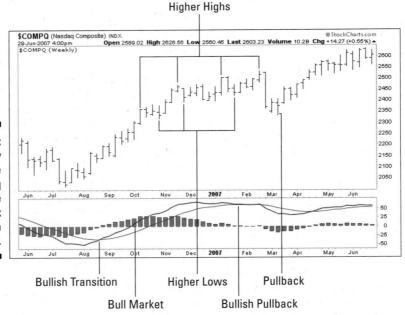

Figure 13-1: Weekly chart of the Nasdaq Composite Index reflects a bull market.

Trend identification tools that we discuss in Chapters 9, 10, and 11 all apply to these weekly charts. For example, you can easily spot the higher highs and higher lows in Figure 13-1 that occurred in late 2006. These higher highs and higher lows correspond to a bull market. You also can easily see the lower highs and lower lows in Figure 13-2; they accompanied the long-running bear market.

You also need to be able to identify the moving average convergence divergence (MACD) crossover points and divergent patterns on these charts. We describe MACD in detail in Chapter 11. MACD signals provide you with additional information to augment the way you categorize current phases of the market.

Using MACD to indicate bull and bear markets is straightforward.

✔ A bull market is indicated when the MACD line is greater than the zero line and greater than the trigger line.

✔ A bear market is indicated when the MACD line is less than the zero line and less than the trigger line.

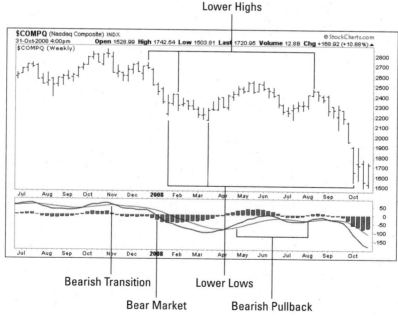

Figure 13-2:
Weekly chart of the Nasdaq Composite Index reflects a bear market.

However, pullback and transition phases are not as clearly defined:

- Either a bullish transition — or a bearish pullback — is indicated when the MACD line is less than the zero line and it crosses above the trigger line.

- Either a bearish transition — or a bullish pullback — is indicated when the MACD is greater than the zero line and it crosses below the trigger line.

Use the bullish percent index, described in the next section, in conjunction with pattern analysis, as described in Chapter 10, to help distinguish between the transition and pullback phases.

Using Figure 13-2, you can see where the MACD indicator on the weekly chart is less than zero and crosses above its trigger line. When the MACD crossed above its trigger line, it suggested the market may have been trying to turn from a bear market to a bull market in a bullish transition phase. You can see two instances in Figure 13-2 where the MACD signalled these bearish pullbacks or bullish transitions in 2008. Both failed, resulting in a dramatic continuation of the bear market.

Using the bullish percent index

You can use the *bullish percent index* (BPI) to fine-tune and confirm trading signals you see on the weekly index charts. The BPI is a powerful indicator that shows the percentage of stocks that have generated buy signals compared with the total number of stocks in a given index. This indicator originally was used to track all the stocks on the NYSE, but it also can be applied to any broad market index, including the S&P/TSX, S&P 500, the Nasdaq Composite, or even the more narrowly defined Nasdaq 100 and sector indexes. BPI provides fewer and better signals when evaluating larger groups of stocks.

The BPI is based on point-and-figure charts — probably the oldest and simplest stock charting technique — and helps you evaluate the strength of the market as a whole. Calculating the BPI is a bit daunting, but fortunately, it's published online. For example, you can find BPIs at StockCharts.com, where the current states of this indicator for the major indexes and several sector indexes are displayed and interpreted. See `http://stockcharts.com/symsearch/index.html?$BP` for details.

As an indicator, BPI works a bit like an oscillator (see Chapter 11). It displays values ranging from 0 to 100 percent to identify oversold and overbought market conditions. For example, when fewer than 30 percent of all stocks are on a buy signal, the BPI shows that the market is oversold and ripe for turnaround. When more than 70 percent of all stocks signal a buy, the BPI shows the market is overbought and ripe for a downturn.

However, like individual stocks, broad market indexes can remain over-bought or oversold for extended periods of time, so by themselves BPI readings below 30 percent or above 70 percent don't necessarily represent respective buy or sell signals. BPI can and does provide readings well above 70 percent and well below 30 percent for extended periods of time.

Changes in BPI levels are triggered by reversal patterns. A 6 percent change in the stocks of a given index is required to trigger any changes (up or down) in the BPI. These reversal patterns are interpreted to describe the state of the market using six unique conditions that roughly correspond with the six phases of the market described in the introduction to this chapter. The six states of the BPI are

- **Bull alert:** Corresponds with the bullish transition phase. It's triggered when the BPI is less than 30 percent and reverses direction when 6 percent (or more) of all stocks change to buy signals.

- **Bull confirmed:** Corresponds with the bull market phase. When the BPI indicator forms a higher high, a *bull market is confirmed.*

- **Bull correction:** Corresponds with the bullish pullback phase. This condition occurs only after the BPI confirms a bull market and a minimum of 6 percent of all stocks change from buy to sell signals. If the BPI is greater than 70 percent, this change may lead to a bear alert (that's up next).

- **Bear alert:** Corresponds with the bearish transition phase. It's triggered when the BPI is greater than 70 percent and reverses direction after 6 percent of all stocks change to sell signals.

- **Bear confirmed:** Corresponds with the bear market phase. When the BPI indicator forms a lower low, a bear market is confirmed.

- **Bear correction:** Corresponds with the bearish pullback phase. This condition occurs only after the BPI confirms a bear market and at least 6 percent of all stocks change from sell to buy signals. If BPI is less than 30 percent, this change may lead to a bull alert.

Although BPI is not a leading indicator, it gives you a good feel for the overall health of the market. When used with broad-based indexes, the BPI doesn't speak often. After all, over 1,800 stocks are traded on the NYSE. For the BPI to register a reversal, at least 6 percent (or approximately 112) of those stocks must change from a buy signal to a sell signal (or vice versa). Actually, the distinction's a bit more subtle than that. A total of 112 more stocks must change to sell signals than are changing to buy signals for the index to change from bull confirmed to bull correction conditions.

The BPI for smaller stock indexes generates considerably more signals. A 6 percent change on the Nasdaq 100 requires only a balance of six stocks to change from buy to sell signals. Although the BPI provides information about the condition of these smaller indexes, you must use the signals with care. We believe this indicator is best used with broader-based indexes such as the S&P/TSX Composite, the Nasdaq Composite, the NYSE, or the S&P 500.

Selecting Your Trading Stock

After you've identified the dominant trend, the leading and lagging sectors, and the current state of the business climate, it's time to select stocks to trade. Beyond general market conditions, two factors drive a stock's price higher or lower:

- ✔ The fundamental condition of a company's business
- ✔ The technical condition of a company's stock

We cover these topics in great detail in Parts II and III of this book, so in this section we highlight only a few important factors for you to consider when selecting your trading stock. On the fundamental side, earnings matter more than any other fundamental data. Traders pay particular attention to the rate of earnings growth as characterized by the earnings per share (EPS) growth rate. In general, the bigger the EPS growth rate, the better the stock price, and vice versa. Stocks without earnings often make very dangerous trading candidates for long-side trades. Although some special situations may merit your consideration, stocks without earnings carry a special risk. Any hint of unfavourable press sends the stock's price reeling. Besides, the downside risk is simply too great for our taste.

Also consider the company's size when selecting a trading candidate. Although small companies can and sometimes do return outsized trading profits, they also present problems for traders. Stocks of small companies usually are lightly traded, which makes them difficult to buy and even more difficult to sell. You can afford to be patient when entering a trade but not when exiting a position, especially when the stock hits your stop-loss price. Lightly traded shares make exiting a position difficult, because the price is likely to fall quickly and dramatically when many traders are trying to exit simultaneously. You're bound to lose more of your precious trading capital (when selling) or spend more of it (when buying) than you intended.

On the technical side, you want to trade the strongest stocks in the strongest sectors. You want to enter positions in these high-relative-strength stocks as they break out of trading ranges or reversal patterns. And you want to hold them as long as they remain relatively strong compared with other stocks.

Exchange-traded funds

Up to this point in the chapter we've mostly talked about trading individual stocks, but at times you may want to consider trading a basket of stocks. For example, say your indicators all suggest a new bullish transition or bull market phase, but few, if any, stocks are showing reliable trading patterns. You want to enter the market with a small position to take advantage of these relatively early signals, but you can't quite identify a good trading stock.

If that's the case, you may want to try an exchange-traded index fund, known as an *exchange-traded fund* (ETF). An ETF is similar to an index mutual fund but is traded on the stock exchanges, just like shares. However, an ETF differs from a traditional mutual fund in several important ways. For example, an ETF order is filled at the price when the trade is executed, not at the end of the trading day like most mutual funds. Also, you can place your ETF order just like any other stock order. You may use market orders, limit orders, stop orders, and stop-limit orders. And, unlike a traditional mutual fund, you may short shares of an ETF. See Chapter 14 for the mechanics of selling short.

ETFs are available for indexes such as the S&P/TSX Composite, Nasdaq 100 (stock symbol QQQQ), the S&P 500 (stock symbol SPY), the Dow Jones Industrial Index, and even many narrowly focused stock sectors. Many brands of ETFs are on the market, and they go by names such as Select Sector SPDR (pronounced "spider"), PowerShares, iShares, and so on. You need to stick with ETFs that trade in high volume. See www.sectorspdr.com or www.morningstar.com/Cover/ETF.html for additional information on ETF trading volumes and on which stocks are included in each ETF. The world's largest family of ETFs is found at www.ishares.ca through Barclays Global Investors. For ETFs with leverage and therefore a bit more horsepower, go to www.hapetfs.com. But be careful — more leverage means more risk.

After you identify, for example, a new bullish transition, you may want to consider the Nasdaq 100 or the S&P 500, or perhaps other ETFs for cyclical and tech stocks. Doing so enables you to take a position in the market while continuing to search for stocks that meet your fundamental and technical criteria.

Trading Strategies

Categorizing the phases of the market enables you to adjust your trading strategies based on current market conditions. The idea: Trade aggressively when you're confident in your market assessment, but protect your capital when you're uncertain. In this section, we present strategies for dealing with various market phases.

Trading the bullish transition

When you first decide the market may be entering a bullish transition phase, use extreme caution when trading — at this phase of the market, your primary goal is preserving your capital. Your secondary goal is getting in on the bull market, if it materializes.

You may take new positions during a bullish transition but the situation is not urgent, so you can be selective. Take small, partial positions rather than full positions (check out the section "A hypothetical trading example"), by

- Identifying the strongest stocks in the strongest sectors
- Looking for trading-range breakouts and other reversal signals

Keep your stops very tight and honour them rigorously. Consider an ETF if you have difficulty finding individual stocks that meet your fundamental and technical criteria.

Trading in a bull market

In a bull market, your primary goal is to become fully invested. Your secondary goal is capital preservation. Emphasize establishing long positions in your trading. You shouldn't take on new short positions. Buy breakouts and take full positions, because your goal is to be 100 percent, or fully, invested. If you have a margin account for leverage, now is the time to use it. (The mechanics of using a margin when trading are discussed in Chapter 14.) You may loosen your stops a bit, because doing so allows for more ebb and flow of higher highs and higher lows.

The most reliable bull market signals occur during the early part of a bull market — after a bullish transition rather than following a bullish pullback. You may want to adjust your strategy to be a bit less aggressive following later-stage bull market signals. For example, you may want to tighten your stops a bit, especially when you're using margin for leverage.

Trading the bullish pullback

A bullish pullback is a consolidation phase within a bull market in which your trading strategy needs to continue looking for high-quality stocks that are breaking out of new or subsequent trading range bases. When you decide the market has entered a bullish pullback phase, you may want to tighten your stops and seriously consider hedging your positions by using options, especially when you're using margin for leverage. Hedging is like buying insurance. In this case, put options can be purchased to protect most of your trading capital in case the market moves dramatically against you. The cost of hedging depends on the amount of protection you buy. Options are discussed in Chapter 18.

A bullish pullback is still a bull market, so you can continue taking full positions on breakouts but you need to be selective. Make sure that your new *and* existing positions are the best-performing stocks in the best-performing sectors. You need to become a bit more cautious when the particular bullish pullback isn't the first to occur during the current bull market.

Trading the bearish transition

A bearish transition indicates the market may be transitioning from a bull market to a bear market. You react to a bearish transition by

- ✔ Tightening stops on all your open positions
- ✔ Monitoring your positions closely
- ✔ Honouring your stops rigorously
- ✔ Exiting any long position at the first sign of trouble

Also consider hedging long positions by using options, as discussed in Chapter 18. If you're using margin for leverage, exiting failing positions quickly is even more important.

If you're so inclined, you can begin looking for short sale candidates, but only nibble at these trades. If you plan to short, take small positions and keep your stops very tight. We discuss the mechanics of selling short in Chapter 14.

Trading in a bear market

When you're certain a bear market has begun, don't enter new long positions. Your open positions are likely to hit their stops and be closed, but for the ones that remain, tighten your stops and exit any existing long positions at the first sign of trouble. Hedge any remaining long positions with put options.

If you're inclined to short stocks, a confirmed bear market is the time to do it. We discuss the mechanics of shorting stocks in Chapter 14. You may want to take full-sized short positions and become fully invested on the short side. (See the upcoming section "A hypothetical trading example" for an example of position sizing.) ***Note:*** A margin account is required for selling short. We rarely use margin for leverage when trading short, but if you're going to do it, now's the time.

Trading the bearish pullback

A bearish pullback is a consolidation phase within a market that nevertheless remains a bear market. As such, a bearish pullback is not a good opportunity for taking new long positions. You need to tighten stops on existing short positions, and consider hedging these positions using call options, especially when you're using margin for leverage. A bearish pullback is an opportunity to take short-side profits and enter additional short positions when you see new or subsequent downside breakout patterns (see Chapter 9). Confirm that new and existing short positions are the worst-performing stocks in the worst-performing sectors.

A hypothetical trading example

Here's a hypothetical scenario. The market is trying to begin a new bull market by entering a bullish transition phase. At this time, your $100,000 example portfolio is 100 percent in cash. Your goal: Establish ten positions by the height of the bull market, which means you plan to allocate $10,000 of your initial capital for each position.

When you begin seeing signs of a bullish transition, you're likely to be champing at the bit to start taking positions, but you haven't found stocks that fit your trading criteria. Still, you'd like to participate in the new bull market, and you're willing to risk a small loss if the bull market doesn't appear.

In this case, you may want to start by taking a small position, perhaps a half-sized $5,000 position, using exchange-traded funds (ETFs) for the broad market indexes and perhaps for a sector fund or two as they break out. For example, you can take a $5,000 half-sized position in the Nasdaq 100 index fund (QQQQ), with a similar commitment to the S&P 500 index fund (SPY), and similarly sized positions in the cyclical and technical sector ETF. In all, you'd have positions totalling $20,000, which is 20 percent of your capital, committed to the market. That kind of commitment is appropriate for a relatively risky bullish transition phase.

As stocks break out of their trading-range patterns, you may add positions, but you need to continue taking small positions until you're certain the market has changed to a bull market. You also need to set an upper limit to the amount of capital that you're willing to commit during a bullish transition phase, perhaps no more than 40 percent or 50 percent of your total trading capital.

If market conditions turn to a bull market, you then can start taking full positions and become fully invested. You may also want to reallocate your positions from the ETFs into high-relative-strength leading stocks. If you plan to use margin as leverage, a bull market is the time to do it. In this case, you could leverage your $100,000 of trading capital into a portfolio of stocks and ETFs worth up to $200,000 or more as your portfolio grows (see Chapter 14 for more about trading on margin). You can either add to existing positions or add new positions in leading stocks as they break out of trading-range patterns. Whatever you decide, keep the number of positions small.

When the market consolidates into a bullish pullback phase, tighten your stops and consider hedging your positions. Doing so enables you to use your stops to get out of underperforming stocks. If you're stopped out of a position, forget about it. If it's a profitable trade, pay your taxes (unless you're using a tax-deferred account or your tax-free account) and be pleased with your profits. If you're leveraged, you want to get out of your margined positions quickly whenever they move against you, so you don't give up your profits.

During a bullish pullback, you must decide first whether to hedge the portfolio, and then whether you want to hedge each individual position or the portfolio as a whole. In general, you're probably concerned more about a marketwide downdraft than you are about a major stumble in any single position. If that's the case, then hedging the whole portfolio with index options makes sense. However, the larger the portfolio, the more sense it makes to hedge your individual positions.

As a bullish pullback reverts back to a bull market, reallocate your capital into the new leaders as they break out. After each bullish pullback, becoming a bit more conservative is prudent. For example, you may tighten your stops, use less leverage, or continue providing a hedge against a significant downdraft.

When the bull market transitions to a bear market, you need to exit your long positions when your stops are hit. You may continue to hold your positions as long as they're not losing money, but don't lose your bull market profits. If you want to sell short, the bear market is the time to do so.

Making profitable trades is significantly easier if you buy during bull markets and sell or sell short during bear markets. Subtleties, of course, may exist. You may, for example, take long positions in defensive stocks, such as utilities and financial companies, during bear markets. Some traders find it profitable to hold a two-sided portfolio, where the best-performing stocks are purchased and poorly performing stocks are simultaneously shorted, even during a raging bull market, but our advice is to keep it simple. Become proficient by trading with the dominant trend before trying to fine-tune your strategy.

Chapter 14

Executing Your Trades

· ·

· ·

*Y*ou've picked your stock and you're ready to enter a position. As long as you're entering the position while the market is open, you have some flexibility in the way your order is entered and executed. However, if you cannot monitor the market during business hours, or if you're entering your order after the market is closed, you need to be much more precise when placing your order and indicating the type of fill (or terms of the order) you're willing to accept. Otherwise, you're likely to run into a nasty surprise when you review your trade confirmation.

This chapter reviews available alternatives when you enter an order to buy, sell, or sell short, and examines how the choices you make can affect the trade. We also review margin requirements, discuss how trading affects your tax return, and identify situations in which you can run afoul of stock-trading regulations.

Entering and Exiting Your Trade

When it's time to enter or exit a trade, you have to tell your discount broker or investment adviser what you want to do. To do that, you enter an *order* that tells the number of shares and the symbol (or at least the name) for the stock or security you're planning to trade. Your order also specifies the type of transaction you'd like to execute and how you'd like to handle your transaction. See Chapter 2 for more about the types of orders available. We discuss your choices for instructing how to handle your order in this section.

Before entering your trade order, you'll probably want to check for a stock quote. Ideally, your quote system provides information similar to that shown in Figure 14-1.

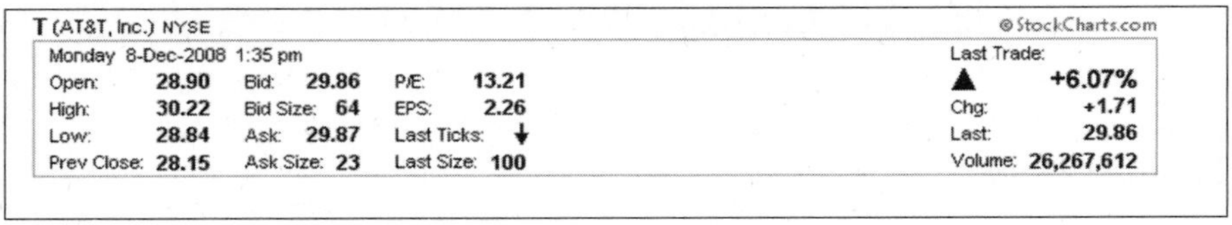

Figure 14-1:
Quote
screen for
AT&T stock.

T (AT&T, Inc.) NYSE						© StockCharts.com	
Monday 8-Dec-2008 1:35 pm						Last Trade:	
Open:	28.90	Bid:	29.86	P/E:	13.21	▲	+6.07%
High:	30.22	Bid Size:	64	EPS:	2.26	Chg:	+1.71
Low:	28.84	Ask:	29.87	Last Ticks:	↓	Last:	29.86
Prev Close:	28.15	Ask Size:	23	Last Size:	100	Volume:	26,267,612

The fields depicted in Figure 14-1 are as follows:

- ✔ **Description:** The symbol and name of the company.

- ✔ **Exchange:** The exchange on which the stock is traded.

- ✔ **Last Trade:** The last trade when the markets are open. (It will be the same as the close price when the markets are closed.)

- ✔ **Chg:** The change in price (+ or –) from the previous close.

- ✔ **Net Percentage Change:** The change in price expressed (+ or –) as a percentage difference between the previous close and the last trade.

- ✔ **Open:** The first trade of the day.

- ✔ **High:** The highest trade of the day.

- ✔ **Low:** The lowest trade of the day.

- ✔ **Previous Close:** The last trade for the previous day.

- ✔ **Bid:** The highest price to buy the stock.

- ✔ **Bid Size:** The number of shares at the bid price.

- ✔ **Ask (or Offer):** The lowest price to sell the stock.

- ✔ **Ask Size:** The number of shares at the ask price.

- ✔ **Close:** The last trade for the day.

- ✔ **Volume:** The number of shares traded.

- ✔ **P/E:** The price/earnings ratio (see Chapter 6).

- ✔ **EPS:** Earnings per share (see Chapter 6).

- ✔ **Last Ticks:** One or more symbols showing the direction of the last few trades in the stock. A plus sign or up arrow indicates a trade higher than the previous trade, or an *uptick*. A minus sign or down arrow indicates a trade less than the previous trade, or a *downtick*. And an equal sign or a dash indicates a trade at the same price as the previous trade.

- ✔ **Last Size:** The number of shares for the last trade.

Understanding bid and ask

To understand the quote system, here's a bit of background and a little history. When you come to the stock market to buy some shares, you need to see what price sellers of those shares are *asking* you to pay — that's why the sell side is called the *ask*. When you come to the stock market to sell some shares, you need to see at what price buyers of those shares are *bidding* for your shares — hence the buy side is called the *bid*.

In the bad ol' days each trader had a stockbroker, each stockbroker had a desk trader, each desk trader had a floor trader, and each floor trader had a market maker. So between a trader selling a stock and a trader buying a stock there were eight people all making a very good living. The market makers also kept the spread between their buying and selling prices way too wide. With the arrival of the Internet, many of those eight people are now driving taxis and waiting tables. Traders who agree on the price and volume at which they both want to trade the same stock no longer need all those intermediaries. Traders themselves have effectively become the market makers by setting the buying (bid) and selling (ask) prices themselves. Sometimes a market maker is needed to balance the buying and selling pressure when it gets out of hand. For most large capitalized public companies, their market makers are often spectators to the action.

A *market order* tells your broker to buy or sell at the current market price. This means that if you use a market order when buying, your order is likely to be filled at the ask price. When selling, your market order is likely to be filled at the bid price. Occasionally, your broker may be able to fill your order between the bid and ask prices — but never count on it, because it doesn't happen very often. Your order can, however, become the highest bid or the lowest ask, if you use a *limit order*. A limit order specifies the highest price you're willing to pay when buying or the lowest price you're willing to accept when selling. If you place your limit order between the current bid and ask prices, your order becomes either the best bid price if you're buying or the best asking price if you're selling. **Note:** You run the risk of having your order not executed at all when using a limit order if the current market price moves away from your limit price. Also, the TSX, NYSE, and Nasdaq each handle this a little differently. Your investment adviser can help you sort through the details if you encounter problems. Your online discount broker might not be so patient.

Understanding the spread

The *spread* is the difference between the bid and ask prices. It's sometimes referred to as the *inside spread,* which is the difference between the highest bid and the lowest ask. Back when stock prices were quoted in increments of eighths (12.5 cents) and quarters (25 cents), the minimum spread was either an eighth or a quarter. Today, with decimal pricing, the spreads tend to be tighter, and can be as low as a penny per share on actively traded stocks.

Many of us veteran traders are so pleased to see shares trading at prices ranging from $20 up to $200 with only a penny between bid and ask prices. Although the major exchanges do not support spreads less than one cent, the TSX and some ECNs (electronic communications networks; see Chapter 2) permit tighter spreads for a small number of securities. Canada was far quicker to adopt the very good idea of trading stocks priced in dollars and cents — unlike the New York Stock Exchange, which insisted on maintaining the units as one eighth of a dollar (and 1/16 and 1/32 and even 1/64, if you can believe it!).

When you place a limit order within the spread, so that your limit price is between the current bid and ask prices, your order will usually become either the best bid if you're buying or the best ask if you're selling. This approach makes sense whenever the spread is particularly wide and the price isn't moving very fast. When the spread is narrow, the way it is in Figure 14-1, using a market order is probably best — that is, as long as the market is open and the stock is widely traded with lots of volume.

The biggest problem with trying to squeeze a profit out of the inside spread is that prices move. Remember that stock quotes are only snapshots of current bid and ask prices. By the time your order reaches the market, these quotes can (and do) change. Even the fastest real-time quote systems lag a bit behind the market, so it's possible that the limit order you just entered between the spread is now outside the spread and won't be filled — and believe us when we say that can be disappointing.

Some markets, such as the Over the Counter Bulletin Board (OTCBB) and the so-called Pink Sheets, do not allow traders to go inside the spread. Ridiculously, market makers are still able to ensure the spread is their nice little profit centre.

Devising an effective order-entry strategy

During trading hours, you can be reasonably confident that a market order will be filled at or near current market prices. But if you're like most people, you won't spend all your time watching the market. As such, you need another strategy for entering and exiting positions. You can use one or more of several alternative approaches to better control the terms and prices that you're willing to accept when your orders are placed in the hope of getting filled.

Using limit orders

If you're buying a stock, choose the maximum price you're willing to pay, and then pay no more. That means you can't use market orders to enter your positions. Instead, you can use limit orders, which enable you to set the highest price you're willing to pay for a stock, making that your *limit price*. If you're selling short, choose the lowest price at which you're willing to sell, and set that as your limit price.

Limit orders are effective for opening a position, but are problematic for exiting a position. For example, if you need to exit your position because the breakout has failed (see Chapter 9), you simply need to exit the position without trying to finesse the price. Failed trades recover infrequently, and they often get worse. You have no reason to be patient when things are going against you.

Similarly, whenever you have a profitable trade and you're trying to protect your profits, a limit order rarely is your best choice for exiting the position. You're better off exiting the position by using either a market order or a stop order after you've identified a reversal pattern.

Using stop orders and stop-limit orders to enter a trade

Traders normally talk about using stops for exiting or trading out of a position, but stops are also effective for opening a position. If you identify the stock you want prior to an actual breakout, you can enter a buy stop at a price above the breakout point. These orders can be entered on a *GTC* (good 'til cancelled) basis, so that even if the trading range lasts a while, your order is poised to trigger a transaction whenever the breakout occurs. Most investment dealers and discount brokers prefer to use "open" orders, which are good for about 90 days. The GTC status can be dangerous if not revisited often.

Most firms limit the length of time orders can remain open to 90 days, so make sure you know your firm's GTC policies — and remember that Nasdaq doesn't have any provisions for handling stop orders. If you're trying to use stops when trading Nasdaq stocks, your broker or adviser has to provide the mechanism for triggering these trades when your stop price is hit. Make sure they can handle the stop orders you want to use.

The downside to this approach is obvious — you're unable to confirm the breakout. If the breakout fails, and you've triggered a buy order on the breakout, you now hold a position that's losing money.

Although we generally recommend waiting a few days to confirm the breakout, using this strategy at some times may be more appropriate than others. For example, if you're convinced the market is in a bull market phase (as described in Chapter 13), the stock's trading range is long and tight, and you can identify an obvious breakout, then entering a GTC buy stop order at a price that's a bit higher than the breakout price is probably okay. However, you need to be much more tentative when the market is only in a bullish transition or pullback phase, or when you're monitoring second and subsequent breakouts. When that's the case, make sure the breakout is confirmed — that means the stock remains above its breakout price for a bullish breakout — within a few days before entering your order. If you have any doubt, wait for confirmation.

Another problem with this approach is that after the stop price is reached, your order is triggered and it becomes a market order to buy or sell. You're in the exact situation you'd be in if you'd entered a market order while the market was closed. You have no control over the fill price after your stop is triggered.

For example, say the stock price gaps higher (Chapter 10) as it breaks out of its trading range and surpasses your stop price by two or three dollars. Your order is triggered and will likely be filled at a price that's much higher than your stop price, and much higher than you had anticipated. If the stock price falls below your fill price, you're now holding a losing position. The only way to avoid this problem is by using a stop-limit order, which means when your stop price triggers the release of your order, the order becomes a limit order rather than a market order and is filled only if the stock price pulls back below your limit price (see Chapter 2 for more on limit and market orders). Again, remember to confirm that your firm permits stop-limit orders on Nasdaq stocks.

You can also use a stop order or a stop-limit order to open a short position. You specify a sell stop or a sell stop-limit order, while designating your trade as a short sale. Again, you must confirm your firm supports these types of orders for Nasdaq stocks.

Using stop orders to exit positions

After your buy or sell order is filled, enter your stop-loss instructions. You need to protect your open positions and simultaneously stay clear of short-term traders trying to *run the stops*. Running the stops is a little game played by short-term traders where they try to find and execute open stop orders before driving the stock price in the other direction. It can be very lucrative for them and infuriating — not to mention expensive — for you. You can try to avoid being run over when they're running the stops by keeping your stop prices away from the most obvious location. For example, if a breakout occurs at $35.75, don't put your stop-loss one cent below at $35.74. Move down a few cents, to $35.69, or even $35.63, to stay away from the obvious stop-loss spots. We discuss stop-loss measures, and the reasons for them, more fully in Chapter 12.

Level 1, Level 11, and TotalView data

The quote screen shown back in Figure 14-1 is called a Level I quote. The bid and ask prices, and their associated numbers of shares, give you a little insight into the current state of the market. However, a Level I quote won't show you the full depth of the market or the number of traders and market makers currently participating in the market for any one stock. For that information you need a Level II quote or display, or its updated cousin, a TotalView display.

A Level II display shows all the outstanding bid and ask prices for a specific stock, the number of shares associated with each price, and the identification of key market makers participating in the stock. Some Level II systems offer a display that consolidates onto a single quote screen all the outstanding bid and ask quotes from all the exchanges, along with all the bid and ask quotes from the ECNs (electronic communications networks; see Chapter 2 for details) where a stock trades. Figure 14-2 shows an example TotalView display for Apple Inc. (AAPL).

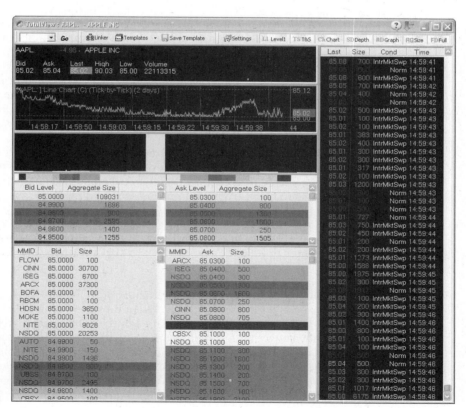

Figure 14-2: Quote screen for Apple stock.

Although interesting, most of the information available on Level II or TotalView displays is unnecessary for a typical position trader. Unless you're swing trading (see Chapter 16), day trading (see Chapter 17), or trading low-volume stocks, you're not likely to need a Level II or TotalView data feed.

Entering orders after the market closes: Be careful

As long as you're entering your trades during market hours, using a market order is fine; however, if you're planning to check your charts each evening and then enter your trades before heading to work in the morning, you must use a different approach. Otherwise, you risk having your orders filled at prices that can differ significantly from the previous closing prices. To make matters worse, you may discover that your position is losing money soon after being filled.

Don't be surprised to discover that many traders trade this way. Because of their daily schedules, they analyze stock charts in the evening and enter orders before the markets open. Unfortunately, common breakout and reversal patterns (see Chapter 9) cause many traders to react in a predicable fashion. When many traders enter buy orders for the same stock, a scarcity of that stock is likely to occur just after the market opens. Scarcity causes prices to rise, sometimes even dramatically, so that all those aftermarket orders are filled at prices significantly higher than the previous closing price. Making matters worse, after the buy orders are filled and buying pressure disappears, the stock price tumbles back toward the previous closing price.

Professional traders — including floor traders, market makers, day traders, and swing traders — exacerbate the problem even further. These short-term traders see the same fundamental and technical analysis signals that you see, and their goal is to profit from your enthusiasm, and perhaps your inexperience, as you try to open your position.

Another concern is automated algorithmic trading using computers programmed to enter orders like a robot. This is also known as *high-frequency trading* (HFT) or *black box trading*.

As a result, you need to think about the tactics these short-term traders employ before you enter any positions. When they see breakout or reversal patterns, short-term traders anticipate a flurry of buying activity in that stock, and they know that few people are going to be eager sellers when a stock breaks out of a trading range. Under those circumstances, the only way buyers can get an order filled is if they bid the price higher or accept whatever price is being asked for the stock. When that happens, the best asking price is going to be relatively high.

Someone will sell the stock to position traders but only at a relatively high asking price. Short-term swing traders and day traders, who may not even own the stock, offer those asking prices, agreeing to provide the stock to the position traders as long as the buying pressure pushes the price of the stock upward. If the short-term traders don't own the stock, they must sell the shares short — in other words, they must borrow the stock before selling (see the section "Selling Stocks Short"). After the short sellers absorb all that buying pressure the rally fades, the stock's price falls back toward the break-out price, and that's when short-term traders buy the stock (at prices lower than they sold it). So, they can cover their short positions — or, in other words, return the shares they borrowed to sell at higher prices to the position traders. How's that for taking a quick profit?

This scenario is at the heart of why being patient usually makes sense. By steering clear of these moments of buying pressure, you're more likely to get a much better fill, and you find out whether enough buying interest is present to keep the stock price above the breakout price. Being patient doesn't always work, of course. Sometimes buying pressure drives the price higher, forcing short sellers to cover at a loss, which in turn drives the price even higher, resulting in a *runaway stock*. When that does happen, you'll probably be left standing on the platform, watching the runaway stock as it leaves you behind. Fortunately, runaway stocks don't happen all that often. Thus, banking on runaway stocks is a poor tactic.

Our advice remains the same: Don't chase these breakout and runaway stocks. When the cycle exhausts itself, as it ultimately must, the stock returns to a more rational price and you can reevaluate whether your position continues to make sense. As a position trader, you can afford to be patient.

Reviewing a week in the life of a trader

To help you get a feel for this, we'd like you to look at a sample trade made by a hypothetical position trader. The idea is to help you understand the rationale and the timing. As a position trader, your week begins during the weekend. You have a few things to accomplish:

- ✔ Evaluate the current state of the market.
- ✔ Evaluate the current state of your existing positions.
- ✔ Find potential replacement candidates for any failing positions.
- ✔ Find candidates for new trading positions.

We'll use the week of December 8, 2008, as the example week.

Before we begin, let's recap the market's recent performance. The broad market indexes peaked in October 2007. Stocks performed poorly over the next year, but they accelerated to the downside in September 2008.

From the October 2007 peak to the trough in November 2008, the S&P 500 Index (SPX), like most broad-market indexes, lost over 50 percent of its value. This downtrend has also seen several short, sharp rallies. The most recent rally in November carried the SPX 20 percent higher over the span of five trading days.

Because the markets rallied 20 percent, the major media declared the bear market over. Rather than taking their word for it, we'll use our analysis to see whether the persistent downtrend has ended.

The technical analysis indicators and fundamental economic conditions show a mixed picture:

- The economy is clearly in recession, possibly the worst economic conditions in our lifetime.
- The Bank of Canada and the Fed lowered rates to their lowest point ever, near 0 percent.
- The consumer staples, utilities, and energy sectors are the best-performing sectors in the market. The sector rotation model (see Chapters 5 and 13) suggests that strength in these sectors often occurs during bear markets, before reaching the bear-market trough.
- The weekly MACD indicator (Chapter 13) for both the Standard & Poor's 500 Index and the Nasdaq Composite Index is far below its zero line. Although the indicator has turned a little higher it remains below its trigger line, suggesting that the market remains in a bear phase.
- The bullish percentage index (BPI, see Chapter 13) for all broad market indexes is signalling a bull confirmed condition.

Given the above factors you cannot conclude that a bull market has begun, as the major media are saying. Instead, the market is most likely in a bearish pullback, but you cannot rule out a bull market transition.

Next, you would analyze your current positions, if you have any. Given the recent volatility of the market, it would not be a surprise if you were stopped out of your short positions. And given your conclusion that the market is probably in a bearish pullback, you have not initiated any new long positions.

Finally, you look for new potential trading candidates. At the time, the news-driven market was waiting for the federal governments' decision about bailing out the Canadian and U.S. auto industries. After the raft of bankruptcy announcements in the United States (including Linens 'n Things, Circuit City, and Lehman Brothers) it's probably best to avoid individual stocks, at least until you see a clear indication of a new bull market. Instead, you'll look at broad-market-index exchange-traded funds (ETFs), as well as sector ETFs, to find trading candidates.

You cannot be certain the market is in a bearish pullback; it might be in the beginning of a bull-market transition. Therefore, you decide to look for both long and short trading opportunities. For long positions, you look at the strongest sectors, including the consumer staples and utilities sectors. For short positions, you look to the weakest sectors such as financial stocks and real estate. You can also look at broad-market ETFs for both long and short trading candidates.

When you search the daily ETF charts it's not surprising that you find few exhibiting a long-lasting trading range (Chapter 9). One that may qualify is the Utilities Select Sector SPDR (XLU). You do find several patterns that might be attractive for short positions (Chapters 10 and 11). For example, you find the Short S&P 500 Proshare Fund (SH) recently made a new high and is in a pullback position. This fund's price rises when the S&P 500 Index falls.

Your final step is to determine the breakout points and your entry prices (Chapter 9) for each of the trading candidates you've found. You may enter buy stop orders for these trades now, or you may monitor the situation and enter the trades as the trading signals occur.

During the trading week, your daily activities are comparatively easy. At the end of each trading day, you must

- ✔ Evaluate the current condition of any new or existing positions.
- ✔ Evaluate the current condition of any trading candidates you identified during your weekend analysis.

The markets gapped higher on Monday, December 8. The Utilities Selector Sector SPDR (XLU) also rallied, but did not break out of its trading range. In fact, it remained in this trading range for the entire week.

The price for the Short S&P Proshare Fund (SH), your short-side candidate, gapped lower at the open, and traded in a narrow range throughout the day on Monday. Over the next several days, trading in SH was within a very narrow range. Although this isn't the classic breakout setup we discussed in Chapter 9, it is very similar. The 60-minute intraday chart for SH looks very much like a long-running trading range. The only difference is that this trading range is over a period of several days rather than several weeks or months. You decided that the SH trade was still viable, and you entered a buy-stop order at US$85.96, just above the high of intraday trading range. This trade was triggered during the day on Thursday, December 11.

Markets gapped lower the following morning, driving the price of SH higher. The opening price was the high price for the day. The ETF traded lower, and ultimately touched the top of the prior intraday trading range, but did not fall back into the trading range, at least not during the week we're discussing.

Using open GTC orders cautiously

You, and you alone, are responsible for monitoring your open orders. It's not uncommon for many stocks to break out almost simultaneously, so you need to be careful not to overcommit. If by some fluke all your open orders trigger simultaneously, or within a short period of time, you must maintain enough purchasing power to adequately fund all your trades. Otherwise, your broker or adviser will call and demand that you pay for all those trades you inadvertently executed. Expect repercussions from your firm, including restrictions on your account, if you don't send the money immediately.

Because we are omniscient (or maybe it's because we are writing this after the fact), we can tell you that this trade did not work out. During the following week, SH fell back into the trading range and hit your stop price, giving you a 4.2 percent loss on this trade.

Selling Stocks Short

When you sell a stock short, you sell something you don't have first and buy it later with a goal of profiting from a falling stock price. To sell a stock short, you borrow shares so that you can sell them in the open market. Your firm gets those shares either from its own inventory or, more likely, from other clients. The proceeds of that sale go into your account. To close that position, you must buy the shares on the open market and return them to the firm. If the price you pay for the stock, or the *buy-to-cover price*, is less than your selling price, you've earned a profit on the short sale. Conversely, if the buy-to-cover price is higher, you've suffered a loss. Instead of buy low sell high, shorting is a case of sell high buy low.

Let's say you borrow 100 shares of Company X and sell the shares short for $100. When the price drops to $80, you buy the shares back (you might also say you covered the shorted shares) and return them. You sold the stock for $100, and bought it back for $80, netting a profit of $20. It's exactly the same profit as if you had purchased the stock for $80 first and sold it for $100 later. Conversely, say you borrow 100 shares of Company Y and sell them for $100. The stock price rises to $120, and you decide to cover your loss. You buy back the shares and pay $120, but you sold them for $100. You have lost $20 on this trade.

Some of the quirks unique to selling stocks short include

- ✔ **Paying dividends to the lender.** If the stocks pay a dividend during the time a short seller holds a position, short sellers pay the dividends on the ex-dividend date to the owners who loaned them the stocks. Short sellers need to keep the ex-dividend date in mind whenever shorting stocks.

- ✔ **Being forced to close a position.** Whenever the original owner sells the stocks you borrowed, your broker can *call away* the shorted shares, which means you're forced to return the borrowed shares by buying them on the open market at the current price. This happens rarely, and occurs only when no shares are available for shorting.

- ✔ **Mandating the execution of short sales from only a margin account.** Short sales must be executed in a margin account, because your firm loans you the stock to sell short, and charges you interest on any margin balance in the account.

- ✔ **Paying margin maintenance requirements.** Your firm can force you to close a short position if you're unable to satisfy maintenance margin requirements.

- ✔ **Having no or only minimal access to selling some stocks short.** Lightly traded stocks may be unavailable for selling short, and when they can be sold short, they may be more likely to be called away (which happens when the original owner sells the stock you borrowed and you are unable to borrow additional shares).

- ✔ **Restricting short sales on certain stocks.** You can't short a stock that's less than $5 per share, and you can't short initial public offerings (IPOs), usually for 30 days following the IPO. And, as we learned during the credit crisis, regulators can prohibit short selling on whole categories of stocks.

- ✔ **Limiting short selling to only stocks without a downtick.** The essence of the rule says you can't sell a stock short in a falling market. Although implemented a bit differently on various exchanges, the result is the same. Short sellers cannot easily pile into a falling stock. You cannot sell a stock short on a downtick. It must be at the last sale price or an uptick.

One unusual aspect of shorting is that it creates future buying pressure. Every shorted sale must eventually be covered, and that means every share that's been shorted has to be repurchased. Future buying pressure can cause the price of a heavily shorted stock to jump dramatically if all the short sellers simultaneously clamour to get out of their positions as the price rises, a situation called a *short squeeze*. You can find out how many others are shorting the stock by looking at short-interest statistics published twice monthly, effective the 15th and the end of each month by the Toronto Stock Exchange and available at www.tsx.com as well as the *Financial Post* www.financial post.com/markets. American short positions are in *Barron's* and *Investor's Business Daily* near the end of each month. From those statistics, you get some idea whether your short position is likely to be squeezed.

Avoiding Regulatory Pitfalls

Several regulatory pitfalls may cause you problems as you trade. You want to avoid running afoul of these regulations. Otherwise, you risk having severe restrictions placed on your account.

Understanding trade settlement dates

The provincial securities commissions regulate when traders must settle their securities transactions. Stock trades, for example, settle three business days after a trade is executed, meaning the buyer must pay for stock trades and the seller must deliver the stock within three business days after the trade is executed. For example, if your trade date is Monday the trade settles Thursday, three business days after the trade date. Short sellers are subject to the same settlement regulations as everybody else. That means the short seller must deliver the borrowed shares to the buyer three business days following the trade.

Most securities, including mutual funds and bonds, settle in this three-day cycle. The shorthand for this settlement period is known as *T+3,* which means *trade date plus three days.* Stock options and government securities, on the other hand, settle the day following the trade date, or *T+1.*

Your firm may insist that the money for all trades be available in your account before allowing you to execute any trades. Firms can exercise this restriction because they're permitted to set more stringent restrictions than regulations require. They can't, however, set more lenient terms. Regardless of your firm's restrictions, the trade settles during the period specified by government regulations. One consequence of this settlement cycle is that you are unlikely to withdraw funds that are part of the trade until the trade settles. However, you might be allowed to trade with those funds as though they are available as long as other trading regulations are not violated.

Avoiding free riding

Whenever you choose to trade in a cash account, you must take care to avoid free riding. Free riding occurs when you buy and sell a stock without depositing sufficient funds before settlement to pay for the transaction. For example, if you have $5,000 in your cash account and you buy 1,000 shares of a $10 stock, for a total transaction cost of $10,000, you receive a money call to deposit $5,000 to settle the trade. Of course, we ignored commission costs in this example.

One way a trader may mistakenly violate the free-riding rules is by trying to use the same capital on two transactions in a single day. Here's the scenario: Say you have $10,000 of equity in your account, and you buy 1,000 shares of a $10 stock. Later that same day, you're stopped out of the position. No problem so far. But if you try to reenter the position on the same day, then you receive a money call for the full price of the second trade. The bottom line: You can't use the same capital to open two positions on the same day in a cash account. That's *free riding*. Note, however, that these trades are permitted in a margin account. Trading in a margin account means you're not at risk of violating free-riding regulations.

If you fail to satisfy the money call within the specified time, your firm either issues a warning or places your account on restricted status. When you're restricted, you have to have enough funds in your account to cover your trade before you execute your order. Restrictions usually are imposed for 90 days.

Avoiding margin calls and forced sales

Although trading on margin is very powerful, it's also potentially very risky. You may recall from our discussion about differing types of accounts in Chapter 2 that a margin account enables you to borrow money which, in turn, permits you to leverage your trading capital. This leverage can improve your total return when things go well, but it can also amplify any losses when a trade goes against you. A margin account is required if you plan to sell stock short.

Before using your margin, you must become familiar with the rules governing its use. Refer to Chapter 3 for more about the use of margin.

Understanding margin fees

Your firm charges interest on the average daily margin balance regardless of whether it's cash or stocks. The margin loan is an adjustable-rate loan for which the interest rate is based on the prime interest rate plus one or two percent. Firms usually quote their respective margin rates dependent upon the quality and the size of your loan.

Understanding margin collateral

Your trading positions represent the collateral used to secure your margin loan. Firms require the value of your collateral to be sufficient to cover any outstanding loan. The amount required, called the *minimum maintenance margin,* can range from 25 percent upward. In other words, your firm requires the equity in your account to be at least 25 percent of the market value of your margined stocks.

If the equity value of your account falls below the minimum maintenance margin, you receive a *margin call,* a demand from your discount broker or adviser to deposit more money or securities in your account. If you fail to satisfy your firm's demand for additional funds, you must liquidate some or all of your trading positions. In fact, your firm may even liquidate your positions before you satisfy the margin call, if the value of the equity in your account continues to fall. Falling stock prices mean falling equity values.

As an example, say you have $10,000 in your account, and you buy 1,000 shares of a $20 stock, which is $20,000 worth of stock. Current margin regulations require that you maintain a deposit of at least 50 percent of the value of that trade in your account to open the trade, and 25 percent of the total value of the position to maintain it. After purchasing the stock, your account has $10,000 of equity and $10,000 in a margin loan. A margin call occurs in our example when the price of the stock falls dramatically the next day from $20 to $12, representing a loss of 40 percent. At this point you still owe the $10,000 margin loan, but the total equity in your account now is only $2,000. The 25 percent minimum maintenance requirement is $3,000 (that's 25 percent of $12,000, or 1,000 shares at $12 each), so you'd receive a maintenance margin call to deposit $1,000 to bring your account up to the $3,000 minimum equity amount.

Notice in the example that you're also dangerously close to owing more than the stock is worth. If the stock's price falls much further, the firm likely will liquidate your position to satisfy your outstanding loan. Firms are allowed to liquidate your position at any time, without your explicit approval. In fact, they're allowed to liquidate any position in your account to satisfy your loan.

This example illustrates the risks of using margin. The value of the stock fell 40 percent in the example, but you lost 80 percent of your equity. Leverage cuts both ways. Earning double profits may be nice, but doubling your losses is very painful. Our recommendation is to never satisfy a margin call — close the offending position instead. In our example, you should have set stops so you'd be able to get out of the losing position long before you got the margin call. But after that margin call is generated, you need to liquidate the losing position(s) immediately to pay off the margin loan.

When you open a margin account you must sign a *margin agreement,* a binding agreement that explicitly entitles your discount broker or investment dealer to liquidate positions to satisfy outstanding margin loans. The margin agreement also permits your dealer to loan any stock in your margin account to another client to provide shares for that client to short the stock. When you short a stock, the shares of the stock that you sell must come from somewhere, and that somewhere is from other clients who own the stock. If you're the one shorting stock, one "gotcha" can accompany this scenario. If the stock you borrowed is sold to someone else, then your discount broker or adviser can call away your short position in a forced sale. Although forced sales like this don't happen very often, they nevertheless are a risk you must assume if you short stock.

The Tax Man Cometh

Trading profits are taxable and half of net capital gains are usually taxed as income at the trader's marginal income tax rate. Check out *78 Tax Tips For Canadians For Dummies* by Christie Henderson, Brian Quinlan, and Suzanne Schultz (Wiley) for more info than most of us will ever need on the subject of taxes. Still, paying taxes is better than losing profits or principal.

One tax trap that snares traders is the *superficial loss rule*. Normally, you can deduct trading losses from trading gains before calculating your income tax burden. However, if you sell a stock for a loss and then repurchase the stock within 30 days, the trading loss cannot be deducted. Fortunately, the loss isn't lost forever. You can use it to adjust the cost basis on the trade by the amount of the loss, which ultimately reduces the amount of tax owed when the position is finally closed. This adjustment effectively raises the cost of a stock purchase for tax purposes, so you owe less tax. A similar adjustment is available when selling short.

Chapter 15

Developing Your Own Powerful Trading System

A trading system is a collection of technical and fundamental analyses tools woven together to generate buy and sell signals. Trading systems often are built using common indicators, oscillators, and moving averages (see Chapter 11). You can combine these various technical-analysis tools to create a virtually unlimited number of trading systems. For the new trader, the advantage to this approach is that you don't need to invent something new to create and personalize a workable system.

The downside, however, is equally obvious. Many traders use these common tools and end up with a system that offers little competitive advantage and only modest (if any) profits. In addition, these systems can be difficult to use, because the signals of one trading system mirror the signals of many others, which makes entering and exiting positions troublesome.

Ultimately, you want to develop or adapt a trading system that closely fits your personality and trading objectives. This chapter helps you methodically develop and add to a trading approach that utilizes your own personalized repertoire of trading systems. It also helps you recognize and avoid destructive and costly habits that can sabotage your trading efforts. In addition, we discuss ways for you to evaluate some of the claims being made by trading systems that are for sale and whether buying someone else's trading system makes sense.

Understanding Trading Systems

Although individual trading systems differ in many ways, thinking about them on the basis of a couple of broad characteristics is helpful. The first characteristic has to do with the two ways a trader interacts with the system. In this case, trading systems are one or the other of the following:

- ✓ **Discretionary trading systems:** A system that presents trading candidates for your consideration, but leaves the final trade execution decision to you.

- ✓ **Mechanical trading systems:** A computer-based system that automatically generates buy and sell signals that will always be traded.

The other way to categorize a trading system is by how it treats trends in the markets. In this case, trading systems are one or the other of the following:

- ✓ **Trend-following trading systems:** A system that tries to identify trade entry and exit points for new or existing trends.

- ✓ **Countertrend trading systems:** A system that tries to identify trade entry and exit points by finding tops and bottoms.

Although these categorizations are not mutually exclusive — discretionary and mechanical systems, for example, can both be trend-following systems — each approach has adherents and detractors. We discuss the strengths and weaknesses of each type of system in the sections that follow.

As you read through our descriptions of the trading systems, understand that *no* system generates profits without any losing trades. Put another way, no system works in every situation. Keep that firmly in mind when you're developing ideas for and designing your personal trading system. Your goal needs to be designing a trading system that is useful to you across a large number of stocks and a large number of situations. Believe us when we say that you will run into trouble whenever you try to tailor a trading system to a specific stock. Additionally, try making your system work across long periods of time and across many different market conditions.

Discretionary systems

A *discretionary trading system* makes you an active participant in all phases of the trades you make and provides you with a great deal of leeway when making trading decisions. With this approach, evaluating the economic data, analyzing the broad market indexes, determining which sectors are showing strength, and identifying high relative-strength stocks that are breaking out of long trading ranges and hoping to catch a new trend all are up to you. You make decisions based on what you see in charts and in fundamental economic data, and you enter and exit (buy and sell) positions based on that information.

A discretionary system requires a great deal of discipline, which can be a source of problems for some traders. This type of system works well for traders who are capable of making good decisions quickly under pressure. But discretionary systems may prove troublesome if you allow your emotions to wreak havoc with your ability to think clearly, act rationally, and make thoughtful trading decisions.

When emotions cloud your trading decisions, you may end up

- ✔ Overtrading
- ✔ Prematurely liquidating your positions
- ✔ Holding positions too long
- ✔ Anticipating trading signals in attempts to get better entry and exit prices

Another problem with discretionary systems is that they're difficult to test, which probably is their greatest drawback. System testing is useful, because it helps you understand situations in which an indicator works well and in which it fails. With a discretionary system you can test the indicators, but you cannot reliably test your discretion.

Controlling your emotions is so important to being a successful investor that one of Canada's largest mutual fund companies gave every investment adviser in the country a "stress control biofeedback card." Even more high-tech is the so-called EmoBracelet, developed by Royal Philips Electronics to limit the emotional response of traders. And the new "trader's mood ring" was developed for Dutch bank ABN Amro, which is now owned by the governments of the United Kingdom and Holland.

Mechanical systems

A *mechanical system* addresses some of the problems that arise when using discretionary systems. Mechanical systems usually are computer-based programs that automatically generate buy and sell signals based on technical and/or fundamental data. You're expected to blindly follow the resulting trading signals. Some mechanical systems actually enter buy and sell orders directly into your account without your intervention.

If your greedy impulses or your fear of losing routinely cause you to make poor trading decisions, a mechanical system may be a better choice for you. An automated approach tends to reduce the stress and anxiety that arise when you have to make difficult decisions quickly. As such, you can make and execute trading decisions in a consistent, methodical way. A mechanical trading system also enables you to automatically include rigorous money management in your trading methodology.

Another benefit of the mechanical approach is having the ability to thoroughly test the system. Through testing you can confirm whether your trading system performs the way you expect it to and explore ways to improve your system before actually committing your trading capital. You can adjust and fine-tune your system after seeing the test results. Unfortunately, fine-tuning your system may lead to other problems. We discuss ways to avoid them in the "Identifying system optimization pitfalls" section later in this chapter.

Trend-following systems

Trend following is favoured by many technicians for one simple reason: Trends offer excellent opportunities for profit. Unfortunately, the popularity of the trend-following approach is one of its weaknesses. Too many of these systems generate many similar buy and sell signals, which in turn makes outperforming the average trader difficult for any individual trend-following trader.

Even the best trend-following systems have a relatively large percentage of failed trades, primarily because they depend on several extremely profitable trades to make up for the large percentage of losing trades. If your trend-following system also is a discretionary system, your discretion (or lack of it) can cause you to miss a few of these profitable trades, and your overall results will suffer.

Trend-following systems typically are based on either moving averages or break-out patterns (see Chapters 9 and 11). Moving average–based trading systems are the most popular and can be quite profitable; however, they work only when a stock is trending. These trading systems depend on long-lasting trends to generate enough profit to outweigh a relatively large number of losing trades. In fact, the number of losing trades can easily outnumber winning trades with this trading system. When a stock is range bound (stuck in a specific price range), a moving-average system generates a large number of losing trades. Because of the large overall number of trades, this system often is accompanied by relatively high transaction and slippage costs (see the section "Accounting for slippage"). Money management is critical when using a trend-following trading system.

You can make some adjustments to a trend-following system that may improve its performance. For example, you can insist that its trading signals be confirmed by another condition before actually entering any positions. If your system triggers a buy signal, for example, you may want to see whether the signal remains in effect for at least a day or two before entering a position. We show some examples of moving-average and breakout systems, along with some ideas to improve the performance of these systems, in the section "Developing and Testing Trading Systems."

Countertrend systems

For many traders, the quest to find a profitable countertrend trading system is all-consuming. *Countertrend systems* appear desirable because their goal is to buy low and sell high. These systems try to identify *inflection points,* or the moments when stocks change direction, so traders can take positions close to when they occur. This approach may work in a few narrowly defined situations, such as in a trading range (Chapter 9) or a trend channel (Chapter 10), but it's likely to fail in a spectacular and expensive way if attempted on a broader scale.

The vast majority of trading systems follow market trends. Trend-following systems tend to outperform countertrend systems, especially for position traders. Swing traders and some day traders sometimes use a countertrend approach, but even then they usually do so in conjunction with a trend-following component.

Countertrend systems usually depend on oscillating indicators, reversal patterns, and channelling strategies to find turning points. Some countertrend systems also are based on cycle theory, and others are based on volatility, expansion, and contraction. We briefly review some of these techniques in Chapter 16.

We discourage you from spending too much time evaluating countertrend systems, at least until you're confident in your ability to use trend-following systems to successfully make your trades. Countertrend systems generate a large volume of trades, and the more you trade the more you spend on commissions and fees, as well as bad fill prices known as *slippage.* These costs alone often swamp potentially profitable systems. Although a countertrend strategy can sometimes work profitably in a trading range or trend channel (Chapters 9 and 10) it's still risky, especially for a new trader.

Selecting System-Development Tools

Conceptually, you can use the back of an envelope to develop your trading-system ideas. However, most traders want some way of confirming that their newly designed systems can perform profitably before they commit real trading capital. That means you need a way to test your system, which further means using computer software to precisely define the system and evaluate its performance. Typically, this requires simulating trades by using historical data.

Regardless of whether you decide on a mechanical or a discretionary approach to trading, your system will benefit from testing. Although thoroughly testing a discretionary system is difficult, you can still test the component indicators to learn when they do and don't provide effective trading signals. To begin, you need a computer, development and testing software, and historical data.

Choosing system-development hardware

Doing the math that's required when testing your system can really slow down your computer, and it can generate a lot of data. Almost any computer will do the job when you're getting started, but if you end up testing many system ideas you definitely need a large amount of disk storage and a fast computer. The computer equipment required to run a proprietary trading platform, including products such as TradeStation or MetaStock, is usually enough for system development and testing. (See Chapter 4 for more information about the hardware requirements for a typical proprietary trading platform.)

Selecting system-development software

Many trading system–development and testing products are on the market. Some proprietary trading platforms, such as TradeStation or MetaStock, include system-testing capabilities. Spreadsheet software, like Microsoft's Excel, also is useful for analyzing simple trading systems and for analyzing the results generated by specialized development and testing software.

Trading system–development and testing software

You need to consider several of the following criteria when evaluating your system-development and testing software:

- ✔ All trading system–development and testing programs use some type of computer language to describe and test your system. Some are terse and difficult to use, others are more intuitive. Traders with strong computer or programming skills have little problem mastering any of these languages, but others may struggle. Pay careful attention to this development language before selecting a system. Be certain you're actually able to use the system you choose.

✔ You need to integrate your trading system with your stock charts. Some system-development software requires you to actually write computer code that enables you to display your trading system and stock charts simultaneously. Avoid these systems if you're uncomfortable writing computer code.

✔ The manner and effectiveness by which your system-development and testing software reports on how your trading system is performing is critical. Some systems provide extremely detailed statistics about the performance of your trading systems. Others, however, list little more than the buy or sell signals. In general, more information is better.

✔ Make sure your system-development and testing programs are capable of exporting the data they generate, historical price data included, into a spreadsheet program for further analysis.

TradeStation is the gold-plated system-development platform. It has many built-in tools that make your development and testing job relatively easy. For those of you on tight budgets, one of the less-expensive alternatives you may want to consider is a charting and system-development program like AmiBroker (www.amibroker.com). Although flexible and powerful, AmiBroker isn't as feature-rich or as polished as TradeStation, and it requires significantly more effort on your part. For example, AmiBroker includes well-known technical-analysis indicators like moving averages and MACD (see Chapter 11), but the number of indicators included is a tiny subset compared with what TradeStation offers. Similarly, you have to use AmiBroker's formula language to create and enter any other indicators that you may be using.

Spreadsheet software

A spreadsheet program is another invaluable testing and analysis tool. Although a spreadsheet program can't do everything that a specialized system-development and testing program can do, it can add quite a bit of analysis horsepower to your system-development tool kit. You can actually code and test simple trading systems directly into the spreadsheet. You can also evaluate the results of your trading-system tests more thoroughly using the spreadsheet's built-in statistical and analysis functions.

You can, for example, copy the price data for a stock into your spreadsheet, calculate moving averages and other indicators, and then configure buy, sell, or sell-short signals. You can also export trading signals from your system-development program and import the results into your spreadsheet for further analysis.

One of our favourite spreadsheet projects is calculating the maximum favourable and unfavourable moves after our system has triggered a buy or sell signal. Simple to do, and it helps you understand the strengths and weaknesses of your trading system in great detail. You can see whether problems with your trading system might be solved by using different exit procedures or tighter (or looser) stop-loss points.

For example, although your entry signals may show promise, your exit signals may be causing you to leave a lot of money on the table. These situations are hard to see when you're working only with charts; however, they sometimes jump out when you're working with raw data during your spreadsheet analysis. You can find an example using this testing technique in the "Working with breakout trading systems" section in this chapter.

Some system-development programs provide a great deal of statistical analysis, so choosing between spreadsheet tools and system-development tools is a trade-off between thoroughness and expediency. After you've been through the testing exercises a few times you get a feel for the strength of each approach. So it's likely that you'll decide to use both a system-development program and a spreadsheet program when creating and testing your new trading systems.

Finding historical data for system testing

When you need to test your system, you can, of course, test it in real time, with real money, and in the real markets. But getting some idea of how your system will perform before risking your hard-earned capital is usually better. Typically, that means testing your system by evaluating how it performs when simulating trading using historical price data. Around 10 to 20 years of historical end-of-day data for the indexes and stocks in which you plan to trade is usually more than enough to properly simulate trades for testing your system.

Many sources can provide the data. You can download historical data from the Internet, and some data are available online free of charge. Some proprietary trading platforms likewise include access to historical data. You may want to get data from more than one source to confirm its accuracy.

Yahoo Finance provides free historical data and permits you to download the data into a spreadsheet. To access the Yahoo data feed, get a quote for the stock and select "Historical Data" under the Quotes menu item. Then click "Download to Spreadsheet."

Many online services offer data in a more convenient format, but for a price. Some sell historical data recorded on CDs. Sources for intraday price data also are available. Here are the URLs for a few of the many sites offering various forms of historical data:

✔ **Historical data:**

- **Yahoo Finance:** `finance.yahoo.com`
- **QP3 Quotes Plus:** `www.quotes-plus.com`

✔ **Intraday data:**

- **eSignal:** www.esignal.com
- **IQ Feed:** www.iqfeed.net
- **Price-Data:** www.price-data.com
- **QuoteTracker:** www.quotetracker.com

✔ **Historical data on CD:**

- **Prophet:** www.prophet.net/satellites/marketData/home/index.jsp
- **CSI:** www.csidata.com

Developing and Testing Trading Systems

The ideas that you may want to include in your system development and testing are virtually limitless. Many new traders begin system testing by combining a few off-the-shelf indicators in an effort to obtain better trading results. Doing so is as good a place as any to begin.

However, we want to caution you to keep your systems simple enough that you can understand not only the system but also the result. Simplicity usually is better when trading, especially when you're first becoming familiar with the processes of system development and testing. We describe the process by looking at a couple of examples in the sections that follow.

Working with trend-following systemsMany trend-following systems use a moving average for their starting points. In this trend-following example the system is designed for position trading, which means we use a relatively long moving average. Short-selling won't be permitted with this simple system.

The first step is defining buy and sell rules for your initial testing. The actual code for defining these rules depends on your specific system-development package. Therefore, trading rules are described as generally as possible. The rules for an initial test may look like this:

✔ Buy at tomorrow's opening price when today's price crosses and closes above the 50-day exponential moving average (EMA).

✔ Sell at tomorrow's opening price when today's price crosses and closes below the 50-day EMA.

To test whether using a moving average as a starting point is a good idea in a trend-following system, apply these two rules to ten years of historical data for the stock or stocks of your choice. After testing this idea, you find that this simple system works fairly well when stock prices are trending, but it's likely to trigger many losing trades when the prices of stocks are range bound. You can try to avoid these losing trades, and possibly improve your overall trading results, by filtering out trading-range situations. One way to accomplish that goal is by changing the buy rule to read: Buy at tomorrow's open when the following conditions are true:

- ✔ Today's closing price is above the 50-day EMA.

- ✔ The stock crossed above the 50-day EMA sometime during the last 5 days.

- ✔ Today's 50-day EMA is greater than the 50-day EMA from 5 days ago.

These added conditions serve as signal confirmation. When you test these rules you find they reduce the number of whipsaw trades for most stocks, but they're also likely to delay buy and sell signals on profitable trades and thus usually result in smaller profits on those trades. Yet this adjustment makes the overall system more profitable, because the number of losses is reduced.

You can find out whether other changes to your simple system actually can improve profitability. You may, for example, test different types of moving averages. Try, for example, a simple moving average instead of an exponential moving average (see Chapter 11 for the types of moving averages). Or you may want to try using different time frames for your moving average, such as 9-day, 25-day, or 100-day moving averages.

Identifying system optimization pitfalls

Most system-development and testing software comes equipped with a provision for system optimization, which allows you to fine-tune the technical analysis tools used in your trading system. You can, for example, tell the system to find the time frame of the moving average that produces the highest profit for one stock, and then ask it to do the same thing for a different stock. Some systems enable you to test this factor simultaneously for many stocks.

Although something is alluring about using this approach, doing so is likely to cause you trouble. If you find, for example, that a 22-day moving average works best for one stock, a 37-day moving average works best for the next stock, and another stock performs best using a 74-day moving average, you're going to run into problems. The set of circumstances leading to these optimized results won't likely repeat in precisely the same way again. We can almost guarantee that whatever optimized parameters you may find for these moving averages won't be the optimal choices when trading real capital.

This is a simple example of a problem that is well-known to scientists and economists who build mathematic models to forecast future events. It's called curve fitting, because you're moulding your model to fit the historical data. You can expend quite a bit of effort fine-tuning a system to identify all the major trends and turning points in historical data for a particular stock, but that effort is not likely to result in future trading profits. In that case, your optimized system is more likely to cause a long string of losses rather than profits.

Testing a long moving average and comparing the results to a short moving average is fine, and so is testing a few points in between a long moving average and a short moving average. As long as you use this exercise to understand why short moving averages work best for short-term trades and why longer moving averages work better for traders with longer trading horizons, you'll be fine. Otherwise, you're probably moving into the realm of curve fitting and becoming frustrated with your actual trading results.

Testing with blind simulation

Blind simulation is a method for setting aside enough historical data so that you can test your system optimization results and avoid the problem of curve fitting. For example, you may test data from 1990 through 1999, and thus exclude data from 2000 through the present. After you've developed a system that looks good enough for you to base your trades on, you can then test your system against the data that were excluded. If the system performs as well with the excluded data as it did with the original test data, you may have a system worth trading. If it fails, you obviously need to rethink your system.

Another approach is choosing your historical data with extreme care. You can expect trend-following systems like a moving-average system to perform well during long, powerful trends. If your stock had a strong run-up during the long-lasting 1990s bull market, that kind of price data can skew your results, magically making any trend-following system appear profitable. Whether that success actually can be duplicated during a subsequent bull market, however, must first be thoroughly tested.

If the majority of your profits come from a single trade, or only a small number of trades, the system probably won't perform well when you begin trading real money. You may want to address this problem by excluding periods from your test data when your stock was doing exceptionally well or when the results of any trades were significantly more profitable than the average trade. This technique is a valid approach to eliminating the extraordinary results arising from extraordinary situations in your historical data. Using it should give you a better idea of your system's potential for generating real profits in the future.

Working with breakout trading systems

Similar to moving average–based systems, a breakout system can take many forms. You may already be familiar with the trading-range breakout system we describe in Chapter 10. To test a different approach, you can define a breakout system as follows:

- ✔ Buying at tomorrow's opening price when today's closing price is above the highest high price that occurred during the last 20 days.

- ✔ Selling at tomorrow's opening price when today's closing price is below the lowest low price that occurred over the last 20 days.

These trading rules are loosely based on the rules for *Donchian channels* (sometimes called *price channels*), which comprise a breakout system developed by Richard Donchian in the 1950s. Donchian was one of the early developers of trend-following trading systems.

A spreadsheet may be helpful for evaluating this system. You can, in fact, configure this system into a spreadsheet, include buy and sell signals, and perform analyses to determine how well the system performs. You also can use the spreadsheet to dig into the system's results to find out what works and what doesn't. Figure 15-1 shows an example.

Re-creating the spreadsheet in Figure 15-1 is straightforward. After you've downloaded the historical price data into a spreadsheet format, all you have to do is encode the formulas into the correct columns. We describe the formulas in the sidebar "Creating the Donchian channel spreadsheet."

If you're like most traders, the first thing you'll do is calculate some statistics about the system. For example, you can use spreadsheet functions to calculate the following:

- ✔ Total gain or loss for the system

- ✔ Average gain (the numerical average)

- ✔ Median gain (the middle result)

- ✔ Maximum gain for any single trade

- ✔ Maximum loss for any single trade

- ✔ Standard deviation

Then you can look at aggregate results to find out whether the system actually made money. In the case of the Donchian channel breakout system, initial results don't look promising. The system lost money during the entire test period.

	A	B	C	D	E	F	G	H	I	J	K	L	M
						Donchian	Donchian	Change					
	Date	Open	High	Low	Close	High	Low	Flag	Buy / Sell	Buy Price	Gain (Loss)	MFE	MAE
	9/4/07	48.93	50.00	48.91	49.68	49.06	44.39	FALSE	-				
	9/5/07	49.56	49.65	48.87	49.18	50.00	44.39	TRUE	Buy	49.56	0.00%	0.18%	-1.39%
	9/6/07	49.23	49.36	48.81	49.14	50.00	44.39	TRUE	-	49.56	-0.67%		-1.51%
	9/7/07	48.53	48.60	47.95	48.23	50.00	44.39	TRUE	-	49.56	-2.08%		-3.25%
	9/10/07	48.62	48.75	47.81	48.20	50.00	44.39	TRUE	-	49.56	-1.90%		-3.53%
	9/11/07	48.51	48.99	48.43	48.93	50.00	44.39	TRUE	-	49.56	-2.12%		-2.28%
	9/12/07	48.84	49.37	48.78	48.94	50.00	44.39	TRUE	-	49.56	-1.45%		-1.57%
	9/13/07	49.29	49.35	48.94	49.18	50.00	44.39	TRUE	-	49.56	-0.54%		-1.25%
	9/14/07	48.80	49.31	48.73	49.22	50.00	44.39	TRUE	-	49.56	-1.53%		-1.67%
	9/17/07	49.00	49.10	48.59	48.81	50.00	45.59	TRUE	-	49.56	-1.13%		-1.96%
	9/18/07	49.09	50.08	48.83	50.04	50.00	46.08	TRUE	-	49.56	-0.95%	1.05%	-1.47%
	9/19/07	50.29	50.59	49.98	50.17	50.08	46.39	TRUE	-	49.56	1.47%	2.08%	
	9/20/07	50.06	50.26	49.92	50.03	50.59	46.71	TRUE	-	49.56	1.01%	1.41%	
	9/21/07	50.28	50.52	50.01	50.36	50.59	46.71	TRUE	-	49.56	1.45%	1.94%	
	9/24/07	50.49	50.96	50.33	50.59	50.59	46.71	TRUE	-	49.56	1.88%	2.82%	
	9/25/07	50.42	51.07	50.36	51.07	50.96	46.71	TRUE	-	49.56	1.74%	3.05%	
	9/26/07	51.36	51.51	51.12	51.32	51.07	46.71	TRUE	-	49.56	3.63%	3.93%	
	9/27/07	51.62	51.65	51.36	51.58	51.51	47.05	TRUE	-	49.56	4.16%	4.22%	
	9/28/07	51.54	51.68	51.18	51.41	51.65	47.75	TRUE	-	49.56	4.00%	4.28%	
	10/1/07	51.45	52.16	51.38	52.00	51.68	47.81	TRUE	-	49.56	3.81%	5.25%	
	10/2/07	52.04	52.06	51.72	52.01	52.16	47.81	TRUE	-	49.56	5.00%	5.04%	
	10/3/07	51.84	52.07	51.50	51.65	52.16	47.81	TRUE	-	49.56	4.60%	5.06%	
	10/4/07	51.75	51.83	51.34	51.77	52.16	47.81	TRUE	-	49.56	4.42%	4.58%	
	10/5/07	52.17	52.90	52.06	52.82	52.16	47.81	TRUE	-	49.56	5.27%	6.74%	
	10/8/07	52.80	53.16	52.71	53.15	52.90	47.81	TRUE	-	49.56	6.54%	7.26%	
	10/9/07	53.27	53.45	53.03	53.38	53.16	48.43	TRUE	-	49.56	7.49%	7.85%	
	10/10/07	53.39	53.57	53.21	53.51	53.45	48.59	TRUE	-	49.56	7.73%	8.09%	
	10/11/07	53.79	53.94	52.28	52.66	53.57	48.59	TRUE	-	49.56	8.54%	8.84%	
	10/12/07	52.90	53.54	52.80	53.53	53.94	48.59	TRUE	-	49.56	6.74%	8.03%	
	10/15/07	53.61	53.71	52.70	53.12	53.94	48.59	TRUE	-	49.56	8.17%	8.37%	
	10/16/07	52.79	53.28	52.68	52.87	53.94	48.83	TRUE	-	49.56	6.52%	7.51%	
	10/17/07	53.62	53.66	52.68	53.55	53.94	49.92	TRUE	-	49.56	8.19%	8.27%	
	10/18/07	53.33	53.89	53.12	53.78	53.94	49.92	TRUE	-	49.56	7.61%	8.74%	
	10/19/07	53.77	53.77	52.39	52.44	53.94	50.01	TRUE	-	49.56	8.49%	8.49%	
	10/22/07	52.16	53.12	52.02	53.07	53.94	50.33	TRUE	-	49.56	5.25%	7.18%	
	10/23/07	53.61	54.21	53.34	54.18	53.94	50.36	TRUE	-	49.56	8.17%	9.38%	
	10/24/07	53.74	53.94	52.60	53.77	54.21	51.12	TRUE	-	49.56	8.43%	8.84%	
	10/25/07	53.89	53.98	52.75	53.05	54.21	51.18	TRUE	-	49.56	8.74%	8.92%	
	10/26/07	54.08	54.20	53.44	53.93	54.21	51.18	TRUE	-	49.56	9.12%	9.36%	
	10/29/07	54.19	54.33	53.84	54.15	54.21	51.34	TRUE	-	49.56	9.34%	9.62%	
	10/30/07	53.94	54.56	53.90	54.26	54.33	51.34	TRUE	-	49.56	8.84%	10.09%	
	10/31/07	54.47	55.07	54.04	55.03	54.56	51.34	TRUE	-	49.56	9.91%	11.12%	
	11/1/07	54.68	54.77	53.97	54.00	55.07	51.34	TRUE	-	49.56	10.33%	10.51%	
	11/2/07	54.42	54.55	53.60	54.42	55.07	52.02	TRUE	-	49.56	9.81%	10.07%	
	11/5/07	53.86	54.40	53.59	54.07	55.07	52.02	TRUE	-	49.56	8.68%	9.77%	
	11/6/07	54.33	54.69	53.78	54.68	55.07	52.02	TRUE	-	49.56	9.62%	10.35%	
	11/7/07	54.22	54.58	53.31	53.35	55.07	52.02	TRUE	-	49.56	9.40%	10.13%	
	11/8/07	53.14	53.33	50.80	51.73	55.07	52.02	TRUE	-	49.56	7.22%	7.61%	
	11/9/07	50.73	51.12	50.00	50.00	55.07	50.80	FALSE	Sell	49.56	2.36%		

Figure 15-1:
Spread-
sheet
analysis for
Donchian
channels.

If you're like most traders, your impulse is to discard the idea and move on to another. But with the Donchian channel breakout system, you need to dig a little deeper before you do. During the time frame of this test, the system triggered 30 trades, 18 of which were losing trades. However, 13 of those losing trades were profitable at some point during the process, and all the winning trades gave back a large part of the profits before the sell signal was triggered. In fact, many of the profitable trades gave back significantly more than half of the profits before the sell signal.

Figure 15-1 shows how a single position from the spreadsheet progressed. The entry trade was triggered when the price of QQQQ closed above the September 4 Donchian high. In this simulated trade, the stock was purchased at the September 5 opening price of $49.56 and then sold on November 9, the day after the price of QQQQ closed below the November 8 Donchian low.

If you look through the last three columns, you'll notice that this simulated trade was profitable, but closed well below its most profitable price. If that happens once during simulated trading you may not need to worry much about it, but if it occurs frequently you need to think of ways to remedy the problem.

In the Donchian channel system, buy signals apparently work better than sell signals. Therefore, you need to consider different types of stops and sell signals. One simple idea that's worth testing is stopping out (selling at a predetermined price) of a position if the stock's low (instead of its close) falls below the Donchian low. Another is to shorten the time frame for the exit signal by using a five- or ten-day Donchian channel. Or you can, for example, use a trailing stop or some completely different criteria to exit these positions.

Creating the Donchian channel spreadsheet

The opening, high, low, and closing prices for the QQQQ exchange-traded fund were copied into columns B through E of the spreadsheet found in Figure 15-1.

You need at least 20 rows worth of data before you can calculate the first Donchian price channels. (These first 20 rows are not shown in Figure 15-1.) The following calculations assume that column headers are in the first row, and the price data begin in the second row. After entering a formula in the following columns, copy the formula for that column to every row that has price data.

The remaining columns are configured as follows:

✓ **Column F** is the *upper Donchian channel*. Use the spreadsheet MAX function to find the highest price value for the previous 20 trading days. Start this calculation in row 22, giving 20 rows of data. The calculation for row 22, Column F is =MAX(C2:C21).

Notice that the formula doesn't include the current row. If it did, the current close would never cross above the Donchian channel line.

✓ **Column G** is the *lower Donchian channel*. Use the MIN function to find the lowest low for the previous trading day. Start this calculation in row 22, using 20 rows of data. The calculation for row 22, column F is =MIN(D2:D21).

As for the upper Donchian channel, the formula does not include the current row.

✓ **Column H** is the *Change Flag* indicator. This flag is a simple way to avoid triggering more than one sequential buy or sell signal. It's also useful for calculating the remaining cells. Simply stated, the cell displays either TRUE for a buy signal or FALSE for a sell signal. If yesterday's close is greater than the Donchian high, turn on the TRUE condition. If yesterday's close is less than the

Donchian low, turn on the FALSE condition. Otherwise, copy the TRUE or FALSE condition from the previous day into this column.

In row 22, column H, type the formula =FALSE(). Then, in row 23, column H, the formula is =IF(E22>F22,TRUE(),IF(E22<G22, FALSE(),H22)).

✔ **Column I** is the _Buy/Sell_ indicator. This column shows when a buy or sell signal first is triggered. It compares the current Change Flag value with the previous value. If they're equal, a dash goes in the cell. Otherwise, the word "Buy" is shown when the Change Flag is TRUE and "Sell" is shown when it's FALSE. The formula for row 23, column I is =IF(H23=H22,"-",IF(H23,"Buy","Sell")).

✔ **Column J** is the _Buy Price._ This column shows the trade entry price. If the Buy/Sell flag indicates a buy, then put today's opening price in the cell. Remember the trading rule is to buy at the opening price on the day following the trade entry signal and sell at the opening price on the day following the trade exit signal. Therefore, the sell signal requires a special case. If the Change Flag indicator is TRUE for either today or the previous day (the special sell signal case), copy the trade price from the previous day to today. Otherwise, the Change Flag is FALSE, so leave the cell blank. The formula from row 23, column J is =IF(I23="Buy",B23,IF(OR(H23,H22),J22,"")).

✔ **Column K** is the _Gain/Loss_ indicator. This column shows a running total of the gain or loss in the trade, assuming the trade closes at the current opening price. The first row after a buy signal always shows 0 percent. The last row following a sell signal is the actual gain or loss from the simulated

trade. The formula from row 23, column K is =IF(OR(H22,H23),(B23-J23)/J23,"").

✔ **Column L** is the _MFE,_ which is short for _Most Favourable Excursion._ This column shows a running total of the best possible outcome for the trade as though it were closed at the high price of the day. This column is useful for what-if analyses but not for estimating your actual gains or losses. You rarely, if ever, sell at the high price for the day, or the MFE for a trade. The calculation is simple. If the Change Flag indicator is TRUE, and if today's high is greater than the purchase price, calculate the percentage gain. Otherwise, leave the cell blank. The formula from row 23, column L is =IF(H23,IF(C23>J23,(C23-J23)/J23,""),"").

✔ **Column M** is the _MAE,_ or _Most Adverse Excursion._ This column shows a running total of the worst possible outcome for the trade as though it were closed at the low for the day. This column is useful for what-if analyses but not for estimating actual gains or losses from the trade. You rarely, if ever, sell at the low price for the day, or at the MAE for a trade. The calculation is simple: If the Change Flag indicator is TRUE, and if today's low is less than the purchase price, calculate the percentage loss. Otherwise, leave the cell blank. The formula from row 23, column M is =IF(H23,IF(D23<J23,(D23-J23)/J23,""),"").

Make sure you have copied the formulas in each column to every row that includes price data.

To evaluate the results, you can copy the trading signals, gain and loss values, and MFE and MAE values from your system to a new spreadsheet. Paste the values using the spreadsheet's Paste Special function. You then can sort and analyze the data in any way you choose.

In any case, this example gives you ideas about how you can use a spreadsheet to test and analyze any trading system. It also provides you with some suggestions about how you can use this kind of analysis to improve your system's results.

Accounting for slippage

Slippage is the term traders use to describe the costs of trading, which is made up of two components. The first is the actual transaction or commission cost for executing your trade. The second is more difficult to measure, because it's the sum of the cost of unfavourable fills. If, for example, you're planning to buy at tomorrow's opening price based on today's closing price, those two prices can be much different. An unfavourable fill is a cost of trading, and accounted for as slippage.

Most trading system–development packages have a provision for estimating slippage costs when testing your trading ideas using historical data. If you know your transaction costs, enter the exact amounts. Otherwise, estimate the transaction cost. You probably need to overestimate the cost of unfavourable fills, because it always seems to end up being worse in actual trading than most traders ever imagine. You may want to start with an estimate of 25 cents per share and adjust it as you gather data on your actual slippage costs.

Keeping a Trading Journal

Keep track of all your trading activities in a trading journal. Doing so eventually turns your trading journal into a reference manual that can become an invaluable tool for helping you recall what you've done to identify what works and what doesn't. A trading journal also can help you analyze your trades and trading systems to determine which aspects of trading you do well and which ones you need to work on.

When you develop a trading system, save ideas and test results in your journal. When you enter a position, record everything about the trade. Include your thoughts as you contemplate making the trade. When you have a what-was-I-thinking moment later on, you can find the answer in your journal.

Using a loose-leaf binder to hold your trading journal is probably best. Print before and after charts for each trade and include them in the journal. Keep detailed notes about each trade, and about the system you used to trigger the trade. At a minimum, your notes need to include the following:

- Trade date
- Stock symbol

- Number of shares, and why you chose that number of shares
- Whether you bought long or sold short
- Which system triggered the entry signal
- Which system triggered the exit signal
- Where you placed your initial stops
- If and why you moved your stops
- What caused you to exit the position and why
- Amount of tax to be paid on net gains
- Percentage gain or loss from the trade
- Amount of slippage
- Whether any economic reports or announcements were made around or during the time of the trade
- Your thoughts, hopes, and fears that you had before opening the position and while the position was open

You can also use your journal to save magazine articles that influenced your thinking. Cut out and save the new high and new low lists from the newspaper. Keep a record showing leading and lagging industries. Save sector charts along with your trade records. Whatever information you use to make trading decisions needs to be in your trading journal.

You can improve only the things that you measure. Record statistics about your trades. Include the duration of each trade, the MFE, and the MAE. After you close a trade, write down what you might have done differently. Find out whether you can identify signals that can help you recognize similar situations in future trades.

Although keeping the journal is important, it is useful only when you review it regularly. Spend a little time every week or month reviewing all your trades, so you can pinpoint consistent mistakes or missed opportunities.

Evaluating Trading Systems for Hire

You'll see advertisements on the Internet, in trade magazines, and in newspapers for foolproof systems that promise amazing returns. Sometimes you'll even see claims for systems that regularly return hundreds of percent with little or no risk.

Although some stocks do actually achieve astronomical returns of hundreds and sometimes thousands of percent, those cases are rare. Consider this: A system that offers profits of 100 percent per year supposedly grows $10,000 into $10 million in only 10 years. ***Be skeptical.*** Experienced traders know that no system consistently returns 100 percent per year. (If you created such a system, would you sell it?)

As the Bernie Madoff scandal taught the world, it's impossible to be involved in trading and not have a bad money-losing year on a regular basis. Those who were suspicious of Bernie Madoff's US$65 billion scandal were tipped off because he never claimed enough money-losing years. Just make sure you don't have too many money-losing years.

When evaluating these systems, the devil is in the details. Advertisements often are unclear about how a system actually works in real-world trading, and some vendors make claims based on nothing more than the results of system testing based only on simulated trades and historical data. In fact, the system's author may never have traded the system using real capital.

Constructing a system that shows great profits when simulating trades with historical data is easy. If you designed a trend-following system and tested it against data during the period 1997 through 2000, or from 2003 through 2007, you can be fairly certain that the system is going to perform well in simulated testing. But that doesn't mean you should use it to trade real money.

If a system sounds too good to be true, well, it probably is. So do your own homework. Find out what works and what doesn't, and save your hard-earned trading capital for trading.

Part V
Risk-Taker's Paradise

The 5th Wave   By Rich Tennant

"I like the faster pace of swing trading. It shortens the agony/ecstasy cycle."

In this part . . .

You discover several alternative approaches to trading, including some of the attractions and drawbacks of swing trading and day trading. We also introduce you to more advanced forms of trading — like options trading, futures trading, and foreign currency trading — and we provide details about the designations and certifications that are required if you plan to do any trading for others.

Chapter 16

The Basics of Swing Trading

In This Chapter

▶ Selecting stocks for swing trading

▶ Understanding the role of volatility in swing trading

▶ Substituting options for stocks

▶ Identifying tax issues and account restrictions for swing traders

Swing trading is a trading strategy that tries to take advantage of short-term opportunities in the market. It occupies the middle ground between position trading and day trading. Swing traders use trend-following and countertrend strategies to participate in trading-range and trending stocks. This turbo-charged trading style requires an exceptional understanding of the inner workings of the markets and excellent analysis capabilities.

In this chapter, we discuss a few of the basic techniques used by swing traders along with the risks that are unique to the discipline. We also talk about tax issues and account restrictions unique to swing trading.

Stock Selection Is Key

Swing trading is a *technical discipline*. Although no hard and fast rule applies, swing traders often trade in 1,000-share increments and usually limit the number of simultaneous positions to ten or fewer. A swing trade can last for as little as a few hours to as long as a few months, but typical swing trades span no more than a few weeks. On this kind of time scale, fundamental analysis has little impact on a stock's price movement; therefore, stock selections are made using technical analysis tools. Careful trade management is crucial to swing trading success.

Stock selection is even more important for swing trading than it is for position trading. When you're looking for a stock to move right away, you base your decisions on selection criteria that are different from when you're positioning for a move that may last for several weeks to several months. A few of the important selection criteria that swing traders use are

✔ **Volume and liquidity:** Swing traders typically focus on actively traded and relatively large stocks. The goal is finding stocks that are easy to buy, sell, and sell short. When trading time frames are short, you need to be able to execute your orders quickly. Unfortunately, stocks with the greatest liquidity and trading volumes are closely followed by the largest number of professional traders, which usually constrains the number of profitable swing trading opportunities, so swing traders often scout opportunities outside of the 25 or so stocks that have the highest trading volume and greatest liquidity.

✔ **Trending:** Trending stocks provide the best opportunity for swing-trading profits. You may use either the methods described in Chapter 9 for identifying trending stocks or the *average directional index* (ADX) indicator. This indicator has three components, the ADX reading, and two *directional movement indicators* — the +DMI and the –DMI. An ADX reading of more than 30 or so indicates a trending stock. A comparison of the two DMIs shows you whether the AMX is trending up or down. If the value of +DMI is larger than the value of –DMI, then the stock is trending higher. If the value of –DMI is larger than the value of +DMI, the stock is trending lower. The ADX indicator is included in most charting applications.

✔ **Volatility:** Swing traders depend on larger, or more volatile, short-term moves for profits. As a result, they want to trade stocks that have histories of making large moves in short periods of time. One popular approach to finding them is keeping an eye on the *average daily ranges* (ADRs, but not to be confused with *American depository receipts*, which are shares of foreign companies trading in the U.S. exchanges), which are simple moving averages that track the day-to-day differences between an individual stock's daily high and low prices. If you're swing trading, you want stocks that show high ADRs. Volatility also can be measured using historical volatility, which is discussed in the "Trading volatility" section.

✔ **Sector selection:** Just like position trading, swing traders try to trade stocks in the strongest sectors, and the weakest sectors are candidates for short sales. Use the techniques described in Chapter 13 to identify strong and weak sectors.

✔ **Tight spreads:** As a means of controlling slippage (see Chapter 15), you need to pay close attention to the difference between the bid and ask prices of the stocks you're considering as swing-trading prospects. Stocks with wide spreads make profitable swing trading difficult. Low-priced stocks rarely are good candidates for swing trading, because the spread, as a percentage of the stock price, is usually too wide.

Swing-Trading Strategies

Swing trading fluctuates between the use of trend-following and countertrend strategies:

- ✔ When a stock is trending strongly, swing traders primarily employ trend-following techniques, but may use countertrend techniques to fine-tune exit points.

- ✔ When a stock is range bound, swing traders use countertrend methods to identify entry and exit points.

Trading trending stocks

Technical analysis patterns that we cover in Chapters 9 through 13 are all applicable to swing trading. Patterns repeat in all time frames. The difference is in how swing traders use and interpret these common patterns. Trend-following strategies are more aggressive for swing trading than they are for position trading. Although swing traders use some of the same indicators and patterns used by position traders, they often use them in different ways. We explain a few examples in the sections that follow.

Trading pullbacks

A *pullback* is another name for a consolidation within a trend. Consolidation patterns include the flags and pennants discussed in Chapter 10. Swing traders use daily charts and intraday charts — ranging from 1-minute bars to 60-minute bar charts — to identify the dominant short-term trend and any pullback patterns within the trend. They try to enter a position when the price of a targeted stock stops declining or pulling back, so they can capture the next move higher in the trend. Conceptually, pullback trading is simple, but in practice, it's trickier than it sounds.

After you identify a trending stock and find a flag or pennant pullback pattern (Chapter 10) by visually examining the daily charts, you must try to enter a position just as the pullback is ending. The classic setup is finding an orderly pullback in which the high of each bar on a chart of the pullback is lower than the previous one. Figure 16-1 shows an idealized example of the type of pattern you're trying to find.

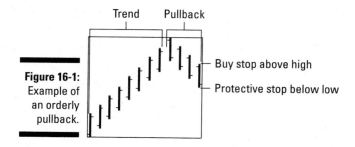

Figure 16-1:
Example of
an orderly
pullback.

Trend   Pullback

Buy stop above high

Protective stop below low

Entering a position is done by placing a buy-stop order. A buy-stop is like any stop order; when the price is hit, the order is executed. See Chapter 12 for details. Entering a position to trade pullbacks is an iterative process, so it's best to use a day order instead of a GTC (good 'til cancelled; see Chapter 14) order. Here are the steps:

- ✔ Select your buy-stop price so it's just above the intraday high price shown in the last bar of the chart.

- ✔ If the stock price trades above your buy-stop price, your order is executed. Otherwise, the order is cancelled at the end of the day.

- ✔ As long as you're still interested in this trade, adjust your buy-stop price to just above the intraday high of the most recent bar on the chart and reenter your order.

- ✔ After your order is filled, place a stop-loss order (Chapter 12) using a stop price just below the intraday low of the lowest bar in the pullback on the chart.

- ✔ As long as the trade is active, continue adjusting the stop price to be just below the intraday low of the most recent bar on the chart.

Figure 16-2 is a price chart of the stock of National Oilwell Varco Inc. (NOV), which is showing a strong uptrend. Several opportunities for trading pullbacks are also shown on this chart.

The first pullback occurred after NOV traded to a new high of $30.44 on January 23, 2007. That new high is labelled Bar #1 on the chart. After identifying the pullback, you begin the iterative process of setting the buy-stop price just above the high of the last bar on the chart. At the end of each day, you reset the buy-stop price, again setting it just above the high of the last bar, and reenter the order.

In this example, the trade is triggered on Bar #2, which occurred January 30. You had set the buy price just above the January 29 high, which was $29.44. NOV opened January 30 at $28.90. The trade was triggered when the stock climbed above $29.45, rising as high as $30.01 before backing off to close at

$29.80. You could expect your order to fill very near your $29.45 buy-stop price. For the sake of our example, we'll assume a fill price of $29.50.

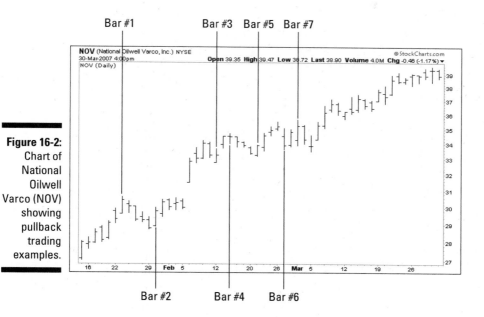

Bar #1   Bar #3   Bar #5   Bar #7

Bar #2   Bar #4   Bar #6

Figure 16-2: Chart of National Oilwell Varco (NOV) showing pullback trading examples.

Immediately following the trade execution, you set a stop-loss order below the low of the previous bar, $28.74 in this case. Or you may set the low at $28.90, the trade day's low. Either approach makes sense, so it's your call. Each day the trade remains active, reset the stop order just below the low of the previous bar on the chart.

The thrust of this trend lasted through February 12, 2007, a duration of ten trading days. This position hit the stop price on February 12, labelled Bar #3 on the chart in Figure 16-2, when the stock traded below the February 9 low of $33.03.

The next opportunity to trade a pullback occurred during the pullback that began after NOV traded at a new high on February 13, labelled Bar #4. The trade was triggered on February 21, shown as Bar #5, when NOV traded above the February 20 high of $33.85. The position hit its stop price on February 27, shown as Bar #6, when the stock traded below the February 26 low of $34.91. Given slippage and transaction costs, this trade was no better than a breakeven trade.

The next opportunity came following the poorly formed pullback that began with Bar #6. You entered the trade on Bar #7 when NOV traded above the February 28 intraday high of $35.00. The trade would stop out two bars later for a loss.

Swing trades don't always work out, of course. Complications and frequent losing trades always are likely.

Surfing channels

Another trend-following approach to swing trading uses a channelling strategy to identify entry and exit points. Chapter 10 explains the channelling strategy and how to construct the channel lines. After a channel is identified on the daily charts, channel lines are treated as lines of support and resistance. Figure 16-3 shows an example.

Resistance Channel Line

Figure 16-3:
Chart of
Jacobs
Engineering
Group Inc.
(JEC) in a
trend
channel.

Support Channel Line

After identifying support and resistance levels for a channelling stock, you can monitor its chart for reversals near the channel lines. As the stock price approaches the lower or *support channel line,* you have an opportunity to take a position in the direction of the trend. After entering a position, your stop-loss order is entered just below the support channel line. As the stock price approaches the upper or *resistance channel line,* that signals when to exit your position.

You can use intraday charts to fine-tune this strategy. As a stock price falls toward its lower channel or support level, begin watching intraday charts for indications that the stock is changing direction and heading higher. If you see an intraday low near the location of the support channel line, followed by a higher high and a higher low, you can use that situation as an entry signal. After entering a long position, you place a stop-loss order just below the support channel line.

You hold this long position until it either is stopped out or the stock approaches its upper channel resistance level. Again, you need to monitor the intraday charts for hints of a change in direction and exit the trade whenever you see the reversal. After that, you wait for the stock to head back toward the lower channel line to initiate a new long trade.

Trading range-bound stocks

Unlike the typical position trader, a swing trader is more likely to use countertrend strategies (see Chapter 15) and actively participate when a stock is range bound. The swing trader tries to make trades based on price movements from the bottom to the top of the range and back down again. You can use either daily or weekly charts to identify the trading range. An example using a daily chart is shown in Figure 16-4.

Your trading approach to range-bound stocks is similar to the one for trading a channelling stock that we describe in the previous "Surfing channels" section. As the stock price approaches the support level, which is just above $59.00 in Figure 16-4, you have an opportunity to take a position. You can use a few approaches to enter a position.

You can, for example, simply choose to place a buy order using a limit price just above the support line. Another approach that may give you a little more control and provide better entry and exit points is to monitor the stock to find pivot points as it trades near the support line. A *pivot point* is a three-bar pattern in which the low price of the middle bar is lower than the lows of the bars on either side of it. The entry and exit points for this kind of trading are similar to the ones used for trading based on a pullback pattern. After identifying a pivot point, you enter an order on the next bar. The protective stop is placed either immediately below the low of the pivot bar or just below the support channel line.

Using intraday charts is another way to fine-tune your entry point. As the stock approaches the support line, you enter a position as soon as you see a reversal pattern on the intraday charts — for example, a higher high and a higher low, or a gap higher (Chapter 10).

You exit these kinds of positions when the stock reverses near its resistance line. You can then take a short position in the stock — using any of the entry techniques described earlier — or wait for the stock to return to the support line to initiate another long position.

If the stock breaks through its upper resistance level, you interpret that condition exactly the way a position trader does — a very bullish indication that the stock is likely beginning a new trend, immediately closing any open short positions and converting to a trend-following strategy (see the earlier "Trading trending stocks" section).

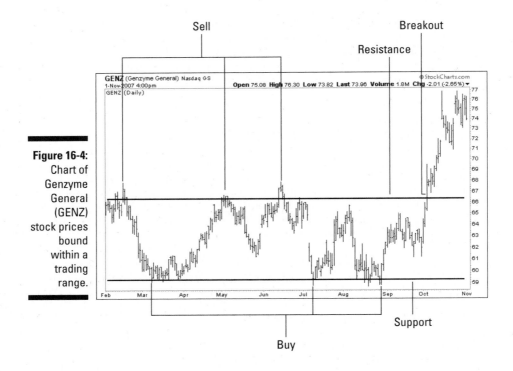

Figure 16-4:
Chart of
Genzyme
General
(GENZ)
stock prices
bound
within a
trading
range.

Trading volatility

Swing traders try to trade stocks that move up and down more than average.
To find these stocks, swing traders spend a great deal of effort measuring
and analyzing volatility, usually in the form of historical volatility. Although
the math required to calculate historical volatility is complex, the concept
is simple. *Historical volatility* measures a stock's price movement. The faster
it moves, the higher the historical volatility. Fortunately, many charting and
analysis programs include a method for calculating historical volatility, so
you don't have to program in the formula.

Historical volatility isn't concerned with the direction of a stock's price
movement. A high historical volatility value doesn't reveal whether a stock's
price is rising or falling. Although swing traders want to know that a stock
trends in one direction or the other, they don't really care which direction.
Downside movement is just as attractive as upside movement to the swing
trader.

Swinging with Gann and Taylor

Swing trading has been around in one form or another since the earliest days of markets. The term itself probably originated with W. D. Gann when he invented the swing chart during the 1920s. George Douglass Taylor popularized the phrase, and a short-term trading technique, when he introduced a now classic three-bar trading pattern in his 1950 book *The Taylor Trading Technique.*

Taylor's ideas serve as the basis for much of today's swing-trading methodology. According to Taylor, trending stocks tend to rally, then rest, and then continue to trend. Swing traders watch for these rest periods and attempt to enter the market just in advance of the thrust of the new trend.

Taylor's method, sometimes called "the book trader's method," was originally developed to trade futures contracts in the grain markets. Taylor theorized that the market cycles through three distinct phases or days. The first phase is the buy day, the second is a sell day, and the third is a sell-short day. Although these three days don't necessarily fall on consecutive days, for the sake of following the discussion we assume they do.

Taylor first determines the short-term trend, finds the position of the short-term cycle within the trend, and then uses this information to determine when to buy, sell, or sell short. The buy day begins the cycle. A typical buy day begins with weakness, and the trader takes a long position near a previously identified support level based on the weakness. This position is held overnight into the next day, the sell day. The sell day typically opens strong, but the strength fades before the close. The trader sells at the early signs of weakness. The final day of the cycle is the sell-short day. The trader watches for any strength near resistance levels on the third day and sells short into this strength. The short position is held overnight and then covered during early weakness the following buy day. The cycle begins in earnest again with the trader initiating a long position after covering the short position.

Taylor's approach is difficult to execute. Like all swing trading, it requires constant monitoring of the market and an excellent understanding of support and resistance levels. It is a discretionary approach that is difficult to test. Few stocks actually follow a three-day script on consecutive days. Many stocks trend for several days before pulling back or rising, so the three-bar method must be adjusted to account for these differences. Nevertheless, Taylor's thinking is evident in much of today's swing-trading methodology.

You can use historical volatility for swing trading in several different ways. One popular approach uses historical volatility for finding stocks that have been very volatile but currently are experiencing quiet periods. These temporarily quiet stocks often return to previous levels of historical volatility, and that presents a swing-trading opportunity. Swing traders identify these stocks by comparing measurements of historical volatility across longer and much shorter periods of time and expressing that comparison as a ratio. The ratio looks like this:

Historical volatility ratio = Short-term historical volatility ÷ Long-term historical volatility

One common ratio compares a 6-day historical volatility with a 100-day historical volatility. Whenever the value of that ratio is less than 50 percent, the stock is a candidate for a swing-trading position.

After this stock takes a short low-volatility rest, it is likely to return to its historical level of volatility with a fast move. Remember that volatility tells you nothing about the direction of price movements, so to get around this limitation be sure to place buy and sell-short stop orders, respectively, above the high and below the low of the current bar. When the stock decides which way it will go, one of your stop orders will be filled and that should get you pointed in the right direction. Using more traditional technical analysis tools is another approach to evaluating a stock's current trend, so you can then trade in the direction of that trend.

Risks accompany both approaches. Using the first approach, the stock may take off in one direction and quickly reverse course, and you may end up holding a position with a highly volatile stock heading the wrong way. This same scenario also can happen with the second approach. Another potential problem occurs when the stock price gaps through your entry order, and your order may end up getting filled at a price that's significantly different than you expected.

Money management issues

Because of the short duration of each trade, swing trading generates a large volume of trades. Execution and slippage costs (Chapter 12) can be very high. Profits are relatively small when measured on each trade, so losses must be carefully controlled.

You need to adhere closely to the money management rules we discuss in Chapter 12. In addition, each swing trade must represent only a small percentage of your trading capital. Ten percent of your capital per trade is too much. Risking less than 5 percent — and perhaps as little as 2 percent — of your trading capital on any one swing trade is a more conservative approach. This approach is similar to the one used by professional traders. When profit potential is small don't take big risks, or you won't be a swing trader for long.

Using Options for Swing Trading

Stock options can be used as substitutes for the underlying stocks when swing trading. A *stock option* is a limited-duration contract that grants the *option buyer* the right to either buy or sell a stock for a fixed price. The *option seller,* usually called the *option writer* or the *option grantor,* is granting the right to the option buyer to either buy or sell a specific stock for a fixed price.

Each option represents 100 shares. A *call* is an option to buy 100 shares of a specified stock. The call buyer is acquiring a limited duration right to buy 100 shares from the option grantor at a fixed price, called the *strike price.* A *put* is an option to sell 100 shares. The put buyer is acquiring a limited duration right to sell 100 shares of a stock to the option grantor at the specified strike price. Options are discussed in more detail in Chapter 18.

You can, for example, substitute a call option for a long stock position or a put option for a short stock position. You realize any profits by selling the options outright, or you can exercise an option and take possession of the shares. Swing traders, however, are more likely to sell the option than exercise it.

Although using options as stock substitutes has several advantages, it also has risks of its own. The primary advantage: An option costs far less than the underlying stock, which enables you to limit your risk to the price of the option.

Each option is a substitute for 100 shares or 100 shares of an exchange-traded fund. One call option, for example, gives you the ability to buy 100 shares at a fixed price for a certain length of time. As an example, assume that the QQQQ exchange-traded fund is trading at $27.10 per share. At the time of the example, you can buy one call option with a $27 strike price for $2.26 per share, or a total of $226, before transaction costs. That one option enables you to buy 100 shares of QQQQ for $27 before the option expires.

Say that the option in this example has approximately six weeks before expiration. Your option position is therefore profitable as long as the QQQQ exchange-traded fund trades above $29.26 (excluding transaction costs) before the expiration date. (We determined the breakeven price by adding the $27 strike price to the $2.26 cost of the option, which totals $29.26.) Your risk is the price of the option. In other words, you can't lose any more than $2.26 per share, or $226, on this trade.

Unfortunately, option pricing is not as straightforward as stock pricing. The pricing example above is merely a snapshot that varies with changes in the price of the QQQQ exchange-traded fund. The following factors affect option prices:

- ✔ Options expire and their prices decay as the expiration date draws closer. This price decay is caused by the option's falling time value.

- ✔ The prices of current-month options decay at faster rates than longer-dated options.

- ✔ In percentage terms, *out-of-the-money* options often move at a faster rate than *in-the-money* options. (An option is said to be in-the-money if it has intrinsic value and out-of-the-money if it has no intrinsic value. For a call option, that means the price for the underlying stock is greater than the specified strike price. For a put, that means the price for the underlying stock is less than the strike price. See Chapter 18 for additional details.) *Note:* Trading options that are far out of the money is rarely a good strategy.

- ✔ Volatility is a component of option pricing. Option prices rise and fall as the volatility of the stock rises and falls.

- ✔ Except in a few unusual circumstances, an option's price doesn't move in lock step with the underlying stock's price. If a stock moves $1, the option, in general, moves some amount less than $1. The more an option is in-the-money, the closer the change in an option's price will be to the change in the underlying stock's price.

Another factor to consider when substituting options for stocks is that the option's *spread,* or the difference between the bid price and the ask price, is extremely wide when considered as a percentage of the option price.

Before you decide to substitute options for your stock trades, make sure you understand the option-pricing model. We discuss it in Chapter 18. And be careful you don't overtrade with options. If you normally buy 100 shares, then you need to buy only one option contract. Although the price of 10 option contracts may be attractive when compared with the price of the stock, 10 option contracts nevertheless represent 1,000. When buying options for 10 times the number of shares that you normally trade, you're increasing your exposure to risk by a factor of 10.

When trading options, you can't make money in as many ways as you can lose it. Being right on the stock's direction but still losing money on an option trade is possible because of pricing issues. That's why gaining an understanding of the option-pricing model is so important before you try to substitute an option for a stock. We discuss options more fully in Chapter 18.

Getting a Grip on Swing-Trading Risks

Swing trading is risky and demands a great deal of time. As a swing trader, you must monitor the market during every trading hour. You also must be able to control your emotions so that you stay focused and trade within your plan.

Ask any swing trader; you're likely to hear that strict adherence to money management reduces risk. The counterargument is that swing trading exposes a great deal of capital to risk but makes only small profits. Some traders are able to swing trade profitably, but you need to realize that the odds are stacked against you. Only you can decide whether it's worth the effort.

Some argue that swing trading combines the worst aspects of position trading with the worst aspects of day trading. Like day trading, swing-trading profits are small and slippage costs are high. Swing-trading positions are held overnight, so swing traders can't take advantage of the special margin provisions that are available to day traders who close all positions by the end of the trading day.

Tackling Taxes

Special tax treatment is available from the Canada Revenue Agency (CRA) for some traders. The benefits enable full-time traders to be taxed as a business rather than an investor, and that means you can deduct the cost of the computer hardware and software used for trading. You can also treat your home-office expenses, including the costs for data acquisition, as ordinary business expenses. Whenever possible within the law, traders should claim their trading gains as capital gains and trading losses as business losses. Consider this example from the CRA's own Web site (www. cra-arc.gc.ca): "Although an adventure or concern in the nature of trade is included in the definition of the term 'business,' it does not necessarily mean that a tax-payer who is engaged in an adventure or concern in the nature of trading is 'carrying on' a business." Make sure you get good accounting advice, because the definitions are not as clear cut as you might think.

Chapter 17

The Basics of Day Trading

Day traders enter and exit trading positions sometimes up to a hundred times within a single day. Day traders may even get into and out of a position within the span of only a minute or two.

Some players compare watching the charts and jumping quickly in and out of positions to the rapid-fire action and excitement of a video game. However, much more is at risk. Instead of merely losing a game, a bad move can mean the loss of your entire portfolio, or maybe even more. Yes, day traders sometimes end up in negative positions, owing money to the firms with which they're trading. We explain how that can happen later in this chapter.

For now, you need to know that day traders rarely hold a stock overnight and that watching a computer screen for hours at a time is a critical part of the day for this high-stress type of trading. Although none of us is or ever has been or even wants to be a day trader, in this chapter we nevertheless explain how this type of high-risk trading works, give you some common strategies used by these types of traders, and show you the high levels of risk day traders face.

What Day Trading Is All About

Day traders try to fashion a career out of buying and selling stocks quickly throughout the day. A certain amount of day trading is critical to maintaining the liquidity of the stock market, because the techniques they use keep the market moving. They're known as *institutional day traders* — specialists and market makers.

Another name for day traders is algorithmic traders due to their trading huge volumes of stock for minute profits using mathematical formulae driven by computers.

Retail day traders, on the other hand, are a different bunch. They make dozens or even a hundred trades a day, but they also close out all their positions at the end of each day. Retail day traders use technological developments that first became available in the late 1990s to get in on the action that used to be the sole province of the institutional day traders.

Institutional day traders and market makers

Market makers, also known as specialists in the U.S., are part of the North American stock exchanges. All are members of an exchange either as an individual, a partnership, or part of a corporation. They're responsible for making markets in certain exchange-traded securities, maintaining inventories of the securities for which they're responsible, and making sure the market for those securities is orderly.

Market makers play a role in maintaining the liquidity and efficiency of TSX Venture Exchange and Nasdaq-listed stocks and stocks that are sold over the counter on Pink Sheets and not listed in a particular market. They're usually part of a firm or bank that facilitates the buying and selling of stocks in these markets. A market maker must be ready to buy and sell stock on a regular and continual basis.

Specialists and market makers used to trade into and out of positions throughout the day, often executing orders in a matter of seconds. More recently, the high-frequency trading from algo traders has replaced the market makers. We discuss market makers in greater detail in Chapter 2.

Retail day traders

Retail day traders try to make money in a totally different way. The playing field of day trading opened for retail day traders in the late 1990s, when computer software was developed that enabled individual investors to have direct access to securities markets in ways that previously were technologically available only to licensed and registered professionals. We talk more about licensing and registration in Chapter 20.

It's all about access

Firms that promote day trading provide their customers with real-time links to the major stock markets, which gives them information not readily available to average retail investors. Firms also provide customers direct entry into their order-processing systems. This direct access enables day traders to send their orders to a particular market and to determine the order route — a task that only licensed professionals previously were able to accomplish. Although other online and traditional firms may provide real-time quotation information, they don't offer their customers linkages to markets. Instead, some have preset algorithms that determine where a customer's order is routed for execution, which may or may not be the cheapest way to go. Many times the algorithms are set based on trading agreements among firms without regard to cost-effectiveness.

Why does direct access matter so much? Speed and, again we say, speed! Systems that provide more and more direct access give day traders the opportunity to execute their trades within seconds. In addition, by using a more direct route, traders can choose bid or ask prices that look the best and fill their orders instantly.

Traders also can post bid or ask prices directly on an ECN, or cancel orders with the click of a button, all because they have direct access. When establishing a position using a limit order through a traditional discount broker, traders must fill out another ticket to cancel their trades — and under those circumstances they can't know whether their orders have been filled until they receive a trade or cancel confirmation.

Day traders aren't looking to make a large profit on one huge sale every day, but instead seek smaller profits on much more frequent changes in the positions they establish during the day. Mere seconds are critical when you're trying to get in and out of a position, trying to make money on small stock price differences which, in trading lingo, translate to dollars in the nontrading world. Although swing traders and position traders seek profits of several dollars with each position they enter, day traders may exit their position after earning a profit of only a few cents. Traders usually buy or sell at least 1,000 shares at a time, so 25 cents translates into a $250 profit for every 1,000 shares traded. *Note:* In a matter of only one second, what looked like a good price to a day trader can be lost.

By controlling where their orders are sent, day traders also gain better control over the costs of their trades. One of the ways that some discount brokers make money on trades they execute for customers is charging a fee called a *payment for order flow.* These fees can be a penny or more per share, providing something of a kickback to the discount firm and enabling deep discount brokerages to charge smaller upfront commissions that barely cover the cost of their trades. Although online discount brokers send trades to particular markets or market makers through which they've established trading deals, day traders have the inside information to select the routes that give them the best prices.

Day-trading firms

In addition to direct access, day-trading firms provide (for a fee of course) their customers with training in how to participate in this rapid-fire, price-sensitive buying and selling and then encourage their trainees to use their strategies and their software. These firms developed proprietary software and systems that day traders use to analyze and chart activity and execute orders. This software usually is available only at on-site trading facilities or downloadable to your computer rather than being used through Web sites.

Day trading through a Web site isn't usually done, because the added seconds it takes to download price information and then send back an order are likely to result in the loss of your order to some other trader. Even when a trader has high-speed Internet access, too much time can be spent waiting for pages to load and sending orders. So to be successful, day traders need the instant access they get through proprietary software.

Settlement: No free rides

An official stock transaction is settled three business days after the date of the trade, meaning that day traders frequently are buying and selling stocks before their transactions are officially settled. Day traders can't *free ride,* meaning they can't buy a security and sell it an hour later without first having enough funds to cover the settlement of the initial trade. If a trader buys a stock or other security, he or she must have the funds to cover the initial trade even if the security is sold for a profit within the same day.

A margin account with leverage of four times excess equity is what enables day traders to get around this rule. To play within these rules, all the trader needs to have is sufficient cash to pay for the shares or sufficient reserve in his or her margin account. Firms can restrict use of margin funds for three days until a stock transaction is settled, but they're not required to do so.

Before trading, be sure you understand the restrictions your firm imposes on margin accounts related to stock transaction settlements. The settlement time for options is the next business day, as opposed to the three-day waiting period for stocks. To trade using options, funds must be in the account before you place the trade or you'll be stuck transferring funds around, which might add to the costs of your trading.

Strategies for Successful Day Trading

As we mention throughout this chapter, day traders trade stocks in lots of 1,000 shares or more, putting large portions of cash at risk with every trade. Although the profit potential is great, so is the risk of losing all your money and maybe even owing money if you use borrowed cash in your margin account.

Before you ever consider day trading, you need to understand the risks you're taking and how to control them. Otherwise, money can flow out of your account very quickly. Studies show that it generally takes six months to learn how to be a successful day trader, and during that learning curve you can count on losing money. Success rates of day traders range from 10 percent to 30 percent of those who try it. In other words, 70 percent to 90 percent of the people who attempt day trading don't succeed and frequently end their day-trading careers in debt. We explain more about risks in the "Risks Are High; Rewards Can Be Too" section later in this chapter, but first we need to review some of the basic strategies that day traders use.

Technical needs

Number one on the list of things you need to become a day trader is a very good computer and Internet setup. They're necessary for successful day trading. Most traders have two or more monitors with a PC built to handle a large number of data feeds at one time. Windows XP or Vista are the preferred operating systems of day traders, because most of the trading platforms are written for these environments and because they're able to handle multiple monitors.

Daily computer maintenance is critical for day traders. Computer problems are the last thing you want to experience in the middle of your trading day, especially when buy positions are left open. You can lose a lot of money if you're waiting for your computer to reboot and a trade goes sour. Traders recommend that you clear the cookies (files that Web sites send to your computer when you're using them) from your Internet cache on a daily basis and that you *defragment* (reorganize your files so the computer runs more efficiently) your computer at least once a week.

Another key step is finding an Internet service provider (ISP) that is reliable and offers high-speed access to the Internet. Many traders have more than one ISP lined up, so they have a backup in case the first one goes down. Again, you don't want to lose even mere seconds when you're in the middle of your trading day, especially when you have open positions.

Trading patterns

Day traders make use of patterns seen in technical analysis that are similar to the ones we discuss in Part III of this book. One common pattern that day traders look for is a price gap in a stock at the opening of the market. They find that prices usually move in the same direction as the opening price gap during the first few minutes the market is open and then the market tends to reverse and fill the gap (see Chapter 10). Trading that doesn't fill the gap during the first five to ten minutes can signal a dominant trend for the day for that particular stock. Some traders watch this action to find their targets for the day and the directions they plan to play them. No consensus on this exists, of course. Others believe early market moves give false signals and that using those moves for planning your trading day can be dangerous.

Traders watch for many of the same patterns they find when looking for breakout signals and signs of reversals (see Chapter 10). The key difference is that a day trader looks for intraday signals, while longer-term traders format their charts for longer periods of time.

Scalping

Scalping basically means you move in and out of a position for a very limited profit in an extremely short time frame, usually just a few minutes or possibly only a few seconds. The scalper's objective is to make profits of only fractions of a dollar on any given trade, rather than the several dollars' profit that most traders seek. Day traders execute their trades in a much narrower time frame, so scalpers look for only 10 to 25 cents per share, hoping to make small gains as often as possible. When scalping with higher-priced ($100 or more per share) or faster-moving stocks, a dollar can be considered a scalp.

For most stocks, scalping doesn't pay if you trade fewer than 1,000 shares. Here's why: A 10-cent scalping profit on 1,000 shares is only $100, before paying transaction fees or commissions. Little profit will remain after fees and commissions if you're trading fewer than 1,000 shares.

Trend traders

Not all day traders use the scalping technique. Some are trend traders. Instead of jumping in and out of a trade for a fraction of a dollar, they look for profits of at least one or two dollars and may stay in a position for minutes or even as long as an hour or two. *Trend traders* make fewer trades than scalpers, but seek higher profits per trade and may trade in blocks of fewer than 1,000 shares because they can make a nice profit as trend traders with considerably less share volume. In fact, traders who look for more than a one-dollar profit sometimes hold a stock for several hours, unless the stock is high priced or its price is moving fast.

Risks Are High (Rewards Can Be, Too)

Reading about trading patterns and the high volume of stock trading, you've probably already figured out for yourself that the risks are high. Within a matter of minutes, trading in and out of stocks in 1,000-share blocks can be costly when a stock quickly moves in a direction you weren't anticipating.

In fact, the U.S. Senate investigated the risks of day trading after a shooting spree at an on-site day-trading facility in Atlanta, Georgia, left nine people dead in July 1999. The shooter, Mark Barton, was a chemist before getting involved in day trading and losing $105,000 in just one month. He killed himself after the shooting spree.

U.S. Senate investigators found that the revenue of the 15 largest firms that specialize in day trading for 1999 was US$541.5 million, or 276 percent higher than their revenue in 1997. Profits went up by more than US$66 million, and by 1999 the 15 firms had opened 12,000 new accounts. Investigators also found that the 4,000 to 5,000 most active traders were borrowing huge sums of money and losing it. In that year traders paid an average of US$16 per trade and made an average of 29 trades per day. Using these statistics, investigators concluded that a trader needed to make more than US$111,000 a year in stock market gains just to break even with that level of costs.

A second study, released in October 2006 by University of California professors Brad Barber and Terrance Odean, who looked at day traders on the Taiwan Stock Exchange, found that 82 percent of traders lost money. Some may profit most days, but end up in a losing position after calculating costs of operations.

Liquidity

To be considered liquid, a trader must have the ability to change holdings quickly into cash. Although you can see that a day trader must trade a large number of shares to make a profit, he or she must also have significant cash and securities in his or her account to be able to continue trading activities.

Slippage

Slippage can cost day traders significantly if they're not careful about how they execute their trades. *Slippage* relates to the difference between what you expect your exit or entry stock prices to be and what you actually end up paying for and getting out of that stock when your order is finally executed. Depending on the volatility of the market, a stock price sometimes can vary by as much as several cents from the time you see the stock quotation until the time your order is actually executed. Traders can control slippage with the right type of order. The three basic ways to enter a position are at market, with a stop order, or with a limit order. Day traders rarely use market orders, which means buying or selling a stock at the market price. Instead they use stop or limit orders to better control when their orders are filled and how much they pay for the stock. We discuss types of orders in Chapter 2.

Most traders recommend you never enter a position without immediately placing a stop-loss order at an exit price you decide is the most you're willing to lose on a particular position. Although a stop order means that when a stock hits the exit price the order changes to a market order and may result in your selling the stock at less than that price, it nevertheless is safer than placing a limit order, which can mean you miss the exit point altogether and possibly lose even more. Stop-loss orders can cause some slippage, but you usually lose less with these types of orders than with limit orders. A limit order can be completely missed when your stock breaks into a downward trend, because the fall in price was too abrupt or rapid for it to be executed.

When buying stock traders use limit orders, because they place limits on the entry prices traders are willing to pay. Traders certainly don't want to end up paying higher prices than they intend, which in turn raises the bar for making a profit higher than is reasonably possible to attain.

Trading costs

Trading costs vary significantly depending on the amount of trading you do or don't do each month. The table below provides a breakdown of the commissions charged by one of the top day-trading firms.

Number of Trades per Month	Commissions
1 to 399	$9.95 per trade
400 to 999	$7.95 per trade
1,000 to 1,499	$5.95 per trade
1,500 plus	$2.95 per trade

The cost of trading is the same whether you have Level I or Level II access (see Chapters 3 and 14 for information on Level I and Level II quoting alternatives). The number of trades you do will affect whether you have to pay for Level II access. To get Level II access for free, you must make at least 20 trades per month; otherwise, the monthly fee for Level II access is $150. Options-trading fees are $9.95 per trade, plus $1.25 per contract. In addition to these fees, per-share charges can range from $0.002 per share to $0.01 per share, depending on the exchange on which you choose to trade. If your computer crashes or your Internet access goes down, phone orders can cost you $15 per trade.

So if you trade 30 times a day for 20 days a month, the number of your trades totals 600. At $7.95 per trade, your commission costs are $4,770 per month, and if you trade 1,000 shares with each trade, that adds up to a total of 600,000 shares per month. Even at the lowest per-share exchange cost of $0.002, that means an additional $1,200 in per-share charges. Thus, your monthly cost for this volume of trading would be $5,970.

In addition to these costs, many traders also pay for newsletters or join trading chat rooms that give them alerts for the best opportunities each day. These services can add another $200 to $250 to your monthly costs. So before you see even one penny of profit, your monthly outlay can be $6,170 (that's $74,040 annually). You can easily understand why so many day traders never see a profit for at least six months and why such a high percentage of day traders actually give up before their businesses turn profitable.

Taxes (of course)

On top of all these costs, you must consider taxes you'll have to pay annually on half of your net capital gains at your current individual tax rate unless you're trading in a tax-free or a tax-deferred account such as a Tax-Free Savings Account (TFSA) or Registered Retirement Savings Plan or Registered Retirement Income Fund accounts (RRSP/RRIF, respectively). If you trade in a taxable account, then the interest expense on any investment loan (known as margin) can be deducted from your income.

Avoiding the Most Common Mistakes

If the risks and costs don't scare you away from day trading, you need to become familiar with some common mistakes that lead to failure for many day traders. Some traders talk about their more common mistakes, especially the ones that cost a lot of money while they were building their businesses. Here are some of the more serious mistakes new day traders make:

✔ **Breaking stop-loss rules:** When a stock starts dropping, newer, not yet disciplined traders tend to panic as their picks begin losing money, so they decide to hold the stock rather than exit when their initial stop-loss is reached. However, traders go broke using that strategy, because they don't stop their losses as planned. You must set your exit prices based on your technical analysis for both losses and profits when you first buy the stock. Follow those rules mechanically when the target price is hit, and don't let your emotions get in the way.

✔ **Chasing trends:** New traders who aren't yet confident in the way they read patterns often wait to see confirmation that they're right before they enter a position. That hesitation causes them to miss planned entry points and, if they're right, can end up forcing them into buying at a stock price that's higher than they intended when an upward trend is expected or selling at a lower price than they intended when a downward trend is expected. By missing intended entry prices, traders end up chasing the trends and finding that their original entry and exit points no longer are valid because many others already acted on the trend and the stock is no longer available at the planned prices. Experienced traders just walk away from that particular trade instead of getting caught up in trading points that don't match technical analysis and thereby chasing a trend.

✔ **Not waiting for the right trade:** A new day trader must exhibit the patience required in waiting for the right trade to match what the technical analysis indicates. Experienced traders know to wait for the right timing instead of forcing a trade, entering at the wrong price, and overtrading their account.

✔ **Not establishing set rules before the trading day begins:** To avoid getting caught up in the emotions of a big win or loss, you need to decide your entry and exit points before the trading day begins and never deviate from them after the day begins. Experienced day traders know that you either focus on your trades or think about your rules. You don't have time to do both, and trying to do so can be a recipe for disaster. Staying objective and following your rules is crucial to maintaining the control a day trader needs.

✔ **Forgetting that fundamentals don't always matter:** New day traders get caught up in the idea that the company whose stock they've purchased is a good company and that when its stock loses ground, it's therefore bound to head back up. Experienced traders know that how good the fundamentals look doesn't matter and that when the market is selling down, even the price of a good stock goes down. Day traders must follow market signs and not worry about how good or bad the fundamentals of the company they're trading may appear.

- ✔ **Averaging down:** Although investors may *average down,* meaning they buy a stock and if the price goes down they buy even more shares believing that it's a good stock that will recover, this technique doesn't often work at all for day traders, and most experienced traders of every variety will tell you that using it is a fatal mistake. Day traders instead believe that you need to set a stop price and get out (called stopping out) of a losing stock and possibly reenter again at a lower price. Doing so gives you time to look objectively at what is happening with the stock and determine whether getting back in is worthwhile. Stopping out also is likely to cost you less than averaging down, and you won't risk getting caught with a margin problem. Averaging down can tie up too much money that otherwise can be used for a more profitable trade with a different stock. The worst feeling, even for an experienced trader, occurs when a stock plunges far below the stop position, because deciding whether to take the large loss is difficult. In most cases, if you're uncertain of your next move, experienced traders recommend you get out of the position before the situation grows worse or out of control.

- ✔ **Not knowing when to take profits:** New traders sometimes make the mistake of either taking profits too early or not taking profits at all. Both can result in unnecessary losses. Most of the time, indecision strikes when traders are afraid they'll lose a profit if they hold it too long or miss a profit if they exit too soon. Just as with losses, exit points need to be determined before entering a position, and rules need to be followed. Remember that as a day trader you must focus either on your trade or on your rules. Day traders who move into and out of positions within seconds or minutes don't have time to do both.

- ✔ **Walking away from the computer with open positions:** Experienced day traders never walk away from their computers when they still have an open position. Although we touch briefly on holding open positions overnight in the introduction to this chapter, this rule is even stricter. Because experienced day traders respond to price changes that occur in mere seconds or minutes, they definitely don't want to be away from the screen while a position is still open.

Day trading is a high-risk career choice that you should consider only after doing a considerable amount of initial research, hunting down good resources for educating yourself about the risks and rewards, and finding all the techniques you need to use to day trade successfully. Even before you get started, be sure to check out the firms you're planning to use as resources by calling up their disciplinary records and complaint histories through the OSC or provincial regulators. You're putting a good deal of money at risk, so take the time to find out all you can before spending even that first dime.

You also may want to consider taking the Canadian Securities Course at www.csi.ca. This course includes the exam all advisers are required to pass. Even though you may never want to work as an investment adviser or discount broker, the information you're required to know for the exam gives you a much stronger awareness of the securities markets and the laws by which they're governed. Studying for the test, you'll also discover more about the various investment products on the market and the risks you take when buying and selling each type. For a closer look at day trading, read *Day Trading For Dummies* by Ann C. Logue (Wiley).

Chapter 18

Doing It by Derivatives

• •

• •

Traders can raise the bar on the leverage they're allowed by opening the door to the derivatives markets. *Derivatives* are any financial instruments that derive their value from another financial security, which is called an *underlier*. The underliers are usually stocks, bonds, foreign currency, or commodities. The derivative buyer or seller doesn't have to own the underlying security to trade derivatives.

You may unwittingly encounter derivatives if you trade those exchange-traded funds (ETFs) that offer to return two or even three times the value of an underlying stock index. Those ETFs use derivatives to amplify the reward — and the risk. And you may recall that derivative trading, especially those derivatives tied to the value of underlying U.S. mortgage assets, exacerbated the mortgage mess that started the financial collapse of 2008 around the world.

Derivatives traders use futures and options, which are the two most common types of derivatives, to make money in a highly risky venture. In this chapter, we introduce you to a variety of derivatives, how they're traded, and the risks involved in trading futures and options. However, you need to seek additional training before jumping into this kind of trading. This is the rocket science of money.

Types of Derivatives: Futures and Options

Derivatives are marketable instruments that over time acquire and relinquish value based on an underlying asset (see the later section on "Options lingo"), including such commodities as coffee or soybeans, bonds, energy prices, and even stocks. They are commonly used by commercial and institutional organizations to *hedge* against the risks of financial losses suffered by the underlying assets that they hold. Buying or selling a derivative, for example, can minimize your financial loss when a major change occurs in the price of an asset that you own. *Hedging* is a popular tactic used by growers, producers, portfolio managers, and users of the commodities.

The two basic and most common types of derivatives are contracts for options and for futures. Traders buy and sell them as a way to speculate on the direction that the volatile prices of underlying assets will take farther down the road. If their hunches are right and the prices move in the directions they expect, traders can make a significant profit. If, on the other hand, they're wrong, they can lose the amount they paid for the derivative — possibly even quite a bit more. Before we explain all the risks, we need to more accurately define futures and options.

Futures

Futures are legally binding contracts between two parties, one of whom agrees to buy and the other who agrees to sell an asset for a specific price at a specified time. The specific price is known as the *strike price*. The specified date is known as the *settlement date*. Futures were first used in the 18th century in Japan as a means of trading rice and silk, but they didn't appear in our markets until the 1850s, when futures markets were developed for buying and selling commodities such as wheat, cotton, and corn.

Futures contracts are one of the most volatile trading instruments. Prices can change rapidly, causing traders to face sudden and sometimes huge losses or gains. Futures contracts are traded based on the prices of underlying commodities, indexes, bonds, and stocks. Most people who enter futures markets do not physically buy and sell the actual goods or underlying financial asset. A futures contract on pork bellies, for example, does not obligate you to fill your garage with bacon. Traders invest in futures contracts either to speculate on or to hedge the risks of the changing prices of the assets that they might or might not hold. A pig farmer uses a pork belly futures contract to hedge his swine breeding. A Saudi prince uses a pork belly futures contract to speculate on the price of bacon.

What's your position?

When people talk about futures, they're bound to say something about their positions. Here's what they mean:

- **Short positions:** The party in the contract who agrees to deliver the commodity, stock, or bond holds a short position. Traders who take short positions are expecting the price of the underlying commodities to go down.

- **Long positions:** The party in the contract who agrees to buy the commodity, stock, or bond in a futures contract holds a long position on the security. Traders who buy long positions are expecting the price of the underlying commodities to go up.

Making money using futures

Traders can make money from trading futures on the daily movements of the markets for the underlying commodities, stocks, bonds, or currencies involved in the contracts they trade.

For example, typical futures contracts for wheat are signed between wheat farmers and bread producers. On one side of this contract, farmers agree to sell a specific amount of the wheat they grow at a specific price and a specified time, and on the other side, producers agree to pay that price for the contracted amount of wheat to be delivered to them by the specified time. Farmers benefit by ensuring they can get a specific price or income from their wheat, and bread producers benefit by knowing how much they have to pay for the wheat they need to make the bread that they, in turn, sell to earn a living.

The value of that futures contract is adjusted daily. Assuming the farmer agreed in February to sell 10,000 bushels of wheat to the bread maker at $4 per bushel in July, and assuming that before the July settlement date the price of wheat rises to $5 per bushel, the farmer holding the futures contract has lost $1 per bushel of wheat, or $10,000. These types of price adjustments actually are calculated daily throughout the duration of the futures contract and that means the farmer's or bread maker's account is credited or debited as wheat prices fluctuate.

The farmer and bread maker will probably never actually exchange their goods. Instead, the obligations of the futures contract eventually are settled with cash. In this scenario, the bread maker will probably buy his wheat at the current price of $5 per bushel when he needs it, but because he speculated correctly on the price, it's only really costing him $40,000 (instead of $50,000 at the current market price) to buy the wheat. Although the bread maker pays $50,000 for 10,000 bushels of wheat, he has saved $10,000 because of the money he made on the wheat futures contract. The farmer, on the other hand, sells his wheat at $5 per bushel and gets $50,000 cash, but actually keeps only $40,000 because he has to cover his loss from the futures contract.

You can see from this example that futures contracts are actually financial positions. This financial position, or the buying and selling of futures contracts, is how traders speculate. If futures traders believe the price of wheat is rising, they buy futures contracts so they can benefit from the gain made by the price. But when the situation is reversed and the price of wheat drops to $3 per bushel, then the trader who buys can be on the losing side of that futures contract and be liable for a $10,000 loss. The cost of buying into a futures contract is called the *premium* paid for that contract, which is only a small percentage of the price of the actual commodity, stock, bond, or currency underlying the contract.

Commodities futures

People who buy commodities futures basically are agreeing to buy a certain amount of a commodity at a set price at a future date. Conversely, people who sell those same futures are agreeing to provide a certain amount of a commodity at the agreed-upon price by the agreed-upon time. Buyers or sellers can enter into futures contracts on many commodities, including farm products (pork bellies, wheat, corn, and soybeans), precious metals (gold, platinum, and silver), and many others.

Traders usually don't get directly involved as buyers and sellers of the actual commodities, because they get out of their futures contracts before the underlying commodities ever change hands. Instead, they're speculators, buying and/or selling futures contracts based on which way they think the commodity price is going to move. Speculation, as you know, is fraught with risk, and the reason the risk is so great is that a commodity contract controls a large amount of the commodity value compared with the relatively small price that it takes to buy or sell the contract. The result is extensive leverage, which means controlling a large position with only a small cash deposit. If the price moves in a direction that's the opposite of what the trader anticipates, he or she may have to take a huge loss to get out of the contract.

Index futures

Index futures are based on the expected direction of the value of indexes like the S&P/TSX Composite Index and the S&P 500 index. They can be the riskiest types of futures. No underlying commodities, stocks, or bonds ever change hands with these futures contracts. Any differences in these contracts must be settled with good ol' cold, hard cash. Leverage also is high on these types of futures. For example, the multiplier on the S&P/TSX 60 contract is $100 per each index point. A Dow Jones Industrial Average contract has a value that's 25 times the value of the underlying DJIA Index.

Smaller index futures contracts, known collectively as *e-minis,* or *mini futures,* are targeted at individual traders. These minicontracts are available for indexes such as the S&P/TSX and the Nasdaq 100. Their respective individual values range from 5 times to 100 times those of the underlying indexes.

The Montreal Exchange (MX) — Canada's oldest exchange, founded in 1832 — has leadership in the financial derivatives market. It is the only foreign exchange authorized by the SEC to manage the technical operations of the Boston Option Exchange (BOX), of which it owns 51 percent. As well as the S&P/TSX Composite Index and the S&P/TSX 60, the Montreal Exchange also trades index futures in gold, energy, financials, and information technology sectors.

The S&P/TSX Composite mini futures contract, for example, is five times the value of the S&P/TSX Composite index. In other words, if a trader takes a position in the S&P/TSX Composite mini futures contract, every time the underlying S&P/TSX Composite index moves one point, the value of the S&P/TSX Composite mini futures contract changes by $5. Another way to think about this is that for every .25 point, the value of the S&P/TSX Composite mini futures contract changes by 5 cents. If you take a long position in the S&P/TSX Composite mini futures contract when the underlying index is at 1,000, and the index moves to 1,010, you have a $50 profit. The trader who took the other side of this trade, the short position, is in exactly the opposite position, losing $50.

Bond futures

The Montreal Exchange also offers bond futures based on the price of future delivery of a specific type of bond in a specific denomination at a specific interest rate on a specified date. Speculators basically are betting on whether the price of that bond goes up or down. Changes in interest rates have a big impact on the values of bonds. In general, when interest rates fall, bond prices go up, and when interest rates rise, bond prices go down. Speculators in bond futures basically enter positions based on whether interest rates will go up or down. For example, a speculator who thinks interest rates will go up sells contracts for the future delivery of bonds. If interest rates indeed go up as expected, the price for the underlying bonds goes down, and speculators can do one of two things:

- ✔ Buy the lower-priced bonds, and in turn earn a profit by selling them to the buyer to settle at the higher price named in the original futures contract.

- ✔ Close the contract to realize a profit.

Stock futures

Stock futures are contracts in which you agree to either deliver or purchase upon delivery 100 shares of a particular stock on or before a designated date in the future (known as the *expiration date*). For example, a trader who enters into a contract to buy 100 shares at $30 a share for a total of $3,000, and who expects the price of that stock to go up, can lock in the lower price and then buy the actual stock at that lower price on the settlement date or close the contract and realize a profit. Traders who enter into this type of contract generally must have about 20 percent of the cash value of 100 shares of the underlying stock in their futures accounts, so a trader in the earlier example would have to have $300 in a futures account.

Foreign currency futures

Future currency contracts are contracts that involve the future delivery of certain foreign currencies. We discuss these types of futures in Chapter 19.

Yes, futures contracts are riskier than options, because you actually have to come up with the underlying commodity, bond, stock, or currency to satisfy the contract, sell the future at a loss before the settlement date, or pay the difference in cash to settle the contract. Futures are binding contracts that require you to fulfill the obligations specified in the contracts. Options are less risky because they're not an obligation to perform. Rather, they instead give the buyer of the option the right to exercise the option, but the buyer is not obligated to do so.

Options

Although futures have been available since the 1850s, it wasn't until 1975 when the old Montreal Stock Exchange became the first in North America to offer stock options for traders. In the United States options did not become available until 1982, when they were part of a government pilot program. The big advantage that options have over futures is that you buy the right to exercise the option, and yet you still can decide to allow the option to expire without ever exercising that right. When you let an option expire, you lose only the amount you paid for the option and not the full amount that otherwise can be lost in trading the underlying asset. Option sellers take the riskier stance, because they can lose the value of whatever asset they promised to sell or buy if the option buyer decides to exercise the option.

Options are financial contracts that give the buyer the right, but not the obligation, to buy or sell a particular asset at a predetermined date in the future at a specified price.

Options lingo

Trading in options has a language all its own, and you'll need to understand it before we get into the mechanics. Some key terms include:

- ✔ **Puts:** A *put option* gives the buyer the right to sell a particular asset at a specified price at any time during the life of the option.

- ✔ **Calls:** A *call option* gives the buyer the right to buy a particular asset at a specified price at any time during the life of the option.

✔ **Option seller:** The person who writes or sells any option is called the *option seller* or *writer*. This seller (sometimes called an option grantor in the United States) must come up with the underlying asset promised in the option, even if doing so means a loss, whenever an option buyer decides to exercise an option. For example, if an option seller agrees to sell you 100 shares of ABC stock for $50 per share on or before May 1, and the stock price rises to $60 on April 20, then the seller must sell you that stock for $50 and take the $10-per-share loss. You get to sell ABC at the current price and reap the profit.

✔ **Covered calls:** If an option seller holds an *equivalent position,* or owns the same number of shares of the underlying asset that is offered in the call, this contract is considered a *covered call.* Options traders selling covered calls are trying to take advantage of a neutral or declining stock. If the option expires unexercised, the seller (writer) of the option keeps the premium. If, on the other hand, the buyer (holder) of the option exercises it, the stock must be delivered. However, because the option seller already owns the stock, the risk is limited. The opposite scenario is an *uncovered call,* which occurs when the seller sells a call for a stock that he or she doesn't own. The seller of an uncovered call is taking virtually unlimited risk.

✔ **Covered puts:** When the seller of a put option also has sold short an equivalent amount in the underlying security, then this option is considered a *covered put.* If the seller has neither established a short position in the underlying security nor deposited a corresponding amount of cash equal to the value of the put, then the put is called a *naked put.* The seller of a naked put also is taking virtually unlimited risk.

✔ **Option buyer:** The person who buys the option is called the option buyer or holder. If the option buyer buys the right to sell an asset at some time in the future, then he or she buys a put option. If the option buyer buys the right to purchase an asset at some time in the future, then he or she buys a call option. The most an option buyer can lose is the amount paid for the option contract.

✔ **Underlying asset:** An option is based on an underlying asset that can be bought or sold such as a futures contract or shares.

✔ **Premium:** The price paid for the option is called the *premium,* which is what the option holder pays to the option seller for the right to either buy or sell the underlying asset. Premiums for options are set by the open market. Option buyers must pay the premium plus a commission and fee.

✔ **Expiration date:** The *expiration date* is the last day that an option buyer can exercise the option. Options based on futures contracts usually expire one month before the settlement date of the underlying futures contract. After an option expires, the option holder no longer has any rights and the option has no value. So option buyers lose whatever premium they paid plus any commission and fee. In that case, the option is said to expire worthless, or out-of-the-money.

- **Exercise:** Option buyers can exercise their rights any time before the expiration date — if, that is, the option they purchased is an *American-style option. European-style options,* on the other hand, can be exercised only on their expiration dates. Exercising a call option means the option buyer buys the underlying asset at the price set in the option regardless of the current market price for the asset. Exercising a put option means the option buyer sells the underlying asset at the price set in the option. An option buyer can always decide not to exercise the rights set forth in his or her option and simply let it expire. The option holder also can sell the option contract at its current market value.

- **Strike price:** The *strike price* is the price of the underlying asset at which the option can be exercised.

- **Offset:** If option buyers or sellers want to realize their profits or limit their losses, they can *offset* their option through a sale or purchase that also is called liquidating or closing an option. When an option is liquidated, no position is actually taken in the underlying asset. Offsetting is usually done on the same exchange where the trader first bought or sold the option. If he can sell the option for more than he bought it, then he will realize a profit. If she sells the option for less than she paid, then she will take a loss.

- **In-the-money:** An option is *in-the-money* when it's worthwhile to exercise the option and buy or sell the underlying asset. A call option is in-the-money when the market price for the underlying asset is above the strike price set in the option. A put option is in-the-money when the price for the underlying asset is lower than the strike price set in the option.

- **At-the-money:** An option is *at-the-money* when the strike price for the option is the same as the market price for the underlying asset.

- **Out-of-the-money:** An option is *out-of-the-money* when it's not worthwhile to exercise the option. A call option is out-of-the-money when the strike price is higher than the market price for the underlying asset. A put option is out-of-the-money when the strike price is less than the market price for the underlying asset.

Option pricing

The three factors affecting the price of an option premium are as follows:

- **Date of expiration:** As the option moves closer to its date of expiration, the value of the option declines, and that's why an option is considered a *wasting asset.* The more time you have until an option expires, the greater possibility you have for the option to reach the point of being in-the-money. Longer options therefore have higher premiums.

✔ **Strike price:** For out-of-the-money options, when the current market price moves more and more out-of-the-money and away from the strike price, the premium price gets lower and lower. The premium for an in-the-money option, on the other hand, rises in value if the underlying asset moves further into the money in relationship to the strike price.

✔ **Volatility:** The more volatility that's in the market for the underlying asset, or stock, the greater the chance that the option will become worthwhile to exercise. When the market for an asset is volatile, premiums for options on that asset are higher.

Option-pricing techniques are considered to be among the most mathematically complex of all applied areas of finance. One common example is the Black-Scholes option-pricing model (named for its developers Fischer Black and Canadian Myron Scholes (Nobel Prize winner Scholes was born in Timmins, Ontario and graduated from Hamilton's McMaster University). The model takes into consideration the stock's price, the option's strike price and expiration date, the risk-free return, and the standard deviation of the stock's return, which are all measures of volatility.

When you get a quote for an option, you can choose from numerous strike prices and expiration dates that are available. When you're thinking about buying a call option, and its strike price is low and yet close to becoming worthwhile to exercise, the premium price (the price you pay for the option) will be much higher than for an option with a higher strike price. If you're thinking about buying a put option, then you'll pay more of a premium for an option with a high strike price than you will for one with a lower strike price.

To get an idea of how the pricing of options is affected by strike price and time check out Table 18-1, which is an options quote for an imaginary stock we call ABC. *Settle* is the time of expiration for the option.

Table 18-1	ABC Stock Sample Option Prices (in dollars)					
Strike Price	*Calls/Settle*			*Puts/Settle*		
	Apr	May	July	Apr	May	July
$50	4.50	4.60	5.40	0.25	0.50	1.50
$52	3.50	3.60	4.40	0.50	1.00	3.50
$54	2.50	2.60	3.40	0.75	2.00	5.50
$56	1.50	1.60	2.40	2.00	3.00	7.50
$58	0.50	0.60	1.40	4.00	5.00	9.50

You can see from the options quotes for ABC stock that a May call with a strike price of $54 commands a premium of $2.60 per share. To buy an option for 100 shares, the premium would be $260 plus fees. Buying a call is much less of a cash outlay than if you were to buy 100 shares of ABC stock at $54, which would cost you $5,400. The premium of $260 is paid to the option seller, minus any fees.

Commissions vary greatly, so be certain you understand all the possible fees before initiating a trade. Some discount brokers charge commissions per trade, but others charge on the basis of a *round trip,* including both the purchase and the sale of the option. Some firms charge per-option transaction fees, while others charge on the basis of a percentage of the option premium that's usually subject to a minimum charge. Investment advisers can offer a flat management fee that allows option trading at large discounts.

Commission charges can have a major impact on whether you're able to earn a profit or have to suffer a loss on an option. A high commission charge reduces your potential for making a profit and can even drive what little profit you make into a loss. So be careful. Know what charges you have to pay and compare them with other discount brokers and investment advisers before you trade.

Options and futures are quoted with bid and ask prices just like stocks, and the spreads with options can grow pretty wide as a percentage of the option's premium — which in turn can have a significant impact on the profitability of your option position. The wider the spread, the harder it is for you to make a profit. As an option trader, you typically buy at the ask, the higher price, and sell at the bid, the lower price. That means any trade must recover the difference between the bid and the ask before you can earn a profit. As with stock trading, you can use a limit order to put your order between the bid and the ask, but no guarantee exists that your order will be filled. See Chapter 14 for more about bid–ask spreads.

Buying Options and Futures Contracts

All types of options and futures in Canada are traded on the Montreal Exchange. Some types of options can be traded on the NYSE and the Boston Option Exchange. The Chicago Board Options Exchange (CBOE) handles stock and several specialized futures options. You can trade stock options and some index options in a traditional investment account. Special risk release forms must be signed, but otherwise the account remains the same. (For more about establishing an account, see Chapter 3.) Covered options and naked short positions require a margin account.

Opening an account

If you want to buy futures or options on futures, you must do so through an individual account that you open with a registered futures trading dealer.

You have the choice of opening either a discretionary account or a nondiscretionary account. A *discretionary account* is an account in which you sign a power of attorney over to your commodity trading adviser (CTA) so he or she can make trading decisions on your behalf. A *nondiscretionary account* is an account in which you make all the trading decisions. You also may want to consider trading through a commodity pool. When trading through a *commodity pool* you purchase a share or interest in a pool of other investors. Any profits or losses are shared proportionately by the members of the pool.

When you open an individual account, you need to make a deposit that amounts to a *margin payment* or *performance bond* for the options or futures you trade. This payment is relatively small compared to the size of your potential market position, and it gives you the opportunity to greatly leverage your money. Small changes in options and futures prices can result in large gains or large losses in relatively short periods of time.

Your futures trader calculates the values of the futures and option contracts in your account on a daily basis, and you need to maintain a margin level that's approximately 75 percent of the amount required when you originally enter your positions. If your holdings fall below that level you'll be asked to come up with the cash to restore your margin account to the initial level, a situation that's known as a *margin call.* If you can't meet the margin call in a reasonable period of time, which can be as little as an hour, your futures firm closes out enough of your positions to reduce your margin deficiency. If your positions are liquidated at a loss you can be held liable for that loss, which sometimes can be substantially more than your original margin deposit.

Custom-designed exchange-traded funds (ETFs) provide traders with many of the features of a futures contract. Traders also can trade options on ETFs — if they have the stomach for it — through the Montreal Exchange.

Calculating the price and making a buy

Before buying an option you first must calculate the break-even price; to do that you must know the option's strike price, the premium cost, and the commission or other transaction costs. With those three details in hand you can determine a break-even price for a call option using this formula:

Option strike price + Option premium costs + Commission and transaction fees = Break-even price

Using the example in Table 18-1, here's the per-share break-even price for buying a May call option with a strike price of $54 and a commission of $25, or 25 cents per share:

$54 + $2.60 + $0.25 = $56.85

To make a profit on this call option, the stock price of ABC has to rise above $56.85. If the stock price doesn't rise above $56.85, you won't make a profit on this option purchase (unless you're somehow able to sell the option for more than $2.85 before the expiration date — see the next section). These calculations are correct only when you have one fee for a round-trip option exchange. If you have to pay fees in both directions, which is common, then you need to double the fee in the calculation. Most firms charge fees in both directions. The fees are the same in each direction, so the cost for trading would be double.

When calculating the break-even price for a put option you subtract the premium, commission, and transaction costs. So, the break-even calculation for a May put option for ABC stock at a strike price of $54 with a commission of $25, or 25 cents per share, would look like this:

$54 − $2.00 − 25 cents = $51.75

In this scenario, ABC stock has to drop below $51.75 for this put option to be worthwhile.

If you expect a stock price increase, you want to consider purchasing a call option, but if you expect a price decline, you want to consider purchasing a put option. In both scenarios, you need to check the fundamental and technical information you gathered on the underlying stock or asset, so you can be certain that any break-even prices you've calculated reasonably match what your analysis indicates.

Options for Getting Out of Options

After you buy an option, you have to decide how you want to opt out of that position. You can choose one of the following three alternatives:

- Offset the option;
- Hold the option; or
- Exercise the option.

Offsetting the option

You offset an option by liquidating your option position, usually in the same marketplace where you bought the option. If you want to get out of an option before its expiration date, you can try to sell it for whatever price you can get. Doing so either enables you to take your profits or reduces your potential loss by the amount you receive for the option. As long as you bought your option in an active market, other investors usually are willing to pay for the rights your option conveys. The key, of course, is how much they're willing to pay.

Your net profit or loss for this option is determined by the difference between what you originally pay in premiums, commissions, and other transaction costs minus the premium you receive when you liquidate the option after deducting commissions and other transaction costs.

Holding the option

If your option is not yet in-the-money but you still believe it may get there, you can continue to hold the option until the exercise date. If you're right, you can exercise the option before the expiration date or liquidate at a later date, which means to buy or sell the option before the expiration date at some time in the future. If you're wrong, you risk the possibility that you won't find a buyer or that you'll have to let the option expire and take a loss that is equal to the amount of the premium, commission, and transaction costs you paid. Some traders take an even more risky position by buying options that are deeply out-of-the-money for just pennies a share. Even if these options never grow any nearer to being in-the-money, as long as they move in the right direction the premiums will rise. Although we don't recommend using this strategy, profits can be made as long as you're able to sell the option before its expiration date.

Options decline in value as they get closer to their expiration dates, so if you think you've made a mistake and the market moves against your position, bite the bullet as soon as possible and try to liquidate your option to minimize your losses.

Exercising the option

You can exercise an option any time prior to its expiration date, as long as you're trading in American-style options. You don't have to wait until the exercise date to exercise an American-style option. (The Montreal Exchange has both European-style and American-style contract types depending on the instrument. Some option contracts sold in the United States are

European-style, which can be exercised only on the expiration date.) Exercising an option means:

- Buying the underlying asset when you own a call
- Selling the underlying asset when you own a put

In general, call options are exercised only when the trader plans to hold the underlying asset, and put options are exercised only when the trader owns the underlying asset and wants to sell it. Option traders are more likely to realize any gains or losses by closing their option positions rather than exercising them.

The Risks of Trading Options and Futures

Trading in options and futures is risky business, and regulations governing those trades are stringent, even with regard to allowing you to open an account. Before opening an account for you, a firm must provide you with a disclosure document that describes the risks involved in trading futures and options contracts. The document gives you the opportunity to determine whether you have the experience and financial resources necessary to engage in option trading and whether option trading is appropriate for meeting your goals and objectives.

Topics that must be covered in the disclosure statement include the risks inherent in trading futures contracts or options and the effect that leveraging your account can have on potential losses or gains. The statement also must include warnings about trading futures in foreign markets, because those types of trades carry additional risks from fluctuations in currency exchange rates and differences in regulatory protection.

Commodities options and futures also can be risky, because many of the factors that affect their prices are totally unpredictable, such as the weather, labour strikes, inflation, foreign exchange rates, and governmental policies. Because positions in futures and options are so highly leveraged, even a small price movement against your position can result in at least the loss of your entire premium payment and possibly even much greater liability for additional losses.

After you begin trading options and futures, you can't close your account until all open positions are closed — if, that is, you're trading through an account with a commodities exchange. This restriction does not apply to options traded in an investment account. Any accruals on futures contracts are paid out daily. Any funds in your margin account that are beyond your required margin or account-opening requirements can be withdrawn, but other such funds have to remain in the account until all your positions are closed. Any restrictions on the withdrawal of your funds are stated in the original disclosure document. Be sure you understand those restrictions before committing your funds.

After opening your account, your firm usually mails or emails confirmation of all purchases and sales, a month-end summary of transactions that shows any gains or losses, and an evaluation of your open positions and current account values. You need to be able to get information from your firm on a daily basis after you begin to trade.

Futures traders must maintain adequate margin in their futures accounts by the process known as *marking-to-market*. At the end of each trading day, margin requirements are adjusted by the change in the price of the futures contracts.

Investment dealers are required to segregate any money you deposit in your account from the dealer's own funds. The amount segregated either increases or decreases depending on the success of your trades. Even when the firm segregates your funds, you still may not be able to get all your money back if the firm becomes insolvent and is unable to cover all the obligations to its customers unless the firm is a member of the Canadian Investor Protection Fund (CIPF) www.cipf.ca.

When problems with your dealer arise that you can't resolve without help, you do have dispute-resolution options. Before deciding how you want to proceed you must consider the costs involved, the length of time it may take to resolve the problem, and whether you want to contact an attorney. You can get more information about dispute resolution by contacting the Investment Industry Regulatory Organization of Canada (IIROC) at www.iiroc.ca/English/Investors/MakingComplaint or by calling 1-877-442-4322. Another useful Web site is www.investored.ca, which is funded by the Ontario Securities Commission (OSC).

Minimizing Risks

In a nutshell, the best way to minimize the risks of derivatives trading is to take the time to find out as much as you can about the inherent risks of the derivatives you're trading and how others have dealt with them. The first step you can take is to check out the firms or individuals with whom you plan to trade. All firms and individuals that offer to trade options or futures must be registered with one of the members of the Canadian Securities Administrators (www.securities-administrators.ca). You can check out firms and individuals online at the IIROC Web site (www.iiroc.ca).

Next, be sure you're familiar with the firm's commission charges and how they're calculated. Compare the firm's quotes with those of other firms you're considering. Whenever a firm has unusually high commission charges, ask for a detailed explanation for the higher charges and what additional services justify the higher cost.

Always make sure you calculate the break-even price for any option you're thinking about purchasing, because you have to know at what point the option you're planning to buy will be profitable and whether the data you've collected justifies the option's premium costs.

You also need to understand the market for the underlying asset of the option or future you plan to buy and what can impact the market price of that asset. Be sure your expectations for the potential profits from the option or futures contract you choose are reasonable.

You don't ever want to buy an option without first coming to a full realization that you can lose the entire value of your trade. If you want to take the riskier position as an option seller, be sure you can accept the possibility that your losses may exceed the premium you initially received for the option. Option selling comes with the potential of unlimited losses, as does futures trading.

Just as with stock trading, you can limit your losses by carefully setting your risk limits before you start to trade. Don't let yourself get caught up in the emotions of futures and options trading. Develop a plan before you buy that first option or future and stick with that plan, and be sure to diversify your holdings not only by asset type but also by time of expiration.

After you determine how much capital you want to put into trading derivatives, make sure you know how much you can afford to lose on just one trade to be able to stay in business. You don't want to overexpose your cash position on one trade and risk the possibility that you won't have the money you need when the next opportunity comes along. By exposing your capital to a variety of markets, you also have a better chance that some of your trades will end up succeeding — how bad can that be?

Be wary of firms that lead you to believe you can make lots of money trading options or futures with very little risk. That's never true. If a firm is using high-pressure tactics to get you to trade that's a sure sign of a problem, so don't allow yourself to be rushed into a trading decision. If you aren't being given enough time to construct your own fundamental and technical analyses before you make a purchase, walk away from the deal.

The risks associated with trading futures and options can be more than you initially paid for the trade, so be careful out there! We've given you an overview of the options and futures trading arena, but before you jump in be sure you get significantly more training.

Chapter 19

Going Foreign (Forex)

In This Chapter

▶ Understanding foreign exchange markets

▶ Using money market instruments

▶ Trading with money

▶ Discovering risks of money trading

*T*rading money in the global markets can be a great way to make more of it, but beware that it also can be a lesson in how to lose money quickly. According to the Bank for International Settlements more than $4 trillion is traded every day on the *foreign currency exchange* (forex), and yet no centralized headquarters or formal regulatory body exists for this form of trade. It is by far the largest and most liquid market in the world. London is the main trading centre, but New York, Tokyo, Hong Kong, Shanghai, Dubai, Zurich, and Singapore are important trading centres as well.

Foreign currency exchange is regulated through a patchwork of international agreements among countries, most of which have some type of regulatory agency that controls what goes on within their respective borders. Thus, the foreign currency exchange actually is a worldwide network of traders who are connected by telephones and computer screens.

Although more international policing of money trading has occurred in recent years, authorities have had some successes exposing scams and frauds that victimize traders, especially newer ones. So if you want to try this wild world of trading, you need to be wary and not depend entirely on what we discuss here in this chapter. Sure, we explain the workings of foreign exchange markets and how the language of the forex and its risks are unique, but you need to obtain a whole bunch more training before you ever consider entering this extremely risky trading arena.

Exploring the World of Foreign Currency Exchange

If you've ever travelled outside of Canada, you've probably traded in a foreign currency. Every time you travel you have to exchange your country's currency for the currency used in the country you're visiting. If you're a Canadian citizen shopping in England, and you see a sweater that you want for £100 (100 pounds — the pound is the currency in the United Kingdom), you'd need to know the exchange rate. In November 2009, for example, the rate was $1.7521 for one British pound. So a £100 sweater would cost you $175.21 in Canadian dollars.

We include this example here to show you how foreign currency exchange is used by the average shopper, but foreign currency traders trade much larger sums of money thousands of times a day. The majority of trades take place in three main centres of currency trading — the United Kingdom, the United States, and Hong Kong. The rest of the trading takes place primarily in Singapore, Switzerland, Japan, Germany, China, Canada, and Australia. According to Euromoney's FX Poll 2009, the United Kingdom manages the largest share — about 23 percent. The United States is second with 21 percent, and Switzerland is third with 18 percent.

Currency trading is ongoing, 24 hours a day, with some countries just getting started as others are finishing up their business day. For example, when the trading day opens at 8 a.m. in London, the trading day is ending for Singapore and Hong Kong. When Toronto, Montreal, and New York open their trading doors, it's already 1 p.m. in London. Thus, traders must be alert around the clock, because a major event at an off hour anywhere in the world can shake the currency markets at any time. Pity poor Vancouver, San Francisco, and Los Angeles, the weakest links in the so-called 24-hour foreign exchange market that spans the globe.

Individual trades in the range of $200 million to $500 million are not uncommon. In fact, estimates indicate that quoted price changes occur as frequently as 20 times per minute, and the most active currency rates can change as many as 18,000 times in a single day, according to the U.S. Federal Reserve.

Types of currency traders

Traders can be grouped into one of four basic types — bankers, investment dealers, customers, and central banks. Each plays a different role in the foreign currency exchange market.

✔ **Bankers, banks, and other financial institutions** do the lion's share of trading. They make profits buying and selling currency with each other. Approximately two-thirds of all forex transactions involve banks dealing directly with each other.

✔ **Investment dealers** sometimes act as intermediaries between the banks, helping them — or other traders looking for a good deal — find out where they can get the best currency trade. Buyers and sellers like working through investment dealers, because they can trade anonymously through intermediaries. Dealers make profits on currency exchanges by charging a spread for the transactions they arrange.

✔ **Customers,** which primarily are major companies, trade currency so they can operate globally or invest internationally. For example, if a Canadian car manufacturer buys parts from a manufacturer in Japan, then the Canadian car manufacturer needs to buy and pay for the parts in Japanese yen. Companies that trade currencies regularly have their own trading desks, while others conduct their currency trading through dealers or banks.

✔ **Central banks,** like the Bank of Canada (BoC) and the U.S. Federal Reserve, which act on behalf of their governments, sometimes participate in the forex market to influence the value of the currencies of their respective countries. For example, if the Bank of Canada believes the dollar is weak, it may buy dollars and even encourage central banks of other countries to do the same in the forex market, to boost, or increase, the value of the dollar. This policy has not been used by the BoC for a long time.

Why currency changes in value

Among the many factors that impact the value of a nation's currency are

✔ Interest rates

✔ Business cycles

✔ Political developments

✔ Changes in tax laws

✔ Stock market news

✔ Inflationary expectations

✔ International investment patterns

✔ Policies adopted by governments and central banks

✔ Employment levels

Traders must monitor all these potential factors so they can stay on top of political or economic changes that impact the value of the currencies they hold. Currency trading, like other forms of trading, is affected by the basic economic principle of supply and demand. When a whole bunch of one type of currency is available for sale, the market can be flooded with it, and the price of that currency drops. When the supply of currency is low and the demand for it is high, then the value of that currency rises. Governments may try to influence the value of their respective currencies by flooding the market whenever they want the value to fall or making the supply scarce (by buying their own currency) whenever they hope the value of their currencies might rise.

What traders do

Currency traders look for a currency that offers the highest return with the lowest risk. For example, if a nation's financial instruments, such as stocks and bonds, offer high rates of return with relatively low risk, then traders who are foreign to that nation want to buy that currency, thus increasing the demand. Currency is also in demand when its country is going through a growth segment in its business cycle highlighted by stable prices and a wide range of goods and services available for sale. Forex traders who speculate on currencies to earn their keep look for specific signs to indicate when exchange rates may change, including the following:

- **Political instability:** Unrest in a country drives up demand for currency in safer markets, such as Canadian dollars, as speculators race to find safe havens. The U.S. dollar used to be the world's safe haven of choice; not so since its recent credit crunch troubles. In fact, during 2009 fifteen of the world's currencies rose in value against the once-mighty U.S. dollar. Only the Japanese yen slipped against the American dollar.

- **Rising interest rates:** Higher interest rates encourage offshore investments in countries where local investors are seeking better rates of return than they can get at home.

- **Economic reforms:** Economic reforms in developing countries may help improve their currencies. As a result, investors see new opportunities for investing in the currencies of those successfully developing countries.

Traders try to predict these moves in advance, so they can get in or out of a currency before others. Correctly guessing where a currency is going and taking a position in that currency at the beginning of the trend can mean huge profits for a trader. Traders make money either by buying the currency at a lower price and then selling it later at a higher price, or by selling their currencies of other countries at higher prices before they have time to react negatively. After the markets for their original holdings fall, they simply reestablish positions at bargain prices.

When a trader purchases a large amount of a particular currency, then he or she is *long the currency.* Conversely, when a trader sells a large amount of a currency, then he or she is *short the currency.*

The forex market is dominated by four currencies, which account for 80 percent of the market — the U.S. dollar, the euro, the Japanese yen, and the British pound. These currencies always are liquid, which makes finding someone willing to buy or sell any of them easy for traders. Other currencies are not as liquid, and as is true with the stocks of small companies, you're sometimes unable to find any buyers or sellers when you're ready to trade for the currency of a smaller country. Currencies of developing countries are softest, usually facing lower demand than the currencies of developed countries. Soft currencies at times can be difficult to convert.

Understanding Money Jargon

The world of foreign currency exchange has a unique language of its own. Prices are quoted two ways, meaning that when one trader talks price with another, they state their respective prices in terms of what *exchange rate* they'll pay to buy it and what they'll take when selling it. Bid and ask price differences, or *spreads,* usually are stated in *pips* or hundredths of a currency unit. Spreads normally are no more than ten pips.

Pips are the smallest incremental price movement permitted in the currency market. Although most transactions deal in thousands or millions of dollars, yen, euro, or other currencies — and a one-cent spread can equal thousands of dollars — most currency price quotes nevertheless are extended out four decimals (1.5432, for example). Many times traders quote only the last two digits, or the small numbers, such as 32 exchange for 22, because the incremental changes are so small only the last two digits matter.

As a trader, you need to think in terms of the host currency when receiving a quote for *direct exchange,* which would be an exchange based on the value of the host country's currency. Quotes for *indirect exchange* are just the opposite. They're based on the foreign currency for which you are seeking a trade rather than on the host currency. For example, if you're in Canada and receive an indirect price quote, you'd be getting a price based on buying a set amount of foreign currency in exchange for Canadian dollars. Most exchanges take place on the interbank market — currency exchanges among the world's banks — and are based on the U.S. dollar. The one exception to the rule is the British pound sterling.

Traders use three different types of trades to exchange currency. They're known as spot, forward, and options transactions.

Spot transactions

Spot transactions account for about a third of all forex transactions and involve trades in which two traders agree on an exchange rate and then trade currencies based on that rate. These transactions usually start with one trader calling another and asking for a price on a particular type of currency without specifying whether he or she wants to buy or sell. The trader on the receiving end of the call gives the caller a two-way price — one if he or she wants to buy and another if he or she wants to sell. If they agree to do business, the two exchange their respective currencies.

Forward transactions

Forward transactions are used when traders want to buy or sell currency at some agreed-upon forward date. A buyer and a seller set an exchange rate for the transaction, and the transaction occurs at the set price at the appointed time regardless of what the current market price is for the currencies. Forward transactions can be only a few days or even years in the future, although most futures contracts are for 30, 60, or 90 days. The two types of forward transactions are futures and swaps.

- **Futures:** *Futures* are forward transactions that have standard contract sizes and maturity dates. These types of transactions are traded on an exchange set up for this purpose.

- **Swaps:** A *swap,* the more common type of forward transaction, is a private contract through which two parties exchange currencies for a specific length of time and then agree to reverse the transaction at a later date, which is set at the time of the initial contract.

The risk that traders take in using forward transactions is that market rates can change, turning the contract to which they've just agreed into a losing trade. They still have to fulfill the contract at the fixed price, because after the contract is signed the price cannot be revised.

Companies that place orders for imported products from foreign firms usually use this type of transaction so they can lock in an exchange rate at some time in the future when their orders are ready. Companies placing these orders don't want to lay out the cash upfront to exchange currencies, but they nevertheless want to be able to budget set amounts for their purchases. As such, they'd rather risk missing a better rate for the currency exchange in the future than a major shift in the price of the product (perhaps brought on by a currency shock) that's going to end up costing them much more than they intended to pay.

Options

Option contracts were added to the forex world to give traders a bit more flexibility than a forward transaction affords them. Like forward transactions, the owner of an option contract has the right to either buy or sell a specified amount of foreign currency at a specified rate up to a specified date. The big difference with option contracts is that traders who hold a contract are not obligated to fulfill the transaction. They can, instead, simply decide to let it expire.

Option buyers have to pay for the right to buy or sell these transactions on or before a specified date. The set price at which the currencies are exchanged is called the *strike price*. When the date for the exchange arrives, the option holder determines whether the strike price is favourable. If it is, the option owner completes the transaction and earns a profit. If it isn't favourable, the option owner allows the option to expire and absorbs the cost of purchasing the original option, which is less of a loss than actually exchanging the currencies. The two types of options currency traders deal with are

✔ **Call options,** to buy currency at some set price in the future, and

✔ **Put options,** to sell currency at some set price in the future.

For example, suppose a trader purchases a six-month call option on one million euros at an exchange rate of 1.39 dollars to the euro. During that six-month period, the trader can (has the option to) either purchase the euros at the $1.39 rate, buy them at market rate, or do nothing at all. As market rates for currencies fluctuate, options in those currencies can be sold and resold many times before the expiration date. Companies operating overseas use options as insurance against major unfavourable market shifts in the exchange rate and thus avoid locking their companies into guaranteed exchanges.

Trades are made using various currency symbols that are similar to stocks when seeking price quotes. We list some of the more common currency symbols in Table 19-1.

Table 19-1	Common Currency Symbols
Currency Symbol.	*Country & Currency Name*
AUD	Australian dollar
GBP	British pound

(continued)

Table 19-1 *(continued)*

Currency Symbol.	Country & Currency Name
CAD	Canadian dollar
CNY	Chinese yuan renminbi
EUR	European euro
GRD	Greek drachma
HKD	Hong Kong dollar
INR	Indian rupee
JPY	Japanese yen
MYR	Malaysian ringgitt
MXP	Mexican peso
NZD	New Zealand dollar
RUR	Russian ruble
SGD	Singaporian dollar
ZAR	South African rand
CHF	Swiss franc
TWD	Taiwanese dollar
USD	U.S. dollar

You can find current exchange rates for most major currencies online at the Universal Currency Converter (www.xe.com/ucc). You merely set an amount, choose the type of currency you want to convert, and select the type of currency you want to convert into. The site tells you the exchange rate and how much your currency is worth when converted. The site won't give you a rate where you're guaranteed to find a trade, but it certainly gives you a decent estimate — to within six decimal points. Billed as "The world's favourite currency and foreign exchange site," the Universal Currency Converter was founded in 1993 in Ontario by Steven Dengler. Although Canada is not a currency trading centre by any means, the site became one of the Internet's first dynamic sites. In many countries xe.com is one of the 100 most popular sites on the Web!

How Money Markets Work

The currency exchange market is made up of about 2,000 dealer institutions that are particularly active in foreign currency exchanges. Most of the players are commercial or investment banks that are geographically dispersed in the key financial centres around the world. Among these 2,000 dealers, around 100 to 200 members carry on the core trading and market-making activities. Major players are fewer still.

As of May 2009, two British banks, a German bank, and a Swiss bank commanded 55 percent of the overall volume of currencies traded. When a dealer buys a Canadian dollar, regardless of where in the world the transaction takes place, the actual deposit is located either directly in a Canadian bank or in a claim of a foreign bank on a dollar deposit located in Canada. The same is true of the currency of any other country.

Different countries, different rules

The actual infrastructures of the various currency markets and how they operate are determined by each separate nation. Each country enforces its own laws, banking regulations, accounting rules, and tax codes. The method of payment and the settlement system also are determined separately by each country. But yikes, doesn't that mean you have to know a lot about international monetary laws to be able to trade? Yup. Especially if you want to be successful.

Luckily, considerable global cooperation exists among exchange regulators, which minimizes differences and helps protect forex traders from fraud and abuse. Governments around the world reach agreements, or *memoranda of understanding* (MOUs), with most other major nations that have active currency exchanges, and these MOUs form a method of cooperation between regulatory and enforcement authorities across international borders that combats fraud and other illegal practices that can harm customers or threaten market integrity.

If you plan to become involved in foreign currency exchange, be sure to bone up on your knowledge of the company you're dealing with and find information about recently exposed scams and other illegal activities. You certainly don't want to get caught up in a fraudulent deal and lose all your money. Some very nasty scams have involved so-called "offshore currency trading."

The almighty (U.S.) dollar

Despite its large decline during 2008–2009, the U.S. dollar still is the most widely traded currency. The euro and the U.S. dollar are the two currencies that are involved in more than 85 percent of all global foreign exchange transactions. The U.S. dollar wears many hats, serving as an investment currency in many capital markets, a reserve currency for many central banks, a transaction currency for many commodity trades, an invoice currency for many contracts, and a currency of intervention used by countries that want to influence the values of their own currencies.

Due to the recent and steep decline of the U.S. dollar, China and some of the oil-exporting countries (such as Venezuela and Iran) have voiced concerns about its default status as the currency of choice. So far it's lots of talk, and we don't know of any major purchases for which U.S. dollars have been refused. Vendors of commodities priced in U.S. dollars have been asking for more and more U.S. dollars to complete their transactions as the U.S. dollar continues to decline. The last Middle East oil producer to export its oil in euros rather than dollars was Iraq's Saddam Hussein. A few months later the Americans and British troops invaded.

The currency in China is the yuan, which is fixed or "pegged" to the U.S. dollar. President Obama wants China to dismantle the currency peg and let the value rise against the U.S. dollar. A rising yuan would assist Canada's export industries looking for Asian markets to replace our dependence on American consumers.

Due to this friction over the value of the U.S. dollar, some executives at the International Monetary Fund (IMF) say the days of the almighty U.S. dollar as the global benchmark are numbered.

Organized exchanges

The money market is largely unregulated as a *defined market*. By that, we mean that a commercial bank in Canada or the United States doesn't need any special authorization to trade or deal in foreign currencies. Securities and investment firms don't need special permission from the OSC or any other regulatory body to carry out foreign exchange activities.

Transactions can be carried out based on whatever terms the law permits and using whatever provisions are acceptable to the two parties, subject to the commercial law governing business transactions. Of course that means the money market can be the closest thing to the Wild West you'll find in some parts of the trading world. Almost anything goes. Institutions that participate are not inspected specifically for their exchange practices, but regulatory authorities nevertheless look into trading systems as part of their regular examinations of financial institutions, just to be sure they're operating under the country's commercial banking or securities laws. They're also inspected in order to prevent laundering of drug money, proceeds of crime, or terrorist financing.

Although no official rules or restrictions govern the hours or conditions of trading on this over-the-counter (OTC) market in the United States, trading conventions developed mostly by market participants are in place in Canada.

The currency exchange market is mostly accounted for by the Big Five chartered banks in Canada, including spot transactions, forwards, and swaps. If you're new to forex trading, starting out is much safer with a large bank, where you can trade currency futures and certain currency options.

Many forex trading Web sites might prove to be for use at your own peril.

The Risks of the World Money Market

Leverage, or margin, which means borrowing money to trade, is the number one risk to your portfolio when trading in money markets. Success on the foreign currency market means having to trade in large sums, because profits are made at differences of only fractions of a cent or pips. Banks or dealers determine the leverage they want to offer you, but you might not find strict regulations like the ones that govern stock margin accounts.

After you're approved for trading, you're given a set amount or allowance on which you can trade on margin. A common starting allowance for trading on margin is 5 percent (see Chapter 14 for more about margins), which means that if you put $100,000 in the bank, you're allowed to execute transactions of up to $2 million. As you gain success with more experience, that margin may be lowered to 1 percent, which means you'd be allowed to trade as much as $10 million on your $100,000 deposit — but you'll be liable for all your losses and your costs of borrowing.

When trading at those high margin levels, even a minor mistake can wipe out your entire deposit.

The most conservative of banks require *full margin,* meaning you have to deposit $1 million to be able to trade $1 million. Be sure you understand the leverage you're being offered and the loss potential you face if your trade goes sour. Just imagine starting with $100,000, which you can use to trade $2 million, and then losing half of that trading maximum with trades that have gone sour. You could end up $900,000 in the hole. Sure, lots of traders can come up with that, no problem. In reality, as long as you stick to trading the major currencies drastic price changes that end up in that type of loss are possible but unlikely — but a loss of 10 to 20 percent of your holding in a matter of minutes can happen. Only trading in third-world currencies could result in losses of the million-dollar magnitude described here, and only if there was a major uprising in the country and the price of its currency dropped dramatically — like what sadly has happened in Zimbabwe!

Types of risk

You also face a number of different kinds of risk, including market risk, exchange risk, interest rate risk, counterparty risk, volatility risk, liquidity risk, and country risk.

Market risk

All traders and investors face market risk. Basically, *market risk* comprises changes in price that adversely impact your trade or investment. Market risk is in play from the moment you enter into a foreign currency position until the moment you exit it. The foreign exchange rate can change any time during that period, so when you're dealing in foreign currency, two key factors can impact the price of the currency — exchange risk and interest rate risk.

Exchange risk

Foreign exchange traders take on exchange risk the moment they buy or sell a foreign currency. Every time you take on a new foreign exchange position, regardless of whether it's through a spot, forward, future, or option transaction, you're immediately exposed to the potential that the exchange rate will move against your position, making it worth less than when you bought it. In only a matter of seconds, a profitable transaction can turn into an unprofitable one.

Interest rate risk

Foreign exchange positions can change in value not only because of the exchange rate but also because of the currency's underlying interest rate. Whenever a country's central bank (think Bank of Canada) raises or lowers the underlying interest rate for its currency, the impact on any positions you're holding in that country's currency can be major.

Counterparty risk

In the currency trading world, a *counterparty* is the other entity involved in a transaction — a bank or banker, a dealer, or another trader. When you buy a currency option or execute a forward transaction, you risk the possibility that the counterparty to your transaction won't be able to meet his, her, or its obligations.

Note: When you buy the option through an exchange rather than directly from the counterparty, this risk is not a factor. When that happens you run into additional replacement costs, because you're forced to enter into another currency transaction to meet your own foreign currency needs. The key to avoiding this kind of risk is entering into contracts with known institutions that have high credit ratings. Additionally, you need to investigate whether the counterparty with which you're trading has had any problems with regulators, insolvency, or questions of ethical conduct.

When evaluating a company, first consider its credit risk. You can find credit rankings for many major banks at the Standard & Poor's Web site (www2. standardandpoors.com). You can research a company's creditworthiness by investigating the requirements and standards it uses when providing credit to its customers. Companies that provide easy credit to their customers run a greater risk of not being able to meet their obligations. Conversely, companies with higher margin limits definitely are safer to do business with when you're entering into a contract.

Volatility risk

Volatility risk relates to the possibility of rapidly changing exchange rates that can impact your positions in foreign currencies. As we mention in the "Exploring the World of Foreign Currency Exchange" section in this chapter, currency prices can change thousands of times per day. Options on currencies are valued according to volatility and underlying changes in the prices of the respective currencies. If a trader sees an increase of 100 percent in volatility, or a doubling of volatility, then the price of the option can increase 5 percent to 10 percent. If you're trading on credit, which is highly likely, your bank or dealer can reevaluate the credit it's extending to you whenever it sees a dramatic increase in the volatility of your holdings.

Liquidity risk

Liquidity risk is not a major factor if you're trading in the more commonly traded currencies, but if you decide to trade in less active currencies it can become a factor when you're unable to sell a currency you hold at the express time you want the sale to take place, especially when the market for that currency is not active — such as the hours when Toronto is closed and Hong Kong is not yet open. You can avoid liquidity risk by buying currency options or futures on an exchange.

Country risk

Country risks come in several different varieties, all of which you need to consider whenever you trade in foreign currencies. Among those aspects are

- ✔ **Political risk:** This variety relates to the political stability of the country in whose currency you're trading. We have seen recent seizures of commercial assets by some nations. For example, Venezuela took control of its oil industry by seizing assets of non-Venezuelan oil companies. American and European governments have seized control of automotive and financial companies. If you trade in currencies of countries that are at risk of possible *destabilization,* the currency you buy can become worthless if the country changes political leaders.

- ✔ **Regulation risk:** This variety relates to what can happen after you establish a position in a country's currency. Its government can change its regulations, and in effect put restraints on the ownership established by your position in the currency and by the position of your counterparty — and that can get messy.

✔ **Legal risk:** This variety relates to which country has jurisdiction to rule on a contract if your counterparty happens to default. Unfavourable contract law in the host country of your counterparty can end up determining that the contract is invalid or illegal, and you can lose your position. Be sure you understand from whom you're buying and under which country's laws any disputes will be settled. Be certain you understand contract law in the country of the counterparty with whom you're trading.

✔ **Holiday risk:** This variety relates to the possibility that the country in whose currency you're trading has different religious, political, or government holidays that can shut down trading in that currency right when you need the money. Be sure you know the holiday schedules for the countries in whose currencies you trade.

Seeking risk protection

Although trading in foreign currencies often is called the modern-day Wild West, forces are in place that can help you minimize the risks — provided you take advantage of them and trade within their boundaries. The primary monitors of foreign currency trading are the world's central banks. They monitor the flow of money between countries and the balance of payments between governments and banking institutions. Regulatory authorities exist in most major currency markets, but if you decide to do business with a nonbanking institution you're transacting your business in unprotected waters outside the safe harbour of regulatory oversight and must do so under the often fateful guise of caveat emptor — let the buyer beware.

Internationally, the Bank for International Settlement (BIS; www.bis.org) is the leading independent agency for evaluating foreign exchange trading institutions on a global basis. BIS created risk-weighted evaluation and capital requirements for institutions that trade in foreign currencies and money market transactions. Be certain that any institution with which you plan to conduct trades meets BIS standards.

A number of common clearing systems assist with the transfer of foreign currencies. The two best-known ones are the Clearing House Interbank Payments System, or CHIPS, and the Society for Worldwide Interbank Financial Telecommunication, or SWIFT. Be sure you're using one of these systems when you trade, because they code transactions to avoid defaults and help you identify the creditworthiness of transactions.

If you're trading in foreign currency futures your risks are much less, because the futures industry is highly regulated. Clearinghouses for futures are efficient, and futures transactions usually are cleared hourly or in some cases even minute-by-minute.

Getting Ready to Trade Money

Your first step as a foreign currency trader is to develop an extensive collection of historical information not only about rate fluctuations for the currencies you plan to trade but also about interest rate fluctuations, economic history, and political stability of the countries whose currencies you're considering. Gathering some background information about the forex market itself doesn't hurt either. You can find more details about trading currency in *Currency Trading For Dummies* by Mark Galant and Brian Dolan (Wiley).

After collecting this information, you need to consider your own trading goals and how much you want to put at risk. Set your risk limits before you start, so you don't get emotionally caught up in having to make these potentially disastrous trading decisions on the fly. Capital that you risk on foreign currency trading needs to be money that you can afford to lose without impacting your lifestyle. Do not, for any reason, use retirement savings, savings for your children's educations, or savings required to maintain your house and lifestyle.

As is true for stock trading, when trading currencies you need to develop a plan that determines what you trade and how much you're at risk. When your plan's in place, stick to it for the entire trading day. You should not be developing the plan and executing it at the same time. Foreign currency trading requires a great deal of focus, and you can't risk breaking that focus to do additional planning in the middle of a trading day. Monitor the successes you have in meeting the goals of your plan. If you're not achieving your objectives, you may want to step back and reevaluate your plan and your decision to trade in foreign currency.

Technical analysis is used by foreign currency traders in a way that is similar to stock trading (see Chapters 9 and 10). Bar charts are the most common tools. The basic bar chart shows the opening, high, low, and closing prices for a given period of time.

The key difference between trading currencies and stocks is that in the foreign exchange market, a daily price chart sometimes shows the opening price in the Pacific Rim and the closing price in Canada. Because the foreign exchange market is open almost 24 hours a day, time periods are different for foreign currency trading than for stock trading. You can play with forex charting online at www.forex-markets.com/charts.htm.

We won't cover the basics of technical analysis for foreign currency trading, because we'd need to take up another entire book to do it right. That's exactly why Wiley Publishing Inc. also publishes *Technical Analysis For Dummies* by Barbara Rockefeller (Wiley). Be sure to check it out, too.

Because we can't say it enough, we repeat: If you truly want to pursue this form of trading, we highly recommend you seek additional training before you begin trading individually.

Chapter 20

Trading for Others: Obtaining Trading Designations and Certifications

As you become more involved in trading, you hear more about getting a designation to trade for others. These designations refer to examinations administered by the Canadian Securities Institute (CSI), which you must pass to be able to work in various capacities within the securities field. After passing these examinations, you can become licensed in the securities markets. What tests you need to take depend on where you plan to work and what you plan to do.

You also may hear an alphabet soup of designations like CFA, CFP, CLU, CMT, PFP, RFP. All are certifications given by different professional organizations to people who have completed coursework, testing, and, in most cases, years of work experience.

Naturally, investment and trading advisers must be licensed. In this chapter, we discuss the various types of licences and certifications and the level of training that is required for each. We also describe the types of tests CSI offers for each of its designations and help you find out about how advisers are licensed and regulated and what requirements you need to fulfill if you plan to make trades for others.

Considering Trading Professionally

The simple fact that you've bought or borrowed this book shows you have an interest in trading securities. At the point when you become a good trader and have confidence in your ability to trade profitably, your success at trading will be limited by the amount of your own capital. If you wish to dedicate yourself toward the profession of trading for others, then your upside is almost without limit. Your rewards can be in the amount of capital you accumulate for yourself and your family, or in the satisfaction of helping others with your trading advice — or both.

For most Canadians, paying their share of taxes is by far the biggest expense they incur every year. Tax advice is as important as medical advice for much of Canada's population. Luckily for us, the government provides many good tax-assisted deals to encourage us to invest in a home, a renovation, an education, a retirement, a major medical expense, or a charitable donation. Remember the RRSPs, RRIFs, RESPs, TFSAs, and IPPs we describe in Chapters 3 and 17? Most Canadian families have several of these pools of tax-deferred money that need to be looked after. Much of this money should be safely invested in government bonds, which are safe and liquid. However, billions of dollars of this money needs to be traded. That's right — other people's money needs to be traded! If you can provide good tax efficiency along with decent trading advice, your services will be in demand. You could translate your interest in trading into becoming eligible to trade for others.

Doctors, dentists, vets, engineers, and lawyers all need to spend at least ten years in expensive university courses and apprenticeships before they are able to command seven-figure annual salaries. Trading for others as an investment adviser requires $1,500 to pay for about eight months of study and only three exams (which we cover in the next section, "Getting to Know the CSI Series"). That's it. Naturally you need to impress somebody enough to want to offer you a job, but it's not rocket science (or medical school). The wonderful thing about these required courses in Canada is that anybody can enroll at any time. You don't need to be sponsored by a financial company, as you do in the United States. No university entrance requirements, no admissions tests, no letters of reference, and your study materials are available online within an hour of payment being received. After only a couple of years, a good trader licensed to trade for others can be enjoying a seven-figure annual income. All doctors, dentists, vets, engineers, and lawyers need trading advice; not all traders need doctors, dentists, vets, engineers, and lawyers.

As of January 2010, more than 200 firms are licensed to trade securities in Canada. If you can prove you're a good trader, and you want to trade other people's money, you'll be offered a position as an investment adviser or a discount broker. The former is much more rewarding for you than the latter.

Perhaps you need to take it one step at a time by temporarily becoming a discount broker to get your foot in the door of the investment industry. That's not such a bad detour on your way to becoming an investment adviser trading other people's money.

With so many investment firms in Canada, you might not have to put on a suit and tie every day and commute to an office tower in the nearest large city. Many different platforms are set up for you to trade for others. Most Canadian investment advisers work for the Big Five bank-owned investment dealers. These employers prefer their recruits to have undergraduate degrees and/or some sales management or networking experience. However, enough independent firms exist for a successful trader to find herself a position trading professionally for others.

Getting to Know the CSI Series

Almost every new career above the clerical level in the Canadian financial services industry includes some time spent at the Canadian Securities Institute Web site (www.csi.ca). This Web site is your first stop when your desire to trade for others turns to action; it's where you can study the required courses, which we cover in the following sections.

Canadian Securities Course (CSC)

Two piles of résumés sit on the desk of every manager in the investment industry. Candidates in the first pile, who have already passed the Canadian Securities Course (CSC), are very likely to get an interview. Candidates from the other pile get a polite form letter recommending a visit to www.csi.ca sometime soon. Some exceptional professionals have begun their careers as clerks, and then worked their way through the ranks while studying to pass the CSC. Today it's generally thought that prospective professional traders should have enough gumption to do the CSC on their own — after all, gumption is one of the key ingredients for success at trading other people's money.

The course costs $880 (at the time of publication of this book), for which CSI issues a tuition tax receipt. Before there were so many useful *For Dummies* books, most of us who studied the CSC considered the textbook alone to be worth the value of the after-tax cost of the entire course. The course involves two exams, which can be written at 65 locations throughout Canada or overseas if required. About 150 hours of study are needed, and you have two years to pass. The recommended pace for the 23 lessons is one lesson a week.

The CSC is a wonderful course to study even when you don't want to trade for others. While trading for yourself, it's useful to know what the pros know. Your own trading skills and self-confidence will grow just from knowing what all the words mean. After all, it's basically one big financial vocabulary test.

Don't be put off by any fear of mathematics — all that's required are the four basic functions of addition, subtraction, multiplication, and division. According to the CSI, only 20 percent of those who take the course are business or commerce graduates.

The table of contents in the CSC textbook is similar to the one in this book. It ranges, as this book does, from the big picture of the global economy to the small picture of corporate balance sheets. You'll learn the merits of analysis from top-down to bottom-up.

The subjects the course covers have grown in value and application since it was first set up. When Christopher studied the Canadian Securities Course soon after Elvis died, it wasn't much more than a mining stock promoter's guide. For example, the phrase "mutual fund" did not appear once in the text or index — which seemed odd at the time, because the man who practically invented global mutual funds, Sir John Templeton, established his Templeton Growth Fund right here in Canada back in 1954.

Conduct and Practices Handbook course (CPH)

This shorter course takes about 50 hours of study and, at time of publication, costs $580. This is where you learn the ropes involved behind the scenes in trading for others. The Conduct and Practices Handbook course delivers the goods from inside the investment industry, and provides lots of technical stuff about the do's and don'ts surrounding handling other people's money. Consider it a guide to the red tape of the trading world.

Other CSI courses

CSI offers several other courses that professionals are required to pass in order to deal in other financial instruments. A sample of these courses all have self-explanatory titles:

- Commodities as Investments (CAI)
- Canadian Insurance Course (CIC)
- Options Strategies Course (OSTC)

The bosses who run the investment dealers where traders look after other people's money have their own set of courses provided by CSI, namely:

- Branch Managers Course (BMC)
- Options Supervisors Course (OPSC)
- Partners, Directors and Senior Officers Course (PDO)
- Chief Financial Officer Qualifying Examination (CFO)

Imagine being paid to do something you really like doing. Imagine turning a hobby into a serious business for which a huge demand exists, and it grows every year. Imagine making money for yourself by making other people happy. Trading for others isn't exactly shooting fish in a barrel. Frustrations do pop up, of course, along with risks aplenty if you lose your focus or your attention to detail. However, you can see how trading professionally can become an addictive pleasure.

The ABCs of Financial Advisers

When you get a business card from an investment adviser or other investment professional, you may see a long list of initials that indicate professional certifications. Some of these require extensive training, education, and testing, but others require only minimal education and testing. In addition to the initial testing, some require continuing education and offer a disciplinary process and ways to check on a professional's status online. The sections that follow break down the key designations for financial advisers and explain what it takes to get — and keep — the designation.

Chartered Financial Analyst

A Chartered Financial Analyst (CFA) designation is issued by the CFA Institute (www.cfainstitute.org). Before you can get this designation, you must meet educational and work experience requirements. Candidates can have either an undergraduate degree plus three years of professional experience involving investment decision making, or four years of qualified work experience.

In addition to the work requirements, candidates must complete 250 hours of self-study for each of these three levels of examination:

- **Level I,** which focuses on investment evaluation and portfolio management

> ✔ **Level II,** which focuses on applying the analytical tools for valuing investments

> ✔ **Level III,** which focuses on the entire portfolio-management process

Many CFA candidates fulfill their work experience requirements while they prepare to take the three required exams.

Certified Financial Planner

A Certified Financial Planner (CFP) designation is awarded by the Financial Planner Standards Council (www.fpsc.org). Candidates must meet work experience and educational requirements. To be recognized as a CFP, candidates must have three years of personal financial experience plus two levels of financial planning exams.

In addition to the work experience requirements, CFP candidates must either complete a CFP board-registered program or qualify to take the final CFP examination by having earned one of the following designations:

> ✔ Certified General Accountant (CGA)

> ✔ Chartered Life Underwriter (CLU)

> ✔ Chartered Accountant (CA)

> ✔ Chartered Financial Analyst (CFA)

> ✔ A doctoral (PhD) degree in business, finance, or economics

Mandatory courses include financial planning process and insurance, investment planning, income tax planning, retirement planning and employee benefits, and estate planning. After earning the CFP designation, planners must complete 30 hours of continuing education every two years thereafter to maintain their CFP status.

Chartered Life Underwriter

The Chartered Life Underwriter (CLU) designation has been issued since 1927 by The American College (www.theamericancollege.edu) and focuses on insurance and coursework. Candidates must complete three years of full-time related business experience, five core courses, and three elective courses. Core courses include insurance and financial planning, individual life insurance, life insurance law, fundamentals of estate planning, and planning for business owners and professionals. The three elective courses can be chosen from courses on individual health insurance, income taxation, group benefits, planning for retirement needs, investments, and estate planning applications. After earning this designation, consultants must take 30 credits of continuing education courses every two years to maintain their status as a CLU.

Chartered Market Technician

The Chartered Market Technician (CMT) is issued by the Market Technicians Association (www.mta.org). Candidates must be a member of the association to enter the CMT program. To become a member, a person must be employed professionally as an analyst or professional investment manager for five years. Membership must be maintained in the MTA to get and hold the CMT certification. Certification includes three exams. The first is a multiple-choice exam on the basic definitions related to technical analysis. The second is also a multiple-choice exam that tests the candidate's ability to apply advanced analytical techniques. The third exam can be satisfied with either a research paper or an essay exam related to portfolio strategies or trading decisions.

Personal Financial Planner

The Personal Financial Planner (PFP) is a professional designation issued by the Financial Planning Standards Council (FPSC). These exams are offered by the Canadian Securities Institute (www.csi.ca). Topics covered on the PFP exam include professional responsibilities, personal financial planning processes, personal income tax planning, risk management planning, investment planning, retirement planning, and estate planning. In addition, candidates must submit references and other documentation that proves their business experience in personal financial planning–related services.

Registered Financial Planner

The Registered Financial Planner (RFP) designation is issued by the Institute of Advanced Financial Planners (www.iafp.ca). In addition to the educational requirement, candidates must meet licensing requirements for securities and life and health insurance. After an RFP designation, planners must complete 30 hours of continuing education each year.

The Designations and Certifications You Need When Trading for Others

If you decide you want to trade for others as well as for yourself, you need to become a registered representative. The most comprehensive test you can take is the CSI's Canadian Securities Course Exam, and you'll need a sponsoring dealer. Then you take the Conduct and Practices Handbook (CPH) exam.

This licence enables you to purchase and/or sell all securities products, including corporate securities, government securities, mutual funds, investment company products, and shares of public companies. Most of the other representative exams are taken whenever you want to sell only a specific type of security rather than the broader options that a CSC designation enables you to market. Professional certifications are not required to sell securities. All pros who seek these certifications do so to show their clients they have attained a level of proficiency and met or exceeded the standards within their specialties.

As you read through the requirements and courses mentioned in this chapter, you may have found subjects that can help you improve the management of your own funds. Many courses that train people for professional designations provide ways for others like you to take the coursework, even if you don't plan to get the licence or certification. You can even study for many of these courses at home online. Two schools that offer online education services in the securities and financial adviser area are the Canadian Securities Institute (www.csi.ca) and Foran Financial (www.foranfinancial.com).

As you probably realize by now, selling securities is a highly regulated field that requires considerable training and probation before you can sell even your first share. Although some people privately trade for others, they risk the possibility of an investigation by their provincial regulators whenever they do so without registering at the provincial level. Be sure the trading activities you do for others fit within the law, or you can end up in a legal mess facing significant fines.

Part VI
The Part of Tens

The 5th Wave   By Rich Tennant

That's the Harrisons. Never have I seen an investment portfolio start so strong and go south so quickly.

In this part . . .

We join in the *For Dummies* tradition of showing you some special lists of ten (or so) important and key factors that help you with your trading. We review ten common and huge trading mistakes and how to avoid them, and we describe ten basic strategies necessary for your survival and long-term financial well-being as a trader.

Chapter 21

Ten (Or More) Huge Trading Mistakes

. . . .

In This Chapter

▶ Trying to trade bottoms and tops (no, this isn't X-rated)

▶ Becoming attached to your trading systems and your stocks

▶ Making decisions on the fly

▶ Losing too much

. . . .

This chapter introduces you to ten (more, actually) huge trading mistakes that befall experienced and novice traders. We offer suggestions for helping you recognize the mistakes and for avoiding and even correcting them.

Fishing for Bottoms

Bottom fishing — trying to catch a stock as it bottoms out — is a great way to get soaked and lose a bucketful of money. In a bear market, stocks get much cheaper than most of us ever expect or want. They won't stop falling until they've run out of gas.

The psychology of a bear market is perverse. As long as traders remain interested in a stock, many are the moments when it seems like the stock may recover. The thing is, stocks rarely turn on a dime and head higher. Only after the momentum crowd loses interest does the stock's downward price slide end. When value investors, who can't resist a bargain, begin nibbling, the stock begins to stabilize; however, it also may spend a very long time bouncing around in a trading range.

Traders have few, if any, reasons for entering the market when a stock is trading in a range. Your best opportunity for profit occurs when the stock breaks out of its trading range. Chapter 9 shows how to identify these trading-range breakout patterns. Instead of risking your trading capital on unreliable bottoming patterns, wait until you're sure.

Timing the Top

Tops and bottoms share something in common. They rarely arrive when they're supposed to. When traders and investors are exuberant, they keep buying even after doing so no longer makes fundamental sense. That's why shorting a stock that's trending higher makes no sense, even if its price is far beyond reasonable.

You don't have to have a lengthy memory or an encyclopedic knowledge of stock market history to remember what happened to Internet stocks in the late 1990s. Those were heady days. Stocks went in only one direction — up. Some of those magically levitating companies had modest revenues, but few had earnings. Remember, Nortel — supposedly Canada's greatest ever company — went from $1,000+ per share to zero! Nevertheless, traders bid hundreds of dollars per share for some worthless junk. Just like the recent housing bubble, Internet stocks were a case of mass hysteria, mob mentality, market madness, or all three.

Call it what you will; when a bubble is inflating definitely is not a time to short related stocks. Sure, these stocks eventually crashed and burned, but not before depleting the trading accounts of a den full of bearish short sellers. Don't guess. Wait for reliable trading signals, like the ones discussed in Chapters 9 and 10, before entering a position.

You might be asking whether reliable trading signals occurred before the Internet bubble burst. Not before; traders aren't fortune tellers (see Chapter 8). However, the risks at the time were well known. And when stocks began heading lower early in 2000, you might have had all the information you needed to protect your profits and trading capital, and begin selling short. Lots of signals that the market was set for another fall were also there in early 2008. Chapter 13 uses the Nasdaq bubble as an example to show how to evaluate market risk and adjust your trading strategy as the market transitions from a rising to a falling market.

Trading Against the Dominant Trend

Trading against the dominant trend in the market leads to costly mistakes. Unfortunately, misidentifying the trend by focusing on the chart in front of you and forgetting to look at the next higher level chart is an easy thing to do. You may see a promising uptrend occur with a pullback on the intraday charts. But on the daily chart, the trend you saw on the intraday chart actually turns out to be a consolidation rally during a strong downtrend. The promising pullback actually is the beginning of the next leg down on the daily chart. If you buy long in a situation like this one, hoping to capture the next leg up, your position will be swamped (and so will your trading capital) by the flood of sell orders coming from traders who recognize the implications of the longer-term stronger trend.

Regardless of the specific indications of the chart you're looking at, always confirm your analysis by looking at charts that are one time period higher. For example, if you're studying daily charts, confirm your analysis on the weekly charts. If you're studying intraday charts, confirm your analysis on the daily charts. Always know which part of the market cycle you're in and what types of industries excel in that part of the cycle. See Chapters 10 and 13 for additional information.

Don't try to buy based on a brief intraday move, when the dominant trend on the daily charts is down. Doing so is a great way of giving up your trading capital to someone else.

Winging It

Traders get into big trouble when they wing it. Maybe you heard the guy on business TV say the stock was hot and heading higher. Maybe you saw the news that a new product was bound to be a big hit. Although that may sound like great information, it's only a reason to look into the fundamental and technical conditions of a company's stock. It's not a reason to buy today.

Devise a strategy. We think that's such great advice, we'll say it again. *Devise a strategy.* Develop and test a trading system that matches your goals and personality (see Chapter 15). Plan your trades and execute your plan. Wait patiently for your signals to trigger your trades. Pick your entry and exit points before entering your order. Have a plan and stick to it.

Traders also get into trouble when they start second-guessing their trading plans. Sometimes, even in the middle of executing a trade, you need to make a decision but won't be sure which decision is right.

When in doubt, close the position. It's easier to think clearly when your money isn't at risk. You can always buy back the stock if further analysis confirms it's the right thing to do.

Taking Trading Personally

A losing trade is bad for your trading account, but you can't let it get to you. Sure, it makes you feel bad, but a losing trade doesn't impugn your honour or disparage your heritage. A bad trade may reduce your net worth, but it shouldn't damage your self-esteem. Entering a losing trade certainly doesn't mean you're a nincompoop or a blockhead — any more than closing a winning trade signals your brilliance and mastery of all you survey.

The market isn't out to get you; it's out to get your money. Don't take trading personally. A losing trade is just another losing trade. You'll have plenty of them. Get used to it.

Falling in Love

Trading is a business. Your stocks are your inventory. Smart business owners don't fall in love with their inventory. It's there to sell, at a profit if possible, at a loss if necessary. And smart businesspeople don't fall in love with their business models. If it isn't working, they change it; otherwise, they'll be out of business before you can say "liquidation sale."

When you fall in love with your stock, you risk large losses. When you fall in love with your trading plan, you risk many more losses. It's easy to fall in love. After doing hours of research and analysis, you want to be right. You want your trades and your trading plans to generate profits, but hoping doesn't make it so.

Be smart. Don't fall in love. Your trading system doesn't have feelings and your stock won't love you back. Be prepared to jettison positions and trading systems that don't do what they're supposed to do. Stocks are not family. They're not even friends. They are tools, just like hammers and wheelbarrows. Love your family and your friends and your faith — do NOT love your stocks! See Chapter 12 for more about trading as a business and effectively managing your inventory.

Using After-Hours Market Orders

When the market opens and it's off to the races, the market order you placed last night before going to bed is going to be swept up in a wave of frantic trading. Bad fills are sure to be the result. You're likely to pay considerably more to buy a stock you want or to sell one for considerably less than you'd planned. You should very seldom place a market order when entering trades after the market is closed (after-hours). Instead, define how much you're willing to buy or sell a stock for by using a stop order, a limit order, or a stop-limit order. Chapter 14 discusses the mechanics of entering these types of orders.

Chasing a Runaway Trend

If you miss the breakout entry point for a stock that you want, waiting is better than entering a position as a trend accelerates. See Chapter 10 for information about identifying and trading a trend. Often, stocks will pull back and test the breakout point. Wait for that point, or wait for the stock to take a short breather after its first leg up. If you're still interested, that's a better entry point than chasing a stock as it accelerates into the trend. Like a fine wine, you sometimes need to let a stock breathe.

On the other hand, if you already have a position in a runaway stock, try planning your exit so that you leave a little money on the table. Capturing every last nickel of the trend is almost impossible anyway, so don't try. Instead, consider trimming your position as the stock reaches for the stratosphere. If you're using margin, consider taking some profit off the table and reducing your leverage a bit. We discuss this strategy further in Chapter 13, and we cover the mechanics of using margin in Chapter 14. When a runaway stock stops going up and everyone wants out at the same time, the speed at which the price falls is remarkable. Be ready to jettison stocks that rally too fast at the first sign of trouble.

Averaging Down

Averaging down is a below-average idea. You sometimes hear advisers suggesting it as a way of reducing your cost basis, but it's merely a technique to throw good money after bad. The logic of averaging down is usually contrary to the logic of trading. Traders sell losers. They don't reward them with infusions of trading capital.

However, averaging up sometimes makes sense. Traders call it *pyramiding*. The idea is to add to your winning positions when your trading system triggers new trading signals in the direction of the trend. Pyramiding is a good way of building a large position in a strongly trending stock. Be aware of the risk, though. The larger your position, the more it hurts when the trend ends and the stock's price begins to fall. Be ready to trim your pyramid position at the first sign of trouble.

Ignoring Your Stops

Talking yourself out of honouring your stops is an easy thing to do. You'll be tempted when a trade goes against you. You'll look at your indicators and the support levels on your charts, and you'll be certain that the stock soon will stop falling. When you start thinking you want to give a position a little room to work its way out of losing territory, you're on your way toward a trading debacle. It's wishful thinking, it's hoping against hope, and it's a good way to lose a lot of money. Unless you're omniscient, close the position when the price hits your stop. Take your loss. Chapter 14 discusses stop orders and how to use them.

Diversifying Badly

Exposing all your capital in one trade is a bad idea, and so is trading hundreds of stocks simultaneously. A happy medium can be found somewhere in between.

You can monitor only so many positions and do it well. You need only so many positions to diversify your risk. And although you can have too few or too many stocks in your trading portfolio, no perfect number — one that is right for every trader — exists. That said, you nevertheless have to figure out what the right number is for you. Start with 10 or 15 positions. You may end up deciding that eight is enough. However, unless you have an extremely large portfolio, imagining why you'd need any more than 20 positions is difficult.

The simple wisdom is this: Don't put all your eggs in one basket. And don't chop your eggs into little pieces and spread them across many dozens of baskets. You want to diversify, just not too much.

Enduring Large Losses

To trade is to lose. No matter how good your trading system is, no matter how experienced you are, and no matter which stocks you pick, you're going to have losing trades. Your success as a trader depends on how you handle those losing trades. If you dispose of the losers quickly, you can become a very successful trader. But if you hold on to those losing positions, you can lose so much money that it may knock you right out of the trading business.

Using margin (see Chapter 14) exacerbates the problem of losing trades. Margin is a wonderful thing, because with careful application it can magnify your profits. But on the flip side, with indiscriminate use it can also magnify your losses. If you want to turn your pool of trading capital into a puddle, leverage a lot of losing trades.

Small losses won't hurt you much, but large losses will. If you use margin and fail to cut your losses, you won't be a trader for long.

Chapter 22

Top Ten Trading Survival Techniques

Trading is not a risk-free activity. Although all traders know that losses are inevitable, they want to minimize those losses and be around to trade another day. In this chapter, we review ten of the top trading survival techniques that can help you enter the world of trading and enable you to continue to trade for a long time to come.

Build Your Trading Tool Chest

Before you buy that first share, that first option or futures contract, or any other security, you need to be certain you have the right mix of trading software, hardware, and Internet access to be successful. You need the right tools to identify trading candidates; display and interpret charts; research trading opportunities; screen stocks for technical or fundamental constraints; and monitor and analyze your portfolio, open positions, market indexes, sectors, and trading statistics. In summary, the proper tools are critical to finding the right trades and then monitoring those positions after you've found and entered them.

Even after you've found them, if you don't have the right tools you may not be able to enter and exit positions efficiently, control or track your orders, track your profits and losses, analyze your trading history, or monitor economic reports, earnings, and other business news.

The proper tools help you evaluate your trading system and test your trading ideas. They enable you to keep logs to review your trading performance. You also can use tools to stay in touch with other traders and exchange ideas that ultimately may help you improve your trading skills and discover new opportunities.

Tools are the core of any good trader's business. Without the right ones, your chances of success drop dramatically. Don't skimp on the tools you select for your trading activities. (For more information, see Chapter 4.)

Use Both Technical and Fundamental Analyses

You may have heard that all traders use technical analysis and believe that fundamental analysis is a waste of time. Don't believe it. Although technical analysis is crucial to finding the right entry and exit points, fundamental analysis improves your ability to make the right stock choices, given market and economic conditions.

You'll find as a trader that knowing the current state of the economy and the state of the market is critical. You obviously want to buy stocks in the bull market and sell them, or short them, in a bear market, but do you know how to recognize when the market is entering a period of transition so you can make your moves when the opportunity for making profitable trades or minimizing potential losses is greatest?

Using a combination of fundamental and technical analyses, your chances of identifying bull and bear markets and finding phases of transition and consolidation improve dramatically. Your best trading opportunities are at the beginning of these phases of change, so be sure you understand the six phases of the market and know which sectors offer you the best trading opportunities within each of those phases. (For more information, see Parts II and III.)

Choose — and Use — Your Favourite Tools Wisely

As you begin sorting out your software and hardware and making contact with other traders, you'll probably find out about the hundreds of tools and charts that are out there on the market. You don't need to learn and use them all. Using too many tools can be as dangerous to your trading system and your sanity as using too few. You'll find you get mixed signals and will probably end up in a state of analysis paralysis trying to figure out which tool is giving you the right signal.

To avoid driving yourself crazy, pick the top two or three trading tools that make sense to you and fit your trading style. Take your time getting to know how they work and how best to interpret the information they generate. Use them to build the types of charts that match your trading style and don't worry about learning all the new gadgets. If your tools are working and you're making a good profit, don't rush to add the newest innovation tool.

Keep your eyes open for new tools that can improve your trading profits, but use caution before making changes to your winning trading system. (For more information, see Chapter 15.)

Count on the Averages to Make Your Moves

You may think that using data from averages to find the right time to enter or exit a position is counterintuitive, but moving averages can be powerful trading indicators. Moving averages actually smooth out the data for you visually and help you identify any trends. Although they cannot predict the future, they nevertheless help you understand the past so you can more effectively extrapolate what may happen to a stock in the future.

Traders use many different types of moving averages in hundreds of different ways. Stock closing prices are the most common data being averaged, but any value on a price chart can be smoothed for interpretation. For example, traders sometimes manipulate the moving averages by using the mid-point between the high and low prices to develop the moving average. Others look for the moving average using the open, high, or low price. It's all a matter of trading style and how the charts you're developing match your trading system.

Be sure to find out how to use moving averages and what they mean. After you understand them and what goes into them, you can manipulate moving averages to your advantage and to coincide with your trading style. Moving averages are powerful indicators, but they're not the only type of indicator you need to use in choosing your trades; use moving averages in conjunction with other indicators. (For more information, see Chapter 11.)

Develop and Manage Your Trading System

You need to have a road map that helps you find buy and sell signals for your trades. A trading system is such a map, because it's developed using a collection of tools created from technical and fundamental analyses woven together to let you know when it's time to enter or exit positions. You can buy trading systems off the shelf, but these systems are available to thousands of others who ultimately will end up with the same buy and sell signals.

To be able to trade outside the pack, you need to develop your own trading system, using your own favourite tools. Although you can use tools provided in off-the-shelf software packages, you want to develop and adapt a trading system that fits uniquely with your personality and trading objectives.

After initially developing and testing your own trading system, your work is not done. You'll need to constantly monitor your system's successes and failures and look for ways to make improvements. (For more information, see Chapter 15.)

Know Your Costs

Trading isn't cheap. Not only do you have to worry about commissions or transaction fees, you also must watch for any slippage in your trades. Even though you may be using stop or limit orders, you rarely end up executing trades at the exact entry or exit prices you plan. Some slippage, or the difference between the quoted price and the actual price for the security, is bound to occur, so you need to be sure you carefully monitor your commission costs, transaction fees, and slippage costs.

In addition, don't forget to consider the tax man. If you're trading stocks, any profits you make are taxed at 50 percent of your net capital gains — unless you use a tax-free or tax-deferred account.

Traders must also avoid being caught by wash superficial loss rules. Most trading losses can be used to offset trading gains and thus reduce your income tax burden, but if you sell a stock for a loss and repurchase the same stock within 30 days, your trading loss for that transaction cannot be deducted. You have to wait until you sell the stock again and use any losses to reduce the cost basis of the trade, which reduces the tax owed when the position is finally closed. (For more information, see Chapters 2 and 14.)

Know When to Hold 'Em and When to Fold 'Em

Knowing when to take your profits and get out and when to accept your losses and close a position before it becomes even more damaging can be among the hardest lessons any trader must learn. All too often you're enticed by the win and want to ride it to the absolute top.

Wise traders plan their exit points at the top and bottom of each position long before they ever enter that position. And, more importantly, they stick to their plan. Getting caught up in the emotions of a winning trade is easy, but don't forget you're operating a business. Take your profits when you reach your goal and get out, so you don't risk turning a winning position into a loss.

When you make a mistake, own up to it quickly, take your hit, and get out of the position. If the stock recovers, you can always reenter the position at a later time. Don't ride a stock to the bottom just to try to prove you were right. Plan your exit points before you buy and stick to them. (For more information, see Chapter 12.)

Watch for Signals, Don't Anticipate Them

After you make a decision to buy a stock, you may find that you're impatient to actually get into that position. You start watching the charts and waiting for the right signal to buy. Often, you'll see charts move close to your planned signal but not actually reach it.

Be patient. Wait for the signal you've designated in your plan. Don't anticipate any moves, even if the stock price is getting close to that point on your charts. You may miss the perfect entry point, but you'll be less likely to make that fatal mistake of entering a position before the signal is triggered only to see your stock reverse course and thus be forced to take a loss. (For more information, see Chapters 10 and 13.)

Buy on Strength, Sell on Weakness

Buy on strength and sell on weakness is a mantra you've probably heard frequently from investment and trading gurus. The reason for its popularity is a good one: It works! And it needs to become your trading way of life.

When you see a stock showing strength and heading into an uptrend, it's time to buy. When you see a stock falling and showing signs of entering a weakening period, it's time to sell. If a weak stock takes a turn for the better, you can always reenter the position. (For more information, see Chapter 13.)

Keep a Trading Journal and Review It Often

One of the only ways you can ever improve your trading skills is by keeping track of what works and what doesn't and trying to gauge why. After each trade, take the time to write down the details of the trade and what went right and/or wrong with that trade. You can improve only what you measure, so measure everything and put it in your trading journal.

Don't forget to review the contents of your journal every week. You may find that reviewing your successes is enjoyable but reviewing your failures is difficult. Failure, however, sometimes is the best teacher. Many people discover more from their failures than from their successes. Try figuring out why your failed trades didn't work and what you could've done to improve your results. Of course, don't ignore your successes. After all, you need to know what works and why and then try to incorporate those winning strategies more consistently into your trading system. (For more information, see Chapter 15.)

Index

• S •

BUSINESS & PERSONAL FINANCE

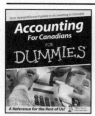

978-0-470-83878-5

978-0-470-73684-5

Also available:
- 76 Tips For Investing in an Uncertain Economy For Canadians For Dummies 978-0-470-16099-2
- Bookkeeping For Canadians For Dummies 978-0-470-73762-0
- Business Plans For Canadians For Dummies 978-0-470-15420-5
- Canadian Small Business Kit For Dummies 978-0-470-93652-8
- Investing For Canadians For Dummies 978-0-470-16029-9
- Wills & Estate Planning For Canadians For Dummies 978-0-470-67657-8

EDUCATION, HISTORY & REFERENCE

978-0-7645-2498-1

978-0-470-46244-7

Also available:
- Algebra For Dummies 978-0-470-55964-2
- Art History For Dummies 978-0-470-09910-0
- Canadian History For Dummies 978-0-470-83656-9
- Chemistry For Dummies 978-1-118-00730-3
- French For Dummies 978-0-7645-5193-2
- Math Word Problems For Dummies 978-0-470-14660-6
- Speed Reading For Dummies 978-0-470-45744-3
- Statistics For Dummies 978-0-470-91108-2
- World History For Dummies 978-0-470-44654-6

FOOD, HOME & MUSIC

978-0-7645-9904-0

978-0-470-43111-5

Also available:
- 30-Minute Meals For Dummies 978-0-7645-2589-6
- Bartending For Dummies 978-0-470-63312-0
- Brain Games For Dummies 978-0-470-37378-1
- Gluten-Free Cooking For Dummies 978-0-470-17810-2
- Home Improvement All-in-One Desk Reference For Dummies 978-0-7645-5680-7
- Violin For Dummies 978-0-470-83838-9
- Wine For Dummies 978-0-470-04579-4

Available wherever books are sold. For more information or to order direct: U.S. customers visit www.dummies.com or call 1-877-762-2974. U.K. customers visit www.wileyeurope.com or call 0800 243407. Canadian customers visit www.wiley.ca or call 1-800-567-4797.

GARDENING

978-0-470-58161-2   978-0-470-57705-9

Also available:
- Gardening Basics For Canadians For Dummies 978-0-470-15491-5
- Organic Gardening For Dummies 978-0-470-43067-5

- Sustainable Landscaping For Dummies 978-0-470-41149-0
- Vegetable Gardening For Dummies 978-0-470-49870-5

GREEN/SUSTAINABLE

978-0-470-84098-6   978-0-470-59678-4

Also available:
- Alternative Energy For Dummies 978-0-470-43062-0
- Energy Efficient Homes For Dummies 978-0-470-37602-7

- Green Building & Remodeling For Dummies 978-0-470-17559-0
- Green Cleaning For Dummies 978-0-470-39106-8
- Green Your Home All-in-One For Dummies 978-0-470-40778-3

HEALTH & SELF-HELP

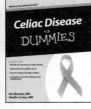

978-0-470-58589-4   978-0-470-16036-7

Also available:
- Borderline Personality Disorder For Dummies 978-0-470-46653-7
- Breast Cancer For Dummies 978-0-7645-2482-0
- Cognitive Behavioural Therapy For Dummies 978-0-470-66541-1
- Depression For Dummies 978-0-7645-3900-8
- Emotional Intelligence For Dummies 978-0-470-15732-9
- Diabetes For Canadians For Dummies 978-0-470-15677-3

- Healthy Aging For Dummies 978-0-470-14975-1
- Improving Your Memory For Dummies 978-0-7645-5435-3
- Neuro-linguistic Programming For Dummies 978-0-7645-7028-5
- Superfoods For Dummies 978-0-470-445-39-6
- Understanding Autism For Dummies 978-0-7645-2547-6